POSITIONING STUDENT AFFAIRS
FOR SUSTAINABLE CHANGE

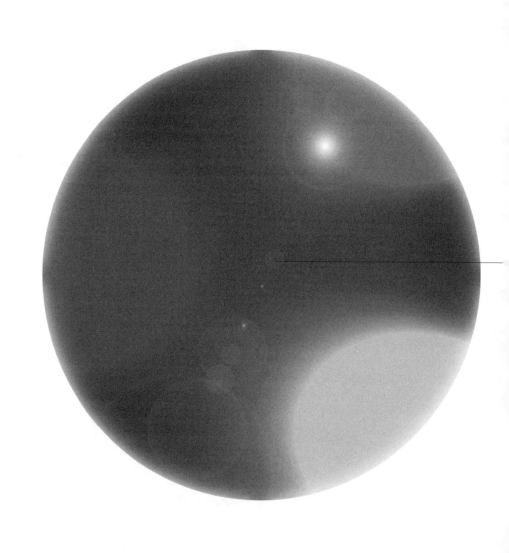

POSITIONING STUDENT AFFAIRS FOR SUSTAINABLE CHANGE

Achieving Organizational Effectiveness Through Multiple Perspectives

Linda Kuk and James H. Banning

Colorado State University

Marilyn J. Amey

Michigan State University

STERLING, VIRGINIA

Published by Stylus Publishing, LLC
22883 Quicksilver Drive
Sterling, Virginia 20166-2102

Library of Congress Cataloging-in-Publication Data
Kuk, Linda, 1950–
  Positioning student affairs for sustainable change :
achieving organizational effectiveness through multiple
perspectives / Linda Kuk, James H. Banning, and Marilyn
J. Amey.—1st ed.
     p.   cm.
  Includes index.
ISBN 978-1-57922-455-4 (cloth : alk. paper)
ISBN 978-1-57922-456-1 (pbk. : alk. paper)
    1. Student affairs services—United
States—Administration.   2. Organizational
effectiveness—United States.   I. Banning, James H.
II. Amey, Marilyn J.   III. Title.
LB2342.92.K85   2009
378.1′97—dc22   2009051682

13-digit ISBN: 978-1-57922-455-4 (cloth)
13-digit ISBN: 978-1-57922-456-1 (paper)

Printed in the United States of America

All first editions printed on acid free paper that meets the
American National Standards Institute Z39–48 Standard.

Bulk Purchases

Quantity discounts are available for use in workshops
and for staff development. Call 1-800-232-0223

First Edition, 2010

10   9   8   7   6   5   4   3   2   1

CONTENTS

ACKNOWLEDGMENTS

We would like to thank Sue Banning, Sharon Boyce, Thom Kuk, Lisa Miller, Leanne Perry, and Dennis Brown for their editorial assistance, counsel, and support throughout the preparation of this book.

PREFACE

T he past decade has presented many new challenges to student affairs organizations. The 9/11 attacks and the Virginia Tech and Northern Illinois University tragedies have increased concerns for safety and mental health issues on campuses. The continuing demands from increasingly diverse students have created expectations for more individualized services and programs. The increased involvement in the lives of students by hovering parents and the increasing amount of intrusion in campus issues by state legislatures and the media have placed greater expectations on campus life, campus services, and the quality of the overall educational experiences for students. All of this has happened in the midst of increasing expectations for high-quality continued services, new residence and campus life facilities, and concern for increasing costs to students. Coupled with the recent economic recession and the resulting decline in available resources, these demands have seriously stressed student affairs organizations. What does the future hold, and how can student affairs organizations adapt to the increasing and changing demands? How can university leaders use existing resources to address these and other emerging challenges with a sense of opportunity rather than dread? How can organizations be redesigned to sustain change while achieving excellence?

Over the years, student affairs organizations have grown and become increasingly complex. Most of the theory and research attention has been devoted to expanding the professional understanding of student development, student learning, and the impact of programs and services on students. Little attention has been given to enhancing the profession's understanding of student affairs organizations or to applying existing and emerging organizational theory to improving organizational effectiveness. Anyone interested in organization-related issues had to turn to business-oriented organizational behavior literature and then translate it to student affairs organizations. As we look to the future, it is increasingly clear that attention to student affairs organizational design and behavior will be critical to student affairs organizational effectiveness. As practitioners and scholars, we need to develop a better understanding of our organizations, how they work, how we interact within them, and how we can better orchestrate and lead within them.

Over the last century, a complex body of organizational theory rich in new ideas has emerged that can be useful to enhancing student affairs organizations. This book grew out of a desire to provide a basic translation of existing and emerging organizational behavior theory to the organizational context of student affairs practice. We, the authors of this book, have all served as practitioners within student affairs and now teach and advise graduate students and future leaders in the field. We, along with our students, have struggled to understand and apply existing organizational behavior and environmental theory to student affairs and higher education organizations. Through these experiences, we have uncovered large gaps in the availability of materials and applications, and have found those that do exist to be focused primarily on business organizations. The few that were useful in the context of higher education were, in many cases, overly complex or ineffective in addressing the unique attributes of student affairs organizations.

This book is intended to provide practitioners, graduate students, interns, and student affairs leaders with an introduction of fundamental theory and applications they might find useful in understanding the organizational world of student affairs. The book is organized by major conceptual areas from within the organizational theory field and presents the major theoretical developments of these constructs over time. Our intent is not to present every theoretical idea or a thorough summary of all related research, but to provide, in an organized fashion, key ideas and concepts related to organizational behavior and change theory so that such theories can be useful to student affairs practitioners. The book also presents fresh ways of approaching organizational assessment so that it might be applicable to your efforts to enhance organizational effectiveness. Where possible, the book also incorporates the work of student affairs and higher education scholars who have provided insights into our understanding of student affairs organizations. Finally, we use a reflective summary process at the end of each chapter to help readers integrate and apply the theory to their own practice.

The foundation of this book is built on values and perspectives that support the human dimension of organizational life. We recognize that organizational dynamics and systems transcend the individual experience and provide an important context for understanding collective and systemic behavior in student affairs organizations. At the same time, we recognize that individuals live their lives within organizations, craft their professional identities within organizations, and trust that organizations operate ethically and humanely. We believe that much of the early theory related to organizations was built on assumptions and values that viewed both the organization and the individual members as units of operating efficiencies and that the basic structures, cultures, and overall systems were built around these mechanistic values and assumptions. We also acknowledge that student affairs organizations and higher education in general were greatly influenced by the organizational developments within business, and many organizational attributes in student affairs have evolved from these theories and practices.

We also hold that innovative thinking, perceptions, and values regarding organizations have moved away from these ideas and now promote values that are more organic, relational, and human-centered, where structure is more fluid and culture is more dynamic and inclusive. We believe that sound and healthy organizational behavior supports professional development and growth, promotes organizational learning, and engages inclusive leadership and change processes. We also recognize the importance of both individual and team contributions to achieving the organization's mission and goals. The theories and approaches presented in this book support these underlying perceptions, values, and principles, with the goal of enhancing organizational behavior and effectiveness from these perspectives.

Individuals live their lives within a variety of organizations, but one of the most critical for many of us is the organization in which we work. For the purposes of this book, we are examining student affairs organizations as work-related entities, and the application of theory to these types of organizations within higher educational settings. We recognize that students are served by these organizations but, for the most part, the focus of this effort is on the work and the employee dimensions of the organizations and not directly on the students they serve.

We also assume that paradox is built into organizational life. We agree that many organizational behavior theories recognize this phenomenon and assert it as a way of being able to manage the complexity within organizations. Understanding the existence of paradox enables one to transcend paradigms and to hold apparently contradictory ideas and assertions in one's mind at the same time. Accepting the existence of paradox within organization theory assumes that the organizational context is everything. It holds that nothing is generalizable and yet everything is applicable to the context (Love & Estanek, 2004, p. 23). This enables us to recognize the unique characteristics of each student affairs organization and at the same time apply theory to practice across the field of student affairs.

Through this lens, we are also able to see the organization from various perspectives and understand the many dimensions of theoretical ideas and applications that simultaneously have relevance. This mindset is possible because "everything is filtered through the experiences and sense making skills of individuals involved in the particular context of application" (Love & Estanek, 2004, p. 23). We recognize that student affairs organizations are not static entities; they are constantly changing and adapting through the ongoing behavior of their members. The perceptions of each organization vary with each member and are different when viewed from different levels of the organization. There is no one way to view an organization and there is no single theory that can adequately explain an organization and its associated behavior.

Our book begins, in chapter 1, by exploring the current state of student affairs and higher education organizations. We discuss why an understanding of organizational behavior theory is essential for addressing current organizational needs and positioning student affairs organizations for the future. We present a snapshot of the organization of student affairs and the various attributes that make it unique as an organization within higher education. We briefly discuss key epistemological perspectives, and we explore some common organizational behavior myths and paradigms and how they affect thinking, acting, and understanding within student affairs organizations.

In chapter 2, we present a brief history of organizational behavior theory through a summary of key constructs that have affected its evolution. We explore relevant broad-based organizational theories, including general systems theory, organizational contingency theory, and social construct theory. We also present the organization reframing theory of Bolman and Deal (2008), which has already been used extensively within student affairs organizations. In addition, we examine the aspect of culture and the key theories that have emerged to explain and frame the concept of organizational culture and its relevance to student affairs.

In chapter 3, we explore the environmental context of student affairs, how the organization interacts with both the internal and external environments. We consider how a successful organization aligns its efforts to respond to changing environmental factors and how it views and supports its understanding of place and space as critical to its survival in a dynamic educational arena. In chapter 4, we examine the human dimension of organizations through a review of individual attributes, human need and motivation, social comparison theory, and organizational learning theory. We discuss the importance of attending to human relations, staff development, and reward and feedback systems. The concept of groups and teams as effective ways to engage participation and improve decision making is explored.

Chapter 5 presents the dimensions of structure and design theory and discusses why student affairs organizations need to think differently about how they organize their resources. We discuss the various principles of design and highlight emerging organic models of structure that support more fluid connections and dynamic interactions with the environment. Chapter 6 focuses on the context and process of organizational change and the supporting theories of organizational development and change. We specifically address the issues of decision making, power and politics, conflict, and communication within student affairs organizations.

The roles of assessment and evaluation are explored as significant components of organizational behavior in chapter 7. A new conceptual framework for organizational assessment is presented as a model and example of the organizational assessment process. Chapter 8 discusses the emerging approaches to leadership in the context of organizational change. Chapter 9 looks to the future of student affairs organizations and how practitioners might use organizational theory to sustain change and enhance their organization's ability to adapt to new and emerging challenges.

Although space limitations have precluded considering the vast number of theories related to organizational behavior, we have highlighted key ideas and theories that we believe have a direct relationship to student affairs organizations. We strongly encourage you to delve into primary sources and the extensive literature in more detail to truly understand and appreciate the rich influence that these theories and their supporting research can have on student affairs organizations. Essentially, this entire book focuses on how student affairs organizations, through a more thorough understanding of organizational theory and behavior, can address emerging issues and sustain themselves in the midst of the changing environment and the challenges they will face.

References

Bolman, L. G., & Deal, T. E. (2008). *Reframing organizations: Artistry, choice and leadership.* San Francisco: Jossey-Bass.

Love, P. G., & Estanek, S. M. (2004). *Rethinking student affairs practice.* San Francisco: Jossey-Bass.

THE STUDENT AFFAIRS ORGANIZATION AS CONTEXT

Dr. Chris Jones sat staring at the organizational chart for the division of student affairs at her institution. The chart appeared as a one-page, multilayer graphic representing operational units, with each unit separated as a functional entity. The boxes of units were shaped into a traditional pyramid diagram with multiple levels; the senior student affairs officer (SSAO) was at the top of the structure.

As the SSAO within the division, Dr. Jones was expected to orchestrate the resources that had been entrusted to her and to guide the division toward meeting the mission and goals of the institution. She affirmed to herself that this operational arrangement had responded to the needs of the students and the institution over the years, and had only received some very minor changes over the past decade or so. Given the increasing demands and the simultaneous reduction in resources, however, she was increasingly concerned that the current organizational design no longer represented what was needed to serve the changing needs of students or the institution. She knew that the current functional unit structures were staffed by competent and experienced directors who, in her mind, managed their limited resources well, and led groups of dedicated staff who provided high-quality programs and services to students.

At the same time, Dr. Jones's observations and instincts told her that these units could be more effective, collaborative, and innovative. And they could be integrating their efforts more strategically across departmental boundaries both within the division and across the institution. She wondered how the organization could become more responsive to the changing demands and more creative in meeting the increasing needs of an increasingly global clientele.

She knew that there was something unique and special about the culture within the various units and that this culture collectively defined the division and set it apart from other academic units within the institution. But she worried that the strengths within this culture were not being crafted and shaped to maximize its strengths and to sharpen and discipline its focus on meeting institution and division goals. She often felt like the division was being burdened with unrealistic demands and was not always the most effective in addressing the challenges coming from the external environment. For too long now, they had taken on more, doing more with less, and not prioritizing or getting rid of programs and services that were no longer productive.

Underneath it all, Dr. Jones was not certain that she had enough knowledge to assess her organization's effectiveness or to implement the changes that might be needed. She admitted to herself that she knew little about the theories and research that had developed within the areas of organizational behavior, especially those related to design, change, and assessment. Most of these areas of study were not included in her professional preparation education, and her attempts to understand and utilize management literature over the years were met with limited success. She often found that the translation from business to education was difficult and sometimes nearly impossible to navigate. She decided that before she could address the fundamental organizational questions she was raising, she needed to know more. She also needed to be able to translate this knowledge so that she could apply it to her student affairs organization. She knew that many, if not most, of her staff members were in the same situation and that they too needed to better understand organizational behavior theory and related research so that they could be engaged in making their organization more effective. She believed that the future was going to present many new and complex challenges and that her organization needed to be staffed and structured to be able to address those challenges head on. How might she attain the knowledge and skills needed to understand her current organization, assess its strengths and weaknesses, and adapt existing resources to enable the sustainable change that would be critical to their future?

Scenarios like Dr. Jones' are routinely faced by student affairs leaders and practitioners within collegiate institutions across the country. Today, they find themselves in the midst of daunting challenges and rapid change. Their organizational designs have served them well over the years, but the issues and expectations that they face are raising questions about their organization's viability in the future. Because the profession of student affairs has moved to a greater focus on administration and environmental change, the ideas and applications that make up the growing fields of organizational behavior and organizational development have become increasingly important to higher education and to student affairs.

Many student affairs practitioners face challenges that are compounded by their own uncertainty about whether they have the knowledge and tools to understand and assess their organization's effectiveness. They have built their practice with a focus on serving students and building effective services and programs to meet the needs of students. They have been trained in student development and learning theory and its application to the student-focused learning environment on college campuses. But as practitioners, they have not had formal professional development, for the most part, in the area of organizational behavior and change theory. Many do not have easy access to this information and/or do not have the time to search for and decipher the enormous amount of organizational behavior literature that has evolved over the last 75 years. Even for those who studied formal organizational development as part of their graduate preparation, the books and materials that were available for use had to be translated from the business environment to the higher education and student affairs environments. This process was not always easy, nor was it always completely successful.

Despite the movement to make higher education operate more like a business, the organization context, the external environment, and the multitude of issues that student affairs organizations face are different than U.S. or multinational businesses. Today, student affairs practitioners increasingly realize that they need more knowledge and skills to manage their organizations and navigate the changes that will be needed to face future challenges. This book is intended to help practitioners begin that journey.

The Organization as a Concept

We begin the exploration of organizational theory and its applications by defining more clearly what is meant by the term *organization*. Organizations are actually abstract, complex entities that exist within a larger external environment (see chapter 3). They consist of units made up of individuals generally organized to address a mission and a set of goals utilizing established work-related behaviors (see chapters 2 and 4). They can be formal or informal in their design and structure. Many are legally constituted entities that have legal and institutional status, with charters and/or bylaws of governance. As conceptual entities, they generally include the intersecting components of structure, culture, social structure, and technology, which are all infused by the concepts of power and influence. Student affairs organizations contain all of these components and the intersection of these components form the unique characteristics of student affairs organizations.

Individuals live their lives within a variety of organizations, but one of the most critical for many of us are the organizations in which we work. For the purposes of this book, we examine student affairs organizations as work-related entities, and the application of theory to these types of organizations within higher educational settings. We recognize that students are the ones served by these organizations, but for the most part, the focus of this book is on the work and the employee dimensions of the organizations and not directly on the students they serve.

We assume that student affairs organizations are part of a larger, loosely connected college or university organization. As a result, these organizations can be viewed as unique entities operating within both the larger collegiate organization and within the external environment. From the perspective of the student affairs organization, both the larger collegiate organization and the external community environment are treated as though they were part of the external environment.

Organizational Studies

Organizations are complex entities, and they can be viewed and understood from a variety of perspectives. Over the years, the study of organizations has been divided into a number of subfields of study. The area or body of knowledge we call organizational behavior essentially studies human behavior in organizations. It is comprised of an interdisciplinary body of knowledge with strong ties to the social sciences. Over the last 75 years, it has evolved into an applied academic discipline that is focused on understanding individual and group behavior, interpersonal processes, team behavior, and organizational dynamics, with the goal of improving the performance of organizations, the individuals and groups within them, and the quality of work life overall.

Another area within organizational studies is the broader area of organizational theory. This perspective on organizations focuses on the overarching attempt to explain, understand, and theorize about organizations. Many would conclude that the field of organizational behavior is an allied area of study within the larger area of organizational theory. For the purposes of this book, some organizational theories are discussed as they relate to structure, culture, design, and the organizational environment. We believe it is difficult to understand organizational behavior without understanding some aspects of key organizational theory and its impact on human behavior.

In the area of organizational study there is another subunit related specifically to organizational change and the change process. It is often referred to as organizational development (OD). Again it becomes difficult to discuss organizational change or OD without an essential understanding and discussion of organizational theory and organizational behavior. Throughout this book, we explore theory and applications from all three areas of organizational study, with the assumption that they are intertwined and nearly impossible to separate without considerable unnecessary confusion and added complexity. Second, all three are important to enhancing our understanding of how student affairs organizations work and how they can become more effective.

Epistemological Perspectives on Organizational Theory

Today, there is a general consensus within the fields of organizational studies that organizations can and generally should be studied from varied perspectives. However, this is a rather new assumption (see chapter 2). Many of the theoretical ideas that have emerged in recent years are the direct result of these expanded ways of understanding organizations. The complexity of organizations and the richness of viewing organizations from multiple perspectives are also seen as advantages in helping to address the multifaceted issues that organizations and their leaders face (Bess & Dee, 2008a, p. 46).

Most organizational theorists recognize at least three general epistemological perspectives for organizing and viewing organizations. Most existing theory has been formulated from one or a combination of these perspectives. (See Bess & Dee, 2008a, and Hatch & Cunliffe, 2006, for a more detailed analysis of these perspectives.) Summaries of their perspectives are presented in the following chapter subsections. We refer to these perspectives throughout this book, and we trust that the readers will come to view organizations from various theoretical perspectives.

Positivist or Post-positivism

This perspective assumes that you can discover what truly happens within organizations from the use of the scientific method through measuring and categorizing behavior. It also assumes that there is a single reality and, through objective statistical analysis, one can dissect the various parts and then examine the parts in relation to each other. The results can then be used to understand, explain, and predict the most effective and efficient ways to organize. This perspective was the only accepted perspective for understanding organizations for most of the 20th century, and it still retains a strong position within academic circles as the most reliable way to study organizations. Although not all positivists agree on what reality is, they all agree that they can discover it and derive models for explaining how organizations work.

Social Constructionist

This perspective rejects the assumption that there is a single reality. It holds that individuals and the communities in which they exist construct their own reality based on their experiences and their beliefs. Because there is no single reality, this perspective seeks to reconcile different concepts of reality through communication and dialogue and by emphasizing flexibility and adaptability. This perspective holds that knowledge is related to the knower and truth is socially constructed and shifts and changes over time. As a result, there is no attempt to define universal principles; rather, there is a reliance on contextual knowledge that may not be generalized to other organizations. At the center of this perspective is the notion that organizations are unique, and what works for one organization may not work for any other organization. This perspective has gained considerable attention and has fostered the development of a number of qualitative approaches to studying organizations.

Postmodernism

This perspective assumes that knowledge is not an accurate reflection of truth because meaning is not fixed and is constantly changing. As a result, those who operate from this perspective do not seek truth and do not commit to any philosophical position. They focus instead on challenging all forms of power as a means of exposing sources of domination and decrying privilege. This perspective holds that there is no certainty, a certain amount of chaos is inevitable, and conflict and the challenges to power are necessary. Traditional approaches to understanding organizations are viewed as repressive, and new inclusive means for understanding are sought as alternatives.

All three of these paradigms have and can be used to understand higher education and student affairs organizations. Bess and Dee (2008a) provide a summary of how these paradigms have been used within higher education related research. The positivist framework has been used primarily to study university governance, leadership, and decision making. The social constructivist perspective reflects some of the new and emerging frameworks for studying culture and symbolic frameworks. The postmodern perspective provides a framework for many higher education critiques and a lens for radically restructuring higher education (Bess & Dee, 2008a, pp. 48–49).

For those who are student affairs practitioners, viewing the organization from one of these three perspectives can create very different views of the organization and are likely to lead to very different understandings of the issues, problems, and strategies to be taken. For example, you are a scholar practitioner and you want to understand your staff's attitudes and values about their work environment. As a result, you seek ways to improve organizational effectiveness and efficiency. However, you would view this issue very differently depending on which epistemological approach you favored. If you viewed the issue from the *positivist perspective*, you would probably view the issue as one that can be assessed objectively. Through careful analysis of variables that affect worker motivation and performance, you would come to an understanding of what needed to be done to address the concern. As a practitioner, you would be likely to research the key variable that would affect worker attitudes and values, and then try to assess these variables within your organization using prescribed research methods and statistical analysis. You might seek to compare and contrast the results of these assessments with benchmarked norms or with findings from previous studies to determine the reality for all the staff members in the organization. Then you would attempt to apply strategies from your research that might improve the situation in the direction of the organization's goals.

But maybe you are a scholar practitioner who views the issue from the *social constructionist perspective*. In this case, you would probably approach the issue as though it were uniquely defined and understood within the culture of your specific organization. You would assume that the members of the organization had their own individual realities related to how they viewed and valued the organization, their work, and their interactions with others in the organization. You would recognize that individuals view the organization from their own organizational perspectives and their "realities" of the organization is influenced by their positions in the organization, their personal experiences, and their biases. You would try to determine what the various perspectives related to the issue were and to find any common ground related to a shared set of attitudes and values. Your approach would focus on communication, listening, and understanding. This would probably be done through individual interviews and/or focus groups in the context of trying to improve communication, and then you would develop a shared consensus about how to enhance and improve the work environment. As a scholar practitioner, you would not assume there was a single best way to improve the situation. Instead, you would try to find the common voice of how to proceed to achieve the organization's goals.

Viewing the issue of attitudes and values related to the work environment from the *postmodern perspective* would result in a third and very different approach to the issue. The postmodernist perspective would be critical of the current organizational structure and culture, and you would seek to deconstruct the basic assumptions of hierarchy and power held by the organization's members. You would be likely to seek to educate current members about how knowledge, power, and control are linked and how hierarchical systems tend to perpetuate certain ideas and values over others. You would probably promote the creation of healthy tensions and conflicts that recognize difference and downplay attempts at consensus, holding that healthy conflict improves creativity and strengthens organizational effectiveness. You would stress the importance of paradox and ambiguity as keys to improving the functioning of the organization, and seek to give voice to traditionally marginalized and silenced groups.

A new research approach, *the multiparadigm approach*, has recently emerged. It focuses on examining and researching organizations from multiple perspectives simultaneously (Kezar & Dee, 2006). These combined approaches provide for a more comprehensive perspective of the organization and enable researchers to examine the complexity, diversity, and depth of organizations (Bess & Dee, 2008a). Because of their combined complexity and the intricacies of design, these approaches have not yet gained wide use, but they do show promise of providing new understandings of organizations.

Throughout this book, we refer to specific perspectives and paradigms. Thus, you will have the opportunity to consider theory from various perspectives. In fact, most theory has a connection to one of the existing perspectives and may have evolved from examining an earlier theory from a new perspective. An important concept to keep in mind is that theories and models are steppingstones for organizing and understanding phenomena, and they are building blocks on which new ideas are built (they also emerged from new ideas, so the process is self-perpetuating). New ideas rarely materialize from thin air; they generally develop from viewing phenomena with a new lens or from a different perspective.

For the practitioner, the intent is not to get caught in classic dualistic thinking of either-or, or new versus old. Rather, as Love and Estanek (2004) so poignantly discussed, it is helpful to view new perspectives as transcending paradigms. Paradigm transcendence is the next step toward thinking differently. The concept of paradigm transcendence is different from Kuhn's (1970) concept of paradigm shift. Rather than a paradigm shift, what has occurred over the last half century is paradigm transcendence. A paradigm shift implies that there is a change from the old to the new, with the old being discredited or discarded. The two paradigms cannot coexist; they are mutually exclusive. In its own way, the concept of paradigm shift is an example of dualistic thinking. To transcend involves rising above, being greater than, going beyond the limits of something and even incorporating it. When applied to paradigms, transcendence implies that there is the old way and the new way. Both exist and both have legitimacy depending on the context (Love & Estanek, 2004, p. 15).

Throughout this book, we intend to build on theory and to portray briefly the evolution of ideas over time. We hope to present theory and ideas as part of a process of understanding that is not static; theory is extended and new elements and ideas are introduced to help us see new connections, and multiple perspectives and ways of incorporating ideas. Our goal is to engage in the process of exploring new ways of seeing and understanding organizations.

Student Affairs as an Area of Organizational Study

Even though student affairs is increasingly viewed as a crucial component of higher education and vital to its mission, little has been researched and written about the nature, functioning, and effectiveness of student affairs organizations. Although there is considerable organization behavior and organizational change theory and research that has been applied to corporations and the business sector, little of this theory and research has been applied to educational organizations, especially student affairs organizations. In recent years, new writing and research has emerged related to higher education organizations (Bess & Dee, 2008a, b; Bergquist & Pawlak, 2008; Birnbaum, 1988; Kezar, 2001), but most of these works have been presented from the administrative and faculty perspectives of collegiate organization cultures. Unfortunately, these works have essentially overlooked the cultural and organizational aspects of student affairs or have buried them deep within their analysis.

We make the assumption that the student affairs organization is a rather unique organizational entity within the greater institution in which it exists.

It exhibits a distinct culture, design, and organizational structure, and generally operates somewhat independently from the faculty and administrative cultures within the greater institution. At the same time, student affairs units are part of a greater institutional system and operate as an organization within an organization. These units are managed, influenced, and at times controlled by the greater organization. The conflicts between and among cultures and the misunderstandings that arise create organizational tensions that are likely to contribute to some of the unique features of organizational behavior in student affairs. As a result, these rather unique organizational dimensions provide an important and often neglected area of organizational study.

Although unique to their institutions, student affairs organizations *do* share some common attributes that make them somewhat similar from one educational institution to the next. Over the last century, the profession of student affairs has emerged with a set of professional standards and ethical practices that have come to guide the practice of student affairs roles and responsibilities. A large group of graduate preparation programs have been developed to train and socialize student affairs practitioners, and these practitioners are hired and move among various student affairs organizations. These shared values, strategies, and benchmarking processes, as well as the definition of roles and responsibilities, have shaped the design and practice of student affairs across the country to create organizations that are consistently similar in many ways.

The Broad Context of Higher Education

Higher education in the United States at the end of the first decade of the 21st century provides an enterprise model of unmatched complexity in size, type, cultural characteristics, and changing demographics. As a major American enterprise or social institution, and despite increasing challenges from abroad, it retains its status as the premier system of higher education in the world, and it also reflects the most diversity. In 2008, there were over 4,500 postsecondary collegiate institutions in the United States. These institutions enrolled nearly 17 million students from within the United States and from across the world. Over 60 percent of high school graduates in the United States enroll in some form of postsecondary collegiate institutions each year. The enrolled students are increasingly diverse in terms of background, gender, race and ethnicity, sexual orientation, age, religion, and socioeconomic status (U.S. Department of Education, 2008).

There are many types of higher education institutions in the United States: research/doctoral, master's, bachelor's, two-year, and professional. Some are institutes and conservatories, as well as vocational technical institutions. These institutions are public, private, for profit, single sex, and/or community-based. Some have historically served Black and Hispanic populations. Some are tribal colleges; some, including military academies, are specialty institutions. Each type has a unique mission and history, and serves different types of students and regions of the country.

Their organizational structures vary depending on the size of the institution, scope and mission, history and desires of the senior leadership. At the same time, they share some of the same goals, values, and organizational structural components and have retained many characteristics of centuries past (Bergquist & Pawlak, 2008; Birnbaum, 1988; Kezar, 2001). Higher education institutions have been found to be a compilation of many distinct organizational cultures (Bergquist & Pawlak, 2008). Despite efforts to control higher education and have it adopt corporate structural components and practices, the system and its units remain loosely allied organizations within a larger institutional framework (Kezar, 2001). Cultural components related to faculty governance, tenure, individually based faculty performance criteria, and discipline-based departments make the culture of higher education institutions distinct from business and government organizations. Within collegiate institutions, the larger organizational cultures are strongly influenced by individualistic work-effort values, and they consist of numerous discipline-based cultural units (Bergquist & Pawlak, 2008). Student affairs can be viewed as one of many distinct cultural subunits within these organizations; as a result, it can be viewed and studied as an organization within an organization.

Higher education institutions today face perplexing challenges in the areas of financial pressures, technological demands, changing faculty, changing pedagogy, and the speed and demands from increasing global changes. The needed change in organizations to address these challenges has accelerated "beyond tinkering" for most institutions (Kezar & Eckel, 2002). At the same time, change has not been easily achieved within collegiate institutions, and few have been successful in dealing with large-scale, transformational change (Kezar & Eckel, 2002).

The Student Affairs Organization

Over the last 50 years, student affairs organizations have emerged as fairly complex entities within higher educational institutions, and they are one of many cultural organizations within the collegiate organization. Their roles and complexities were initially propelled by the tremendous growth in numbers, diversity, and needs of students accessing higher education after World War II. In recent decades, the demands of consumer-oriented students and their families for greater access, additional educational and service amenities, and services for diverse populations of students have pushed institutions to add services, programs, and facilities to lure and retain students (Kuk, 2009; Manning, Kinzie, & Schuh, 2006). These organizations reflect the same components as other organizations: structure, culture, social structure, and technology; yet these components reflect some distinctive characteristics.

Student Affairs Organizational Structures

Today, student affairs organizations consist mainly of functional hierarchical structures, with unique characteristics and organizational practices that are distinct from other academic units in the collegiate institutional structure. They are essentially administrative and service-oriented in focus and mission. Some version of this entity exists in most higher education institutions, but its title, the units comprising it, and its structure may differ. Budgets and resources may come from tuition and fees, but they may also be provided as part of student fees or fees for services. The programs and services they provide to students, families, and other constituents are varied and complex, with no uniform definition of what units and services constitute a student affairs organization (Ambler, 2000; Hirt, 2006; Kuk, 2009; Kuk & Banning, 2009).

What is common to these organizations across different collegiate settings is that they share a mission that focuses on serving the needs of students by providing services and programs that support the academic success and the social and personal development of students, and by creating campus environments that support the specific educational mission of the institution (Kuk, 2009). These collections of programs and services appear to be increasingly organized to meet the institutions' missions and goals and may reflect many structural characteristics of similar higher education institutional types. Student affairs organizations at research universities are increasingly structured like those at other research universities, and student affairs organizations at community colleges are increasingly structured more like those at other community colleges (Hirt, 2006; Kuk, 2009; Kuk & Banning, 2009). These student affairs organizations are generally hierarchical and multilayered, and even when they report through academic affairs, they generally operate as "siloed" structures, that is, independent of other units within the collegiate organization. Teams and committees are essential components of student affairs practice, but these structures are fleeting and not generally built into the fabric of the division's organizational design.

Culture of Student Affairs

Student affairs is often viewed, both internally and externally, as a "cultural island," distinctly different from other academic and administrative units. Historically the focus of these units has been on serving and interacting primarily with students, and only more recently in partnering with faculty and other campus units to focus on student learning (Manning et al., 2006). The cultures of student affairs organizations generally revolve around the values of inclusivity, student development, and broadly defined student learning and success. They view the educational experience as one that is holistic, multidimensional, and focused on integrating student experiences both in and outside the classroom. These organizations often sit at the epicenter of the campus diversity, social justice, student engagement, and environmental sustainability issues and programs. The underlying values and the efforts to engage students in these issues (Cook & Lewis, 2007) have not always been viewed as consistent with the academic and curricular mission of the institution as viewed by faculty. As a result, these issues have generally been addressed within the cultural domain of the co-curricular component of campus life and are seen as tangential to the core academic mission of the institution. Over the years, student affairs has been charged with managing campus life, and the faculty have focused on curricular and intellectual development. More recently, there have been attempts to partner around the values associated with student learning, but these efforts have been inconsistent and have not been incorporated into the ongoing structure and culture of the institution.

Over time, student affairs units have become viewed as more critical for ensuring the overall success of the students served by the institution. At the same time, these units are not consistently viewed as partners and colleagues with faculty in the teaching and learning role of the institution. Student affairs is rarely considered an essential part of the fabric of the institution's organizational structure and has increasingly been placed outside the executive decision-making structure of the organization, reporting through academic affairs.

In the context of shrinking institutional resources, student affairs organizations are often considered more expendable than academic units. Collaborations with academic and administrative units are generally initiated by student affairs staff with infrequent and inconsistent reciprocity from academic units. Despite efforts to build bridges between the two parallel cultural worlds of academics and student affairs, they remain distinct and different.

Within their functional administrative structures, various student affairs units also develop unique subcultures, with their own operating practices, values, norms, and ways of interacting with each other and the rest of the campus. Because of their specific functional foci, they often view the institution through the lens of their roles, and they are often isolated from interaction with other parts of the institution that are not directly related to their specific responsibilities.

For example, individuals who work as housing professionals are responsible for students who live in campus residence halls. These operations are often the largest units with student affairs and operate with the largest budgets, especially if they operate as an auxiliary unit. Because they focus on students who live in campus housing and this focus requires attention around the clock, staff members generally do not engage with other units within the institution on a regular or ongoing basis. It is not unusual for these units to have duplicate programming, advising, and other service units. For example, they may have their own technology and maintenance staff as well as human resources and educational programming components.

These units often develop their own culture, norms, and practices and often view themselves as housing professionals rather than student affairs professionals. They attend housing- and residence-life-related conferences and professional development activities and bond with other housing professionals at other institutions. They generally view the rest of the collegiate organization in terms of housing-related issues and, because of time constraints, they probably limit their interactions to housing-related concerns. They generally have little interaction with faculty and other student affairs staff members who are not directly related to housing activities unless they are assigned to a division or campus committee.

The varied cultural nuances created by organizational unit subcultures often play out within student affairs organizations and may contribute to a perceived isolation and an internal focus of the student affairs organization activities. These distinct organizational characteristics present some interesting challenges both within the larger context of the institution, as well as among and between the various units and departments within the student affairs organization itself.

Social Structure of Student Affairs

The social structure has a strong and almost dominant focus within student affairs organizations. Interactions, staff meetings, and social programming are central to the working of student affairs organizations. The social interactions within student affairs organizations are generally casual and informal in nature, although the organization itself is hierarchical in structure. Titles are not generally used in day-to-day interactions, and socializing among staff at various levels within the organization occurs frequently. It is also very common to employ students as part-time workers, and they are often treated more as colleagues than students. Celebrations, recognitions, and social events are viewed as essential components of working with students and developing staff.

As nonfaculty professionals, student affairs staff generally do not have a voice in the campus governance process and rarely have vesting and employment rights comparable to tenured faculty. Some staff may have annual or multiyear contracts or belong to a faculty or professional union, but the lack of employment security and equality with faculty can be a focus of staff concern. Despite a stronger focus on collaborative efforts in recent years, staff members may still perceive that they are second-class citizens. Status and governance concerns outside their immediate unit or outside the broader student affairs arena are a focus of interest and concern among many student affairs staff, but internal student affairs equity and fair treatment are critical issues for most student affairs staff members. Staff members generally talk among themselves and seem to know the nuances of employee treatment, salary, and workload issues. In many public institutions, salaries are public information and are often hot topics of discussion among staff members. At all levels of the organization, staff members view their peers within student affairs as the group with which they actively compare themselves, even though they may have concerns about comparisons more broadly across the institution.

Rewards and recognition are important to the social structure of the student affairs staff. Although the staff members may value group efforts, they also value personal recognition. Given limited fiscal resources, rewards are generally limited to personal recognitions and sometimes staff development opportunities. Titles and internal promotions are often viewed as important vehicles for rewarding and recognizing staff effort and longevity. In light of the hierarchical structure of student affairs organizations, as well as a larger organizational expectation that most position replacement openings be posted publicly, the opportunities to utilize internal promotions as rewards are limited and can be very political. Cross-training and lateral opportunities for growth and change can serve to keep staff members engaged in their roles and committed to the organization. Given the focus on job specialization and experience, this approach has not been utilized very often.

Within the last 25 years, student affairs staffs have increasingly been hired with professional training and expertise. Professional staff members are generally expected to have a master's degree, and ongoing professional development is increasingly held as a professional expectation. And the changing needs of increasingly diverse students and the realities of community expectations and increased responsibilities continue to mean ongoing training, education, and more effective mentoring. Staff development efforts are an important collective social interaction within student affairs organizations, and attendance at professional association conferences has become a primary vehicle for supporting these efforts. Resources for professional development are often the first resources to be reduced in times of budget tightening, and lost resources are not always replaced when the financial picture improves. Over the years, student affairs staff members have increasingly been expected to cover the costs of their professional development and memberships in professional associations.

Although the personal and professional rewards of helping students achieve academic and personal success are great, staff turnover and burnout is an ever-present reality in many student affairs organizations, especially at the non-managerial levels, and many worry about the ability of these organizations to sustain effectiveness in the face of increasing expectations.

Technology of Student Affairs

The technology, the methods for engaging the work of student affairs, has been both individual- and small-group-focused since its inception. It has been a labor-intensive field with hands-on direct services and program delivery. Over time, the focus has shifted from counseling, advising, and providing direct services to one that also focuses on creating learning and cultural environments that support student success. General programming, trainers to train paraprofessional student facilitators and advisers, and triage methods of intervention have become standard practice in the delivery of programs and services.

Electronic technology within student affairs organizations has become increasingly sophisticated and attuned to the desires and needs of students who have been raised in a technology-focused culture. Clearly restrained by costs and the availability of resources, technological applications for serving students have been generally infused in most aspects of the student affairs programs and services. From recruiting to admissions, registration, development of social networks, student climate assessments, podcast programs, residence halls and student centers equipped with technology, online counseling, and educational efforts, the use of technology has permeated student affairs organizations. Few areas of student affairs service and program delivery are not integrated with both technology applications and face-to-face interactions. Student affairs departments have hired students to assist in the development and management of these efforts in order to both manage costs and to stay cutting-edge wherever possible. The integration of technological applications with a focus on novel and creative approaches at low cost has become a centerpiece of student affairs organizational efforts. At the same time, this emphasis on the use of cutting-edge technology has also created generational communication and performance tensions, and differences among student affairs staff members.

Debunking Organizational Myths

Before considering new organizational theories and applications, we would like to utilize a component of Kurt Lewin's (1951) classic change model process and "unfreeze" some existing myths that may have guided our understanding about organizational behavior within student affairs organizations. These ideas may have been part of an earlier theoretical position, but research and applications have proven them not to be as absolute as originally thought, or they have been expanded given the changing environmental demands on higher educational organizations. In other cases, the ideas may have been seriously limited, but reliance on them over time and the lack of sound theoretical understanding and research may have ingrained them into the fabric of our organizational understanding. In any case, these ideas have made their way into the study of organization behavior, and they continue to dominate our understanding. Thus, they can present false and/or limiting understandings, stymie change, and stifle organizational effectiveness.

The following ten organizational myths are examined to challenge your thinking and "unfreeze" your perceptions. Through examining these examples of organizational ideas, we hope to begin the process of considering and constructing new and emerging ways of understanding student affairs organizations.

Myth 1: Organizations Are Machines

From the initial discussions of organizations (Durkheim, 1893/1894; Taylor, 1911; Weber, 1924/1947), organizations have been viewed and designed from the Newtonian images of the universe.

We manage by separating things into parts, we believe that influence occurs as a direct result of force exerted from one person to another, we engage in complex planning for a world that we keep expecting to be predictable, and we search continually for better methods of objectively measuring and perceiving the world (Wheatley, 2006, p. 7).

For a number of early theorists, organizations and the people within them were seen as machines. The focus was on obtaining efficiency and effectiveness through control; conformity; and a separation of the human dimension of work, family, and community. Through the ideas and principles found in New Science, some theorists (Wheatley, 2006) are beginning to understand and design organizations differently than in the past. Organizations are being seen as open, holistic systems that can self-organize into new forms. They see change as a natural process that leads to renewal through chaos and conflict and that requires a focus on relationships, empowerment, and teaming as key elements in achieving organizational effectiveness.

> Our concept of organizations is moving away from the mechanistic creations that flourished in the age of bureaucracy. We now speak in earnest of more fluid, organic structures, of seamless organizations without boundaries. We are beginning to recognize organizations as whole systems, constructing them as learning organizations or as organic and noticing that people exhibit self organizing capacity. My own experience suggests that we can forego the despair created by common organizational events such as change, chaos, information overload, and entrenchment behavior if we recognize that organizations are living systems, possessing the same capacity to adapt and grow that is common to all life. (Wheatley, p. 15)

Myth 2: Structure Is Semipermanent

Organizations have long been designed with the notion that they are like a fortress, built to last. Structure has been viewed as the physical framework of the organization, essential for separating components for work production. Work has traditionally consisted of specialized tasks, organized as jobs or positions, performed by different people with different levels of authority and decision making. For example, the director of a career center has a different position, is in a different department, and is at a different level in the organizational structure than a food service worker in the student cafeteria. The theory and practice held that, through the use of structure, the work of an organization could be managed and understood. If a student needed career counseling, he was usually sent to the career center and not to food service. Having structures that were viewed as permanent made the organization of work predictable, seemingly efficient, and easier to locate within the institution. A permanent structure enabled those within and outside the organization to know where and at what level the work would be done. Within this conceptual mind-set, changes in structure were viewed as very disruptive and often avoided unless absolutely necessary. This has led to the thinking that, if change in structure is to be successful, it must be done early in the tenure of institutional leaders. Once set, the structure enabled the work to be performed effectively and efficiently.

This worked well when the organizational work flow was predictable and the outside environment presented few challenges that would require changes in the way things were done. Because the external environment has become more demanding and has created greater challenges to the organization, this old notion of structure has not worked as well as it did in the past.

Current organizational theory has shifted away from the notion that organizational structures should be fixed or permanent. In fact, newer organizational theories focus on organizational structures that are more fluid, adaptable, and seamless (Ashkenas, Ulrich, Jick, & Kerr, 2002; Galbraith, 2002; Goold & Campbell, 2002; Helgesen, 1995; Wheatley, 2006). Having structures that are more pliable and responsive enables the organization to be able to respond to changing needs and demands more quickly and to make better use of human and physical resources across the spectrum of work needs. Having fewer boundaries fosters collaboration and less turf protection. With a more fluid structure, organizations can shift gears and reposition resources more quickly and efficiently to address new and changing demands and challenges. Creating more fluid and adaptive structures can be achieved in a number of ways, for example, training some student affairs practitioners to be generalists rather than specialists or cross-training staff, and integrating programs and services beyond functional units when addressing student needs. Not associating pay or title with hierarchy and flattening the organizational structure, or having written job descriptions that define positions in narrow and specialized ways can help make adaptation to change a routine part of the organizational dynamics.

Myth 3: Functional Hierarchy Is the Best Way to Organize

The functional, hierarchical organizational model has been the way student affairs organizations have always been structured, just like other administrative units within collegiate organizations. What is most interesting is that academic department units in higher education generally operate successfully as flatter, more democratic organizations.

The hierarchical model was adopted from the industrial model of the early 20th century. It focused on creating vertical efficiency and control where information, work flow, and authority ran up and down the organizational ladder and decision making stayed at the top of the pyramid. The president and senior-level managers planned and made decisions; everyone else did what they were told to do. Work was distributed within the administrative organization based on functionality. Housing provided housing, counseling provided counseling, and financial aid provided financial aid. Rarely did anyone from financial aid deal with housing issues, or vice versa. This model was believed to create efficiency and consistency and to provide desired control. This model was especially necessary when organizations were growing beyond the face-to-face management of smaller, more personal organizations and becoming too complex for senior management to know everything that was going on in the organization. Financial systems and personnel systems were established to support the hierarchical model, ingraining them into the fabric of the organization and making it difficult to organize any other way.

As student affairs organizations have become more complex, the levels of hierarchy simply grew and expanded. As new demands emerged, new functional units were created and added to the hierarchical structure. When the number of units became too many or too cumbersome for the senior administrators to manage, midlevel administrators were added to provide additional oversight. In time, status, power, and rewards became associated with where on the pyramid a position resided and how many units were part of a manager's oversight. In most student affairs organizations, a common career goal was to climb the hierarchical ladder and eventually be at the top of the pyramid. Many career development conversations have been focused on how to navigate the maze of hierarchical levels to reach the top of the pyramid.

What is ironic is that academic units within collegiate organizations did not adopt the hierarchical model that appeared in administrative units. They did respond to the need for specialization, but the academic organizational response developed flatter, more collegiate, and more discipline-based structures with collective authority and governance processes. Department chairs are members of the faculty who are coordinating and conducting the needed administrative tasks of the department. They are not viewed as the supervisors of faculty or managers of the organizational unit in the same way that administrative units view the authority structure of their hierarchies. As collegiate organizations have taken on more corporate structural models, administrative organizations have been overlaid on top of discipline-based departments and have added some interesting, and at times conflicting, organizational dynamics to the collegiate culture.

It is not likely that hierarchical organizations are going away any time soon. They still possess many positive and essential dimensions in the way student affairs units need to be organized. At the same time, organizational design theory, research, and corporate practice has signaled that flatter, less hierarchical organizational structures are better able to address the emerging needs of most organizations. These new models are enabling organizations to be more resilient and responsive to the increasing speed of environmental demands on their programs and services (Goold & Campbell, 2002). These new approaches facilitate cross-unit collaborations that are currently blocked by functional fiefdoms. They also promote more efficient and effective communication, place decision making closer to the situation, and as a result provide more focused and timely responses (Galbraith, 2002).

A number of these emerging models attempt to combine the best outcomes of hierarchical, functional models with some new design elements to produce hybrid organizational models. Matrix organizations and lateral organizations are two models that are produced when some design elements are added to hierarchical models. These types of models are beginning to appear within student affairs organizations and show considerable promise for the future. (Organizational structure and design theories are discussed in chapter 5.)

Most student affairs organizations are also structured functionally. In a recent study (Kuk & Banning, 2009), all of the SSAO respondents indicated that they had a functional structure, and no one mentioned any other structure, even though some actually had elements of other designs as part of their structures. Functional structures have had some advantages for student affairs organizations, especially because their organizations have grown and increased in complexity. Functional organizations permitted gathering together similar types of work and enabled specializations, which created a level of efficiency. Specialization was viewed as necessary given the complexity of many of the issues and needs that were emerging in student affairs organizations and functional units. This rearrangement enabled specialists to be grouped together to provide the service and programs. Within student affairs administrative units, individuals and unit teams became experts in managing their assigned services and programs.

Functional structures have a number of weaknesses. First, they work best in small, less complex organizations where they are focused on a single service or a few services and have long operating cycles, and cross-functional communication and processes can be managed easily and most often face to face. Second, functional structures in larger organizations have a tendency to concentrate their focus within their specialization and on vertical communication up and down the organization. They find it cumbersome to collaborate across organizational boundaries, resulting in the development of organizational silos. Duplication of programs and services can appear as a result of isolation and the vertical focus within the functional units. These types of behavior and duplications are quite common in student affairs organizations, especially large organizations.

Many student affairs organizations have outgrown the utility of functional hierarchical structures. For the most part, student affairs organizations are increasingly complex, multifocused organizations that need to be able to respond to students, parents, the external community, and other constituent groups quickly and from multiple perspectives simultaneously. Collaboration and sharing information, resources, and expertise are critical components of everyday life. It is no longer effective to stay within one's functional unit and expect to meet the demands and challenges that are being presented.

Current organizational theories suggest that other organizational structures, such as *matrix structures* or *structured networks* can serve "as a means of achieving multi-dimensionality" (Goold & Campbell, 2002, p. 330). Multidimensional structures involve units that have responsibilities that cut cross unit boundaries. They require collaboration; staff members learn from each other and seek to create learning organizations (Senge, 1990). They create flatter, decentralized, fluid structures that minimize or eliminate hierarchy and place decision making and self-organizing in the hands of frontline staff (Goold & Campbell, 2002).

Myth 4: Control Is Essential

Control of behavior within organizations has been central to the study of organizational behavior and organizational design. It was an essential component in the mechanistic models of organizations espoused by early organizational theorists. This concept is strongly reflected in the desire for organizational leaders to control and manage individual and collective group behavior and, as a result, control productivity and quality. It is also reflected in the decision-making processes and levels of decision making, as well as the accountability mechanisms that occur in organizations. In early organizational theory, the application of control was a very visible component of how employees, work, and productivity were managed. Decision making was a top-down process and organizations sought to control work flow, productivity, and organizational culture so that behavior within the organization reflected the values, norms, and goals of the organization's leadership.

Wheatley (2006) stated that we have created problems for ourselves in organizations because we have confused control with order and continue to view organizations as machines.

> If people are machines, seeking to control makes sense. But if we live with the same forces intrinsic to all other life, then seeking to impose control through rigid structures is suicide. If we believe that there is no order to human activity except that imposed by the leader, that there is no self-regulation except that dictated by policy, if we believe that responsible leaders must have their hands into everything, controlling every decision, person and moment, then we cannot hope for anything except what we already have—a treadmill of frantic efforts that end up destroying our individual and collective vitality (p. 25).

Within student affairs organizations, control mechanisms have not been as overt as in other administrative organizations. But decision making, human resource issues, time accountability, and information related to finances and resources have often been kept centrally controlled as a means to maintain levels of organizational control.

In current and emerging organizational behavior theory, control gives way to enabling and supporting as the central management focus. The process of decision making is viewed as more efficient and effective if it is conducted closer to the situation or issue requiring a decision. Decision making is increasingly being placed in the hands of those closest to the problem and viewed as a more open and collaborative process.

The leader's new role is to provide staff members with the resources and information they need to make sound decisions, and the senior leader's role is to coach and enable staff members rather than control them. Improving communication, involving all levels of employees in setting goals and designing accountability measures, enables staff members to control their work flow and work process to the greatest extent possible. These new values are replacing the old focus on uniformity and control within organizational culture. Performance assessments are becoming two-way conversations more and more often, and they are used to enhance performance outcomes rather than punish negative performance. These dimensions of organizational culture are discussed in chapters 4 and 5. The changing nature of leadership and leadership roles are discussed in chapter 8.

Myth 5: Leadership Is a Top-Down, Solitary Activity

In traditional hierarchical organizations, leadership is at the top and is often the focus of organizational decision making. Senior leaders are viewed as the key players in an organization, taking credit for organizational success and the blame for mistakes and failures. Leaders make the decisions and convince others to carry out their vision and plans.

Current organizational leadership theories argue that this conception of leadership is misguided. Some believe that separating thinking from the doing is inappropriate and does not work effectively in most organizations. However, this approach to leadership and hierarchy is not easy to change because it is firmly tied to organizational power and authority, which have been central to organizational life, even in student affairs.

Helgesen (1995) introduces the metaphor of the web of inclusion as a means of describing the successful modern organization and its approach to leadership. "Inclusiveness draws on leadership from throughout the organization" (Helgesen, 1995, p. 110). The web of inclusion, with its decentralized structure, multiple lines of communication, and emphasis on the value of those who have not achieved top rank, provides an extraordinary means by which an organization can redefine the role of those on its frontlines, and so begin to coax the best from them. The inclusive nature of the web redistributes power throughout the organization, not least by broadening the range of connection and blurring the line between those who decide and those who act on those decisions (Helgesen, 1995, pp. 128–129).

Others present new approaches to organizational leadership as cultural enhancements that support pervasive leadership (Love & Estanek, 2004) and support risk taking, building relationships, and leadership capacity building. New approaches related to organizational leadership are discussed in chapter 8.

Myth 6: Change Is Predictable

Change is rarely predictable, but organizations spend a great deal of time, energy, and resources in an attempt to predict, understand, and control change. In early organizational theory, change was seen as a disruptive intrusion and/or a problem that had to be addressed. The behavior of individuals was seen as resistant to change and assumed to be reacting against change.

During organizational change efforts, organizational members often reacted to change by increasing resistance and trying to fend off change. This type of behavior has been cited as contributing to the failure of most organizational change processes. Yet resistance is not necessarily an innate response to change. Some new theories suggest that components within the organizational culture, such as job descriptions, hierarchical titles, and the status associated with these concepts, have locked in the idea of resistance and made it appear natural for staff members to resist change. If change is associated with loss, fear, and uncertainty, why would anyone want to change? This notion of resistance has been built into our understanding of how organizations work and the alleged dread many employees feel about trying to implement change.

Today, change is increasingly viewed as necessary and constant, and a vital part of everyday organizational behavioral life. Adapting to change is an increasingly expected norm in organizations. In fact, change theorists hold that organizations must be designed to change if they are going to survive and be successful. "[O]rganizations have to be built to change, not merely changed as a result of a special change program or effort" (Lawler & Worley, 2006, p. 19). Organizations are more successful if they are designed to be flexible and adaptive, and if individual employees are comfortable with the reality of constant change. This is not easy to do. Change theory and OD processes are discussed in more detail in chapter 6.

Myth 7: Staff Would Much Rather Be Doing Something Else

Human resources, the student affairs staff members, are the most vital resources within student affairs organizations, yet they do not get the attention and development to be truly effective. It seems ironic that a profession that centers on human development, learning, and personal growth related to students does not direct the same values, principles, and processes to its staff. Within student affairs, practitioners are often asked to do more with less; to work long hours and on weekends; and address complex and life-threatening issues with positive, engaging attitudes and high levels of professional expertise with little support and debriefing after an incident. At the same time, they are rarely adequately valued by the organization outside student affairs. These professionals are generally not highly compensated for their time or expertise, and rarely do they have job security similar to faculty tenure or multiyear contracts. Yet their loyalty and commitment is boundless, and they bring a level of energy and creativity to their work that is exceptional.

In the midst of financial downturns, professional development resources are often the first to be given up. Even in good times, student affairs professionals are often required to cover the costs of their professional development and professional association memberships. Some of these staff members burn out; some find that the work is not what they thought it was and move on to other professions. But for many, the work becomes a passion that is contagious and fulfilling, and despite the negative and unsupportive elements in the organizational environment, they most assuredly do not want to be doing anything else.

At the same time, student affairs organizations could do a better job of paying attention to the needs of the human resources entrusted to them. Understanding the culture and how to make it healthy and supportive can greatly enhance the effectiveness of the overall organization. Focusing more intentionally and strategically on staff development and the mental and emotional health of staff, and fostering growth and opportunities for staff are important to organizational effectiveness. It is also important for leaders to ensure that staff members have time to engage their lives outside work in order to keep both the individuals and the organization healthy. The theory related to the human resource dimensions of organizations are discussed in chapter 4.

Myth 8: We Must Stop Doing Stupid Things

Stupidity within an organizational context can be viewed from a number of perspectives. Generally, it has been viewed as not making mistakes in the first place or not repeating mistakes once they have been committed. In many organizations, thinking outside the box and taking risks were not always supported. Generally, taking risks and doing things differently were feared because they could lead to mistakes, and mistakes were viewed as costly to the organization. Organizational leaders have often publicly penalized individuals who made mistakes. When something went wrong, it was easier to find someone to blame than to focus on solving the problem.

Doing stupid things can also be seen as continuing to do the same thing over and over without any indication that it works or that it is effective.

Doing stupid things often results from not understanding how systems work and not knowing how to utilize organizational assessment tools to create response loops that focus on measuring organizational progress and effectiveness. Assessment is only now becoming a tool used within student affairs organizations. Yet some recent reports indicate that it is also one of the areas, along with staff development, that is being eliminated in the recent resource reductions.

Systems theory (Allen & Cherrey, 2000; Senge, 1990, 1999) and new approaches to organizational assessment (Miller, 2007) have provided theory and tools to help understand these processes. By understanding organizations from a systems perspective, one begins to understand that things may not work because there are systemic problems that are not attributed to an individual or small unit, yet they need to be addressed. Focusing on the system helps steer the organization toward solving a problem rather than punishing people. For example, blaming and subsequently firing an admissions director for the downturn in campus enrollment does not fix the campus enrollment problem. Focusing on what is going on within the entire system that may have resulted in the enrollment downturn will probably isolate the problem and lead to a real solution.

An enhanced understanding of the dynamic nature of organizations now encourages risk taking and exploring new ways of doing things in order to prevent organizations from becoming static and losing their creative and competitive edge. Taking the example discussed in the previous paragraph, if the entire campus system is assessed to better understand what may have affected the enrollment downturn, solutions that are outside the normal response may be developed and employed to turn the enrollment situation around. Blaming does not lead to learning or to effective solutions; it just makes the organization members more isolated and the organization itself less innovative. This is the type of stupidity that should be prevented.

Myth 9: Student Affairs Staff Members Share the Same Values, Get Along, and Work Effectively Together

Despite the general congenial nature and heartfelt humanitarian values shared by most student affairs staff members, individuals in these organizations do not always see the world the same way, value the same things, or get along without disagreements and conflict. But this reality has not easily been acknowledged or embraced within the student affairs culture. Conflict and dissent are generally avoided and frowned upon. The unspoken expectation is that people should get along and that conflict is a negative reflection of not being able to get along with others. Those who disagree or confront issues and behavior head on are often labeled as troublemakers or as not acting as team players.

Supervisors and senior staff members have not always been trained to deal with conflict as a healthy and enhancing mechanism within an organization. They often go out of their way to avoid having to address it. Research has demonstrated that this can lead to long-standing feuds and discontent festering under the surface for long periods of time. Sabotaging behavior and passive-aggressive communication both vertically and horizontally within the organization are likely to result and can have a very damaging impact on the workings of a student affairs organization. In some cases, staff members are not given honest performance feedback and have no idea why they are being treated a certain way or why their performance feedback does not match the raise or reward they were provided. Honest and transparent communication is one of the most critical attributes of sound, healthy organizations, yet it is surprising how rarely it occurs.

On a larger scale, the projected attitude that everyone must get along and that disagreement is not tolerated often leads to the perceived repression of values and perspectives that do not go along with the majority. Although student affairs organizations claim to be inclusive, those who do not reflect the values and perspectives of the majority may feel marginalized and undervalued, yet believe they cannot articulate their differences without retribution. Group think and intragroup superiority can easily result from these types of cultural norms. The notion that there is a single student affairs perspective or that everyone shares the same values is not the way healthy organizations operate effectively. The ability to deal with and at times promote conflict and truly encourage differing values and perspectives enriches an organization and enables it to bring varied and critical issues and solutions to the table. More discussion about culture, norms, and values are discussed in chapters 2 and 4.

Myth 10: Money Fixes Everything

Money has been viewed as the solution to most problems, yet it rarely fixes anything. This is true when it comes to organizational issues, too. Most organizational issues in student affairs have very little to do with money. When they do, it is not generally about having more money, but how the institution's leadership and practitioners choose to prioritize where the money goes and what it supports. It is true that student affairs organizations are generally the first to receive reductions during economic downturns, and they often do not receive new resources when new resources become available. At the same time, practitioners often stagnate and limit creativity by focusing on what resources they do not have rather than focusing on the resources and strengths they do have within their organizations.

Most organizational issues are really about values, attitudes, and the paradigms we use for viewing and understanding organizations. They are about how existing resources are assigned and assessed. They are about relationships and culture in the context of human interactions and how work is assigned, performed, and rewarded. Changing these organizational dynamics does not generally require new resources, but it does require human energy and the commitment to understand and view organizational behavior differently. Most important, it requires a desire to make the organization more effective in achieving its mission and goals and to be open to adopting the change that is required.

As you read the remaining chapters of this book, reflect on some of the same questions faced by Dr. Chris Jones in the chapter-opening vignette regarding your understanding of student affairs organizations.

Reflective Summary

1. What do we need to know about organizational behavior theory and application?
2. How can we integrate new information and understandings with the existing knowledge and the paradigms we use for understanding organizational behavior and change?
3. How can we apply organizational behavior and change theory within the context of the student affairs organization in which we work?
4. How can we use organizational behavior, organizational development, and assessment tools and techniques to enrich the organization and make it more effective?

References

Allen, K. E., & Cherrey, C. (2000). *Systemic leadership: Enriching the meaning of our work.* Lanham, MD: University Press of America, Inc.

Ambler, D. (2000). Organization and administrative models. In M. J. Barr & M. K. Desler (Eds.), *The handbook of student affairs administration* (2nd ed., pp. 122–133). San Francisco: Jossey-Bass.

Ashkenas, R., Ulrich, D., Jick, T., & Kerr, S. (2002). *The boundaryless organization: Breaking the chain of organizational structure.* San Francisco: Jossey-Bass.

Bergquist, W. H., & Pawlak, K. (2008). *Engaging the six cultures of the academy.* San Francisco: Jossey Bass.

Bess, J. L., & Dee, J. R. (2008a). *Understanding college and university organizations: Theories for effective policy and practice. Volume one: The state of the system.* Sterling, VA: Stylus.

Bess, J. L., & Dee, J. R. (2008b). *Understanding college and university organization: Theories for effective policy and practice, Volume two: Dynamics of the system.* Sterling, VA: Stylus.

Birnbaum, R. (1988). *How colleges work.* San Francisco: Jossey-Bass.

Cook, J. H., & Lewis, C. A. (2007). *Student affairs and academic affairs collaboration: The divine comity.* Washington DC: NASPA.

Durkheim, E. (1893/1894). *Division of labor in society* (W. D. Halls, Trans.). New York: Free Press.

Galbraith, J. R. (2002). *Designing organizations: An executive guide to strategy, structure, and process.* San Francisco: Wiley.

Goold, M., & Campbell, A. (2002). *Designing effective organizations.* San Francisco: Jossey-Bass.

Hatch, M. J., & Cunliffe, A. L. (2006). *Organizational theory* (2nd ed.). New York: Oxford University Press.

Helgesen, S. (1995). *The web of inclusion.* Washington, DC: Beard Books.

Hirt, J. B. (2006). *Where you work matters.* San Francisco: Jossey-Bass.

Kezar, A., (2001). *Understanding and facilitating organizational change in the 21st century. ASHE–ERIC Higher Education Report, 28*(4). San Francisco: Jossey-Bass.

Kezar, A., & Dee, J. (2006, April). *Conducting multiple paradigms analyses of higher education organizations: Transforming the study of colleges and universities.* Paper presented at the annual meeting of the American Educational Research Association (AERA), San Francisco.

Kezar, A., & Eckel, P. (2002). The effect of institutional culture and change strategies in higher education: Universal principles or cultural responsive concepts? *Journal of Higher Education, 73*(4), 435–460.

Kuhn, T. (1970). *The structure of scientific revolutions* (2nd ed.). Chicago: University of Chicago Press.

Kuk, L. (2009). The dynamics organizational models within student affairs. In G. S. McClellan & J. Stringer (Eds.), *The handbook of student affairs administration* (3rd ed., pp. 313–332). San Francisco: Jossey-Bass.

Kuk, L., & Banning, J. H. (2009). Designing student affairs organizational structures: Perceptions of senior student affairs officers. *NASPA Journal, 46*(1), 94–117.

Lawler, E. E., & Worley, C. G. (2006). *Built to change: How to achieve sustained organizational effectiveness.* San Francisco: Jossey-Bass.

Lewin, K. (1951). *Field theory in the social sciences.* New York: Harper & Row.

Love, P. G., & Estanek, S. M. (2004). *Rethinking student affairs practice*. San Francisco: Jossey-Bass.

Manning, K., Kinzie, J., & Schuh, J. (2006). *One size does not fit all: Traditional and innovative models of student affairs practice*. New York: Routledge, Taylor and Francis Group.

Miller, B. A. (2007). *Assessing organizational performance in higher education*. San Francisco: Jossey-Bass.

Senge, P. M. (1990). *The fifth discipline: The art & practice of the learning organization*. New York: Doubleday.

Senge, P. M. (1999). *The dance of change: The challenges to sustaining momentum in learning organizations*. New York: Doubleday.

Taylor, F. W. (1911). *The principles of scientific management*. New York: Harper.

U.S. Department of Education. (2008). *Digest of Educational Statistics, 2007* (NCES 2008–022). Washington, DC: U.S. Government Printing Office.

Weber, M. (1947). *The theory of social and economic organization*. Glencoe, IL: Free Press. (First published in 1924).

Wheatley, M. J. (2006). *Leadership and the new science: Discovering order in a chaotic world* (3rd ed.). San Francisco: Berrett-Koehler.

2

SEEING STUDENT AFFAIRS ORGANIZATIONS THROUGH THE LENS OF ORGANIZATIONAL THEORY

Vice President Robert Wilson is hosting his first set of roundtable meetings with his new student affairs staff. He has been in his new role as vice president for student affairs for about a week, and he feels it is time to reach out across the division to meet his staff members face to face. He decided that an ideal format for this meeting was to host roundtable discussions with the staff members in each area to find out what roles they each played and to learn a little about them individually, as well as learn more about the workings of their units.

He was surprised to learn that the professionals within the division of student affairs saw themselves as housing professionals, admissions counselors, and counseling center psychologists and not necessarily as part of a broader student affairs organization. Many openly admitted that they had no idea that they were part of a larger organization, and others were not sure why it mattered. Over time, they had built strong, unit-based programs and services that were often duplicated in other units, had developed policies and procedures as though they operated in a vacuum, and rarely sought out cross-unit collaborations. Wilson was baffled by this finding because the units were clearly found as part of the university organization on the institution's organization chart, and he knew that the directors had met with the vice president on a regular basis.

During the conversations, and afterward in meetings with the various directors, it became increasingly clear why they thought and behaved the way they did. Historically, the various units were permitted to operate fairly independently of each other. Each unit, especially the larger units, had developed their own norms and emphasized professional values aligned with their functional responsibilities and roles. They had developed strong operational units and performed their roles as highly competent professionals. Most of them were known for serving their students with high-quality programs and services.

Although the directors met regularly, they were treated as independent units and rarely asked to collaborate or share resources across unit boundaries. Most of their communication was vertical, going to the vice president and/or through to the president and other vice presidents as needed. Because most of them were funded on separate student fees or fees for service, they did not have to deal with competing issues related to funding, and each relied on their individual connection to securing new and/or additional resources for their operations. The director meetings did serve as a forum for announcements of upcoming programs or reaction to issues that came from other units outside student affairs. Occasionally the vice president had to act as an arbitrator when the actions and policies of one unit conflicted with the needs and policies of other units, but these were rare because most units had learned how to stay clear of the concerns and issues of other units and thus avoided conflict.

Given the changes within the institution and decreasing resources, the vice president knew that this way of organizing and behaving could not continue for long. Units were going to have to learn to become more collaborative and to share resources and ideas across unit boundaries. The demands from external entities were demanding greater accountability and quicker responses to issues, and the old ways of each unit doing for itself would no longer work.

The division was being asked to develop a set of shared goals and strategies that would require an interdependent sense of identity and cooperation, and to view themselves as part of a larger organizational system. The vice president knew that he needed to focus on helping the divisional staff understand their connection to each other and their need to collaborate with other units throughout the institution. He also knew that changing the history and the culture of functionally siloed behavior, in which each unit acted like an individual and vertical one, would not be easy, that it would require additional education related to organizational theory and behavior.

The study of organizations is a rich, diverse, multidisciplinary area of inquiry with many branches and approaches. Although relatively new as a discipline, its origins in the social sciences and the study of human behavior trace back over a century both in the United States and Europe. Its development as a field of study parallels the expansion of epistemological perspectives and also the development of student affairs as complex administrative organizations in collegiate settings. This chapter provides a brief historical development of organizational studies, epistemological expansion related to understanding organizations, and the evolution of student affairs organizations. It also presents a variety of broad-based organizational theories, including systems theory and contingency theory, and a discussion of the concept of organizational culture and how these ideas and perspectives are useful in understanding student affairs organizations.

Student affairs organizations grew out of the expansion of higher education after World War II. Like many growing organizations, the student affairs division was not conceived as an operational entity in its current form; it grew into its roles and responsibilities as needs changed and demands for student services increased. As new responses to student needs emerged and new services were required to meet those needs, new services and programs were created and added to the array of existing student support services. By the mid-1960s, student services, or student affairs organizations, as they eventually were generally labeled, became stand-alone divisions within existing collegiate organizations. As unique entities focused on student development, non-curricular student life, and the provision of student support services, they have continued to evolve into complex organizations. As part of this evolution, they became separate and distinct from other academic and administrative units.

Along with complexity came specialization and identification of staff members with subunits, such as housing, student activities, college unions, counseling, admissions, advising, and orientation. Each area developed its own professional and organizational identities. To this day, identification with various subcultures within student affairs organizations has framed practitioners' understanding of organizational behavior, at times limiting the ability of practitioners and their units to see the larger issues and context of the institution. Professional associations have developed around these functional subgroup identities and fostered the specialized organizational culture and structure of student affairs organizations.

The hierarchical structures and organizational cultures within student affairs that have evolved over the years were influenced by the understanding of organizations that existed at the time. The early mechanistic and hierarchical understandings of early organizational theory are quite evident in the development of student affairs organizations. Student affairs organizations grew into present-day entities over decades of time. They were fashioned by the values, theoretical perspectives and understanding of organizations that emerged during their formative years. In their current state, they face the challenges of changing to meet new demands and uncertain futures. In this light, they find themselves being evaluated and redesigned in the context of emerging knowledge and the understandings from a rich and growing field of organizational studies.

We begin our exploration of organizational theory from a broad historic and theoretical framework, essentially from the perspective of the big picture. In subsequent chapters, we focus more specifically on theory and approaches that address organization-specific components and attributes. It is important, from our frame of reference, to understand the broad interconnections of history and theoretical perspectives, and their application to existing organizational behavior, as well as how new and emerging ideas and perspectives can influence the future.

This chapter presents a brief history of organizational theory. It highlights and discusses key holistic organization theories, and notes the parallel development of epistemological frameworks that provide rich application to student affairs organizational behavior.

A Brief History of Organizational Theory and Behavioral Study

Over a century ago, as a result of a growing interest in the study of management, researchers began to apply scientific methods to the study of the working conditions and administrative practices in factories and other work settings in the United States and Europe. These early researchers and theorists had a profound effect on the development of our understanding of organizations and the practice of management. The subsequent development of student affairs organizations was greatly influenced by these early ideas, and much of the present-day culture, structure, and processes are a reflection of these early theories. Initially, the study of organizations emerged from the work of German sociologists and eventually became independent areas of study. The following historical summary includes theoretical ideas from a number of important early organizational theorists.

Emile Durkheim, a French sociologist, discussed in his book, *The Division of Labor in Society* (1893/1894), the ideas of specialization, organizational hierarchy, and interdependence of work tasks brought about through the shift from an agricultural economy to an industrial one. In his book, he made a distinction between informal and formal organizations and placed an emphasis on the importance of a worker's social needs. His work was important to organizational behavior, and his ideas related to informal organizations are at the foundation of the current concept of organizational culture. The idea of staff socialization and the importance of social connection are important elements in student affairs cultures.

Max Weber (1924/1947), another German sociologist also attempted to understand the impact of industrialization on society. He developed the theory of bureaucracy, which is based on the ideas of authority and rationality. Weber held that bureaucracy provided rules and processes for managing organizations. He believed that, through the use of bureaucracy organizations, one could achieve efficiency and avoid ongoing conflict for authority and power. These ideas about bureaucratic organizational structures and the assumption that they would lead to organizational efficiency dominated the thinking of organizational theorists for most of the 20th century. In fact, the ideas surrounding bureaucracy are still pursued in some organizational research circles. This concept has greatly influenced the administrative structures of higher education organizations, including student affairs, and has led to the reliance on functional hierarchical organizations currently utilized in student affairs organizations.

The area first attributed to organizational study was the scientific management approach spearheaded by Fredrick W. Taylor (1911). This approach sought to apply scientific methods to the study of how to make the people who performed specific jobs more productive. Through these early efforts, productivity greatly increased and the use of these mechanistic approaches to job performance and productivity became the centerpiece of understanding and constructing work organizations.

At around the same time, the industrial psychology movement, fostered by the desire of the U.S. government to select personnel for World War I, began to develop. These efforts were refined even more extensively during World War II. After the war, they were applied to training workers for the postwar economy. From these initial interests in management and worker productivity sprang the interest and development of organization-related theory and the study of behavior in organizations.

The development of the entities that comprise student affairs within collegiate organizations came from a desire to provide counseling and career-related education, with an emphasis on professionalization within what had been the predominantly liberal arts educational process. The expansion of access to higher education after World War II as a means to professional education also increased the need for and desire to provide new services, create campus housing, and address the campus life issues brought by increasing numbers of diverse students.

During the 1920s, researchers began to focus on the activities of managers. The ideas related to management behavior and the development of managerial principles grew into a body of knowledge called administrative theory. Through observation studies, researchers, including the French theorist Henri Fayol (1919/1949), attempted to develop guiding managerial principles that could be used to improve workforce performance. From these efforts emerged the managerial principles of planning, organizing, and controlling, as well as a number of organizational design principles that fostered hierarchical and vertical management practices. Many of these ideas are still viewed as fundamental to administrative roles within higher education and student affairs.

Mary Parker Follett (1923) was among the first to propose management theory based on principles of self-governance and workplace democracy. Her work on organizations as communities is often viewed as the predecessor to organizational cultural studies and the more recent scholarship of knowledge and learning within organizations (Hatch & Cunliffe, 2006, p. 34). Her work had an influence on the formation of shared governance and the development of collective decision making that is prevalent in collegiate organizations today.

Chester Barnard, in his 1938 book, *The Functions of the Executive*, suggested that managing the informal organization was a key role of managers. He proposed organizing employees into social systems, with a focus on communicating goals and paying attention to worker motivation. Barnard is believed to have been an early pioneer in the development of current research and theoretical perspectives on organizational culture, meanings, and symbolism (Hatch & Cunliffe, 2006, pp. 35–36).

As a reaction to the neglect of human dimensions found in the early classical theories, behavioral sciences were introduced into the study of management. These theories became known as neoclassical theory and evolved into two areas of study, the human relations perspective, which focused on interactions and relations within groups, and the behavioral school, which focused on individual behavior within organizations (Bowditch, Buono, & Stewart, 2008).

The human relations perspective of organizational behavior emerged as a result of the Hawthorne studies that were conducted at the Western Electric Plant in Cicero, Illinois, in the late 1920s. These studies resulted in a concept that became known as the Hawthorne effect, an observation that worker treatment made a difference in performance outcomes. These studies led to increased attention on leadership behavior and the impact of work-groups and peer pressure on employee satisfaction and performance. Subsequent research demonstrated that financial incentives were not the primary performance motivator, supporting the idea that performance motivation is complex and individually determined. By the 1940s, this line of research had become extensive and began to include a focus on human factors research dealing with worker attitudes, group dynamics, and relationships between workers and managers. The current use of work climate surveys and assessments are directly related to these early efforts.

Contemporary Organizational Study

Organizational behavior as a field of study emerged in the late 1950s and early 1960s. At this time, two distinct but related approaches to the study of organizations evolved: organizational theory and organizational behavior (see chapter 1). Both approaches are believed to be important to understanding current organizational behavior. We view them as essential for understanding behavior in student affairs organizations and, as a result, we will discuss theories from both areas of study.

A number of early contemporary theorists helped shape the focus of organizational study. James March and Herbert Simon (1958), advanced Barnard's ideas of organizations as social systems. Emphasizing individual decision making, they developed a more complex motivational theory. Lawrence and Lorsch (1969) concluded that organizations in a stable environment are more effective if they have more procedures and centralized control of decision making, and organizations in an unstable environment are more effective if they have decentralized and more participatory decision making (Tosi & Mero, 2003).

The behavioral school, growing out of the human relations perspective, focused on personal growth and individual development. This approach to understanding behavior fostered a number of ideas about the individual and the human dimension of work and management in organizations. Abraham Maslow's (1954) theory of hierarchy of needs is one of the most well-known models of human motivation. The model stated that human need, which underlies all human motivation, could be ordered into a hierarchy of five levels: physiological, security, social, self-esteem, and self-actualization needs. David McClelland (1965) found that people have three basic needs: achievement, power, and affiliation. These theories continue to have a significant influence on our understanding of student affairs organizations and the behavior that occurs within them.

Douglas McGregor (1960), in his Theory X and Theory Y, proposed that most managers make incorrect assumptions about the people they manage. He argued that Theory Y was a more correct way to view employee attitudes and behavior. From this perspective, employees were viewed to be trustworthy and self-motivated, and there was no need for a rigid, controlling, centralized administrative structure. Chris Argyris (1957, 1964) also questioned the need for organizational control and bureaucratic structures. He held that these forms of organization were unhealthy and unsupportive of the needs of human beings and that they actually were counterproductive to the goals of greater efficiency and effectiveness. Fredrick Herzberg's motivator-hygiene theory (Herzberg, Mauser, & Snyderman, 1959) suggested that motivation is composed of two types of factors: those that prevent dissatisfaction but do not encourage people to grow and develop, and job-related factors that actually encourage growth and productivity. Many of these theories, and the ideas and theories that emerged from them, are discussed more extensively in chapter 4.

Current Organizational Theory

At about the same time as organizational theories and behavior were coalescing as areas of study, theorists and researchers were beginning to develop alternative ways of viewing and understanding the world. The positivist epistemology and its use of the scientific method to measure behavior and categorize phenomena through objective analysis began to be challenged as the only means of understanding the world. Today, it is widely assumed a number of different epistemological frameworks can help us understand the world, and these perspectives have influenced the development of organizational theory, too. Through the lens of these expanded epistemological frameworks, different perspectives and theories related to organizations have emerged, and older theories have been transformed and expanded to widen the understanding of organizational complexity.

The study of organizations has come a long way since the late 1960s. The number of theories and ideas related to this area has grown substantially. Many of these theories have been built on early theory, and some have taken initial ideas in very new directions of thinking and application. Some of the theories grew out of the positivist perspective, now also called post-positivist, while others have been framed from the social constructivist or postmodern perspectives (see chapter 1). Over the last 50 years, the preponderance of these ideas and their supporting research have focused on business organizations, yet their implications and applications for higher education and student affairs are numerous. It is also appropriate to borrow from this body of literature to apply its richness and insight to understanding how student affairs organizations work. The following discussions highlight some of the broad organizational theories that apply to student affairs organizations.

General Systems and Social Theory

Systems Theory

Ludwig von Bertalanffy (1968) first proposed systems theory as a way of generalizing all scientific theory into orderly hierarchies of building blocks, which he called systems (Hatch & Cunliffe, 2006). Systems consist of interrelated parts called subsystems. Systems have boundaries that separate one system from another, and they interface with other systems and with the environment, which consists of everything outside the system. This concept has been widely used as a way of understanding organizations.

Organizations are systems. With regard to organizations, systems theory helps explain the two fundamental institutions in society: the organization and the individual. A number of theorists have contributed to the development and expansion of systems-related ideas over the years, including Kenneth Boulding (1956), Walter Buckley (1967), Barry Oshry (1995), Eric Schein (1985, 2004), and Margaret Wheatley (2006). The following discussion is a general summary of the ideas formulated by these theorists around the concept of organizational systems.

Organizations are comprised of tops (executives), middles (managers), and bottoms (workers). Each of these groups exists in their own environment, with their own culture, rules, and perspectives, and they see the organization from the part of the system that they occupy.

Student affairs organizations are also systems. The position at which a staff person works in the student affairs hierarchy determines how and from what perspective that person sees and understands the organization. No one can clearly see all the perspectives of the organization. Leaders need to have others from throughout the organization contribute to the common knowledge about how the organization is functioning. They need to use well-thought-out and timely communication up and down and across the organization, and they need to include different voices in the decision-making process. Understanding the organization as a system that depends on open communication and collective input in decision making enhances the effectiveness of the organization. Organizations can be healthy only when they are viewed as a collective whole, and when organizational leaders understand that organizations operate as systems.

What happens in one part of the organizational system affects what happens in other parts of the system. Individuals see their part of the organization as a subsystem of the whole organization, but they often do not see the whole organization. They do not always understand the impact that change in one part of the system has on another. Organizational members often blame others when it is the system that is responsible. This blaming creates organizational conflict and can lead to both individual and organizational failure.

Understanding the phenomenon about what happens in one unit of the organization affecting what happens in other units of the organization can help student affairs organizations prevent unanticipated problems. They can be proactive by being collaborative and seeking out input before actions are taken or policy is implemented. Problems or failures are not always the fault of a person or a student affairs unit; they may be related to problems in the system. Understanding this dynamic can help focus on addressing problems and finding solutions rather than blaming others.

Systems are highly differentiated because each subsystem performs a different function. Differentiation provides the system with the benefit of specialization, yet specialization also creates a need for integration at the system level. The system is composed of a hierarchy of systems, from the simple to the more complex. Analysis of the system can occur at any level, or it can occur between subsystems and/or between the subsystems and the environment. Organizations are generally composed of four major subsystems: structure, culture, social, and technology. Student affairs organizations are often highly differentiated as functional structures, with varying degrees of specialization, and they are composed of the four major subsystems. Within student affairs organizations, these subsystems may vary by type and size, yet they have some common components, as well as a mission and focus.

Individuals often suffer from both spatial and temporal blindness, and this creates problems within organizations. Spatial blindness is when one thinks he knows when in fact he does not know. Myths, prejudices, and erroneous beliefs often blind individuals to the truth of the whole system. Temporal blindness results from one's lack of understanding of the history of current events. All events have histories, and this lack of understanding can cause conflict and problems. Events do not occur in a vacuum. Their histories are probably tied to events, beliefs, and actions within other parts of the system and/or the system as a whole and clearly have influenced the culture of the organization.

Student affairs organizations also have histories, and their culture and the resulting behavior are shaped by events within the context of the larger system. For example, resistance to student affairs–academic affairs collaboration is probably not just the result of lack of time or resources. It may also be related to past efforts to achieve such initiatives. If collaboration has been successful in the past, it may be easier to achieve in the future. If student affairs organizations have been viewed historically as not essential to the core academic mission of the institution, it may be difficult to change this perception among faculty members and it may be harder to persuade them to spend their time on collaborations.

Boundaries separate the system from other systems and from the greater environment. They act as structures that help define identity, provide protection, and act as a point of exchange and/or contact with the greater environment (Bess & Dee, 2008). Boundaries are not necessarily physical, but they delineate the functions that the system performs. Systems can be either open or closed. An open system is one that is open to other systems and the greater environment, and a closed system is one that is closed to other systems and the greater environment and must rely on its own resources to carry out all of its functions.

Environments consist of everything beyond the boundaries of the system. These can include other systems and also the greater external environment. Inputs to the organization system originate from these environments, and outputs are developed and directed toward these environments. Student affairs organizations interact with other systems within the collegiate structure, such as academic and administrative systems, as well as with the greater community outside the collegiate organization. They receive input in the form of new students, funding, information, and so on, and also direct their output in the form of services and the growth, learning, and change they provide to students as they move into the outside environment.

Systems expend energy both internally and externally to maintain balance or equilibrium in the system. Stasis exists when the parts of the system are in balance. The system is dynamic when the parts are temporarily out of synch. According to theory, the dynamic state has a natural tendency to more toward equilibrium (Berrien, 1980). Student affairs organizations exhibit this behavior when they seek to update policies and practices that no longer work or seek to redirect resources and energy to address growing issues and concerns that have emerged from the diverse needs of new students.

Equifinality (Gresov & Drazin, 1997) is a principle, strongly embedded in systems thinking, that holds that organizations can reach the same results but do not have to achieve them using the same structure or means. There is not necessarily one best way or set of processes. This enables organizations to set their own course and to follow their own mission and vision to achieving success. Ironically, this goes against the current best practice model used by many higher education and student affairs organizations in which they benchmark policy and practice against other institutions as a means of both improvement and assessment.

Entropy (Katz & Kahn, 1978) is another concept closely tied to systems theory. This concept claims that as systems grow, they differentiate, but as they become large, there is a tendency to lose energy and focus and to become disconnected. This process leads to disorder, duplication, waste of energy, loss of focus, missed communication, and eventually decay and death of the organization. Organizations can reverse this trend toward decay through continual revitalization and restructuring.

Open systems appear to have a self-organizing dynamic that adapts as needed to create structures that fit the immediate need. These systems are process structures that reorganize to protect the organization's identity. Open systems stay fluid and use teams that can be easily changed and adapted to ever-changing needs. These types of systems are open to new information, especially information that is new and disturbing. The organization intentionally seeks to keep the system off-balance so that it can be responsive to needed change.

An open organization doesn't look for information that makes it feel good, that verifies its past and validates its present. It is deliberately looking for information that might threaten its stability, knock it off balance, and open it to growth. This is so different from the way information is handled in well-defined organizations (Wheatley, 2006, p. 83).

Self-organizing systems are also strong partners with the external environment, which creates greater autonomy vis-à-vis the forced changes brought on by the external environment and also permits them to develop new capacities that make them more resourceful. Second, self-organizing systems are self-referencing: They change to address needed shifts in ways that allow them to remain consistent. Change is not random. Like a living system, they change to preserve themselves (Wheatley, 2006).

General systems theory has often provided the logical basis for many other organizational theories. Many organization theories have systems theory concepts as a basic assumption in their foundation. It also provides a lens for viewing organizations as a whole. These ideas focus on how the various subsystems relate to or work together or how they collectively affect organizational performance.

Social Systems Theory

Social systems theory (Lewin, 1938) is closely related to general systems theory. It states that all human behavior is a function of the interaction of a person with his or her environment, $B = f(P, E)$. In other words, it is important to take into account both the individual and the environment if one wants to understand the behavior within organizations. Social systems generally vary in their emphasis of one of these dimensions over the other. For example, student affairs organizations have generally placed more emphasis on individual development and have not always understood or focused on the impact of the environment as it relates to student development and learning. Through the use of the campus ecology model (Banning, 1978) more attention has been given to the importance of the campus environment and as it relates to the person–environment interaction. This theory and supporting ideas are discussed in more detail in chapter 3.

Organizational Contingency Theory

Organizational contingency theory holds that the best way to design an organization depends on the situation in which the organization finds itself (Donaldson, 1985). The focus is to align the various elements within an organization, including environmental factors, goals, technology, people, and unique characteristics so that they maximize efficiency and effectiveness. Researchers try to identify the best approach for this alignment depending on the specific contingencies that are being faced by the organization. This theory is increasingly being used with student affairs organizations that seek to align their mission, goals, structure, and available resources with the mission of the institution and its interaction with the greater external environment.

Student affairs organizations face many challenges in their efforts to provide programs and services for diverse needs and interests. According to contingency theory, different needs and challenges facing the organization demand that various organizational elements be aligned to best address them. No one way of orchestrating or structuring services can effectively serve the needs of every organization. Student affairs organizations must be creative, flexible, and adaptive to be able to align their resources to best serve the needs and challenges that they face. This may require unique approaches that are not found among benchmarked best practices.

Social Construct Theory

Our social world is constructed through our interpretation of what is happening around us. Through interaction with others, human beings produce their individual identities and experience reality. Reality is socially constructed by individuals. Through sharing, these realities become both personal and shared and find their way into the culture of organizations. These shared realities become objectified and normalized within a group and organization. The group then socializes new members in line with the group's social constructs, which are internalized and then externalized as shared reality. Through this process, the shared social construction of reality is sustained (Berger & Lukmann, 1966; Weick, 1979).

Within student affairs, professional socialization occurs both through professional membership in student affairs and its organizations, but also through orientation and experience with the unique characteristics and culture of a particular student affairs organization. On a professional level, student affairs practitioners—both individually and through shared professional values, ideas, and experiences—create a student affairs reality. This reality is shared through professional development activities and informal ideas shared within campus programs, professional associations, and graduate preparation programs. As professional norms and values become part of the common student affairs experience, they are shared through a variety of professional socialization processes for new student affairs practitioners. They find their way into the fabric of most student affairs organizations through professional socialization and migration of staff from one organization to the other (Tull, Hirt, & Saunders, 2009).

Within the larger social group are subgroups that have their own sociocultural context. They create shared realities through externalization of their personal experiences, and objectification and internalization of these shared realities. Student affairs organizations are actually a variety of functional subgroups, such as housing, student activities, orientation, admissions, financial aid, and so on. Each of these subgroups has its own professional associations and has developed its own professional identity, norms, values, and ways of viewing its student affairs world. Although these subgroups may be part of the larger organization, their professional reality may be more focused on the subgroup. As a result, housing professionals may identify with housing more than with the larger student affairs organization.

Change occurs when members externalize something new through borrowing or acting different and the new idea or behavior is taken up by the others in the group. Student affairs, like many other professions, have trendsetters, both professionally and within collegiate organizations. These trendsetters are usually change agents that bring new ideas or practices to the organization. They may borrow from other professions or organizations, or they may infuse ideas from other sources to create new models and approaches that are then incorporated into the organization. Within student affairs, this behavior may come from an organized effort to adapt new approaches or policies, or it may come from individuals who are viewed as bringing new and useful ideas and practices to the organization. Professional conferences, newsletters, and other media also help stimulate the transfer of new ideas and the socialization of professionals.

Karl Weick (1979, 1995) brought social construct theory into organizational theory with his theory of sensemaking. He held that organizations exist largely in the minds of members, and they exist in the form of cognitive maps, or images of experiences. These maps regarding the organization are created through social interaction and are used as tools to help make sense and bring order to their reality. According to Weick, the organization's environment does not exist independently of the organization. In other words, it is socially constructed and reconstructed based on the actions of people gathered together who act as an organization. This theory and varying approaches to its application are discussed in more detail in chapters 3 and 4.

Reframing Organizations

Bolman and Deal (2008) organized and synthesized organizational theory into four frames or areas for the purposes of understanding the various dimensions of complex organizations more clearly. They have added to and refined their model over four revisions of this work, which began in 1984. These frames are organizational structure, human resources, political systems, and symbolic representation. Each lens captures an important slice of organizational reality, but alone each one is incomplete. The basic premise of their model is that, to fully understand the organization, one must view it from all four perspectives.

Structural Frame

The structural frame views the organization as a rational system. It stresses the importance of designing structural forms that align with an organization's goals, tasks, technology, and environment. Differentiation of work roles provides for clarity of purpose and contribution, but it also leads to the need for appropriate coordination and integration mechanisms.

Human Resources Frame

The human resources frame explores the interactions between and among organizations and people. Due to increased complexity, organizations are often not healthy places for human beings, and the talents, creativity, energy, and commitment of human effort is often wasted and lost. This frame attempts to look at core concepts such as human need, interpersonal dynamics, and management practices that seek to improve the human dimension within organizations.

Political Systems Frame

The political systems frame views organizations as political arenas that constantly address varied individual and group interests. Conflict is central to organizational dynamics, and power is the most important resource because decision making in organizations focuses on the allocation of scarce resources. Organizational goals emerge from bargaining and negotiating among different coalitions within the organization. This frame also explores the political behavior in an organization.

Symbolic Frame

The symbolic frame interprets and highlights the issues of meaning and values that make symbols powerful aspects of the human experience within organizations. It assumes that events have meaning and can have different interpretations from different people. Ambiguity and uncertainty, which are increasingly common in current organizations, often result in the creation of symbols that create clarity and predictability. This frame explores the impact and meaning of symbolism in organizations.

The Bolman and Deal (2008) frame theory has been widely used in student affairs and has considerable use in its application to student affairs organizations. It provides a lens for viewing both the entire organization and its specific components. But more specifically, it provides a vehicle for understanding the interconnection of the four frames as they relate to viewing the organization from different perspectives, especially the idea of organizational culture.

Organizational Culture Theory

Organizations possess cultures and subcultures, and both have a profound impact on how the organization works and how people within the organization behave. A great deal about human behavior has been learned through the study of organizational culture. Elliot Jacques (1952) is credited with conceptualizing the idea of organizational culture. He felt that much about the emotional life of organizations had been ignored because of an emphasis on organizational structure, and so he began to apply the concept of culture to organizations. Like the concept of culture, organizational culture refers to a set of shared beliefs, assumptions, and expectations held by organizational members. It includes a unique approach to perceiving the organization's artifacts and environment, and its norms, roles, and values as they exist outside the individual (Bowditch, Buono, & Stewart, 2008). Within larger organizations there are also subcultures, which are distinct subsets of organizational members, who view themselves as a "distinct group within the organization and routinely take action on the basis of their unique collective understandings" (Hatch & Cunliffe, 2006, p. 176).

Organizational culture, much like culture in general, has a lasting and encompassing impact on the behavior of individuals and groups within an organization. These influences have both positive and negative effects on the organization. Culture often serves as the glue that holds the organization together; it provides a sense of identity, and it helps shape and define the ways of achieving the goals of the organization. Organizational culture is formed over time through member interactions and the development of shared common beliefs and values and a common sense of reality. New members to the organization are socialized within the culture to adhere and adapt to the culture of the organization. The organizational culture, by its nature, is both symbolic and emotional, and is distinctively different from structure. Structure is discussed in chapter 5.

Organizational culture also has a dark side: Its organizational members come to distrust and resist new ideas, values, and ways of doing things, especially those brought in from outside. This can make change or adapting new ways of doing things difficult and, at times, nearly impossible. Cultures are laden with contradictions and paradoxes and are not a tangible concept to view and to grasp. The emotional and symbolic nature of culture can easily shift in dysfunctional and obstructive ways that can have a negative effect on both the organization and the individual members.

Research has shown that organizational culture is unique to an organization, although some aspects of culture may be similar across an industry or profession. This is believed to be true across student affairs organizations. Research has also differentiated between subjective and objective culture. The term *subjective culture* refers to the shared patterns of beliefs, assumptions, and expectations held by organizational members and the group's ways of perceiving the organization's environment and its values, norms, and roles (Bowditch et al., 2008). It also includes the managerial culture, which in turn includes the leadership styles, orientations, and frameworks for addressing and solving problems that are valued by the organization. The term *objective culture* can be understood through observing artifacts, space, art, decorations, logos, and so on, that are created by the organization to reflect that organization's culture and values (Bowditch et al., 2008).

Multiple cultures often exist in organizations, and most have one or more subcultures. This generally occurs in organizations that are functional in structure. Although most organizations have a dominant culture, a subculture is likely to have a more pronounced impact on the members who are part of the subculture. In higher education, the faculty culture might easily be considered the dominant culture, although many would argue that there are a number of faculty cultures (Bergquist & Pawlak, 2008). Student affairs could be considered a subculture of the larger organization, distinct from faculty cultures. It has many characteristics that share attributes of many of the faculty cultures and has other attributes that are unique to student affairs.

At the same time, student affairs has a number of subcultures within its organization, too. Directly connected to the functional structure and high levels of specialization, these subcultures have a strong tendency to act as silos, which resist coordination and collaboration among organizational units. In some cases, a subculture might evolve into a counterculture, a culture that rejects what the larger organization stands for and works against what the greater organization is trying to achieve. These types of behavior can be conscious or unconscious.

Although a number of theories have contributed to our understanding of organizational culture, one of the most notable theories related to organizational culture was developed by Edgar Schein in his book, *Organizational Culture and Leadership* (1985, 2004). According to Schein, culture occurs at three levels. The deepest and most basic level consists of assumptions. These basic assumptions represent truth and/or the organizational member's reality of truth. They are taken for granted and are dominant in the thinking and actions of members. At the next level of culture are values, which are the principles and goals that the members hold as having intrinsic worth. They define what is cared about and guide ethical behavior within the organization. Although values are not always central to the mindset of members, they can be recognized and often become important when the organization's culture is challenged.

Values are often expressed through organizational norms, the unwritten rules and expectations that govern the behavior of the organization's members. They might be exhibited through the ways that information is shared, or the clothes that are worn, or how one addresses others. These rules and expectations can be written as policy, but they are more likely shared through more informal modeling behavior. The third and more visible level of culture is reflected in activities that produce and reflect artifacts. Artifacts are symbols and representations of the underlying norms and values of the culture, but they may not directly reflect the values and assumptions that created them.

Schein (2004) viewed culture and leadership as being two sides of the same coin: One cannot be understood without the other. Organizational culture defines who will be chosen and viewed as successful leaders, and leaders create, manage, and change culture. The creation and changing of culture distinguish leaders from managers in Schein's view.

Diagnosing an organization's culture is an important step in understanding its dimensions and strengths. Not all organizations have strong cultures. Depending on the strength of a culture, the behavior and attitudes of members are influenced differently. Organizational culture can be distinguished between thick and thin cultures, depending on the degree of shared beliefs, the influence the culture has on member behavior, and the level of ambiguity among members regarding the importance and priority of shared values (Schein, 2004).

According to Bowditch, Buono, & Stewart (2008), a number of interpretive and diagnostic models have been proposed by researchers of organizational culture, but several aspects of culture are commonly the focus. A summary of their analysis appears in the next subsections.

1. *Visible cultural artifacts*

These artifacts are visual and symbolic manifestations of the organization that reflect the organization's values. They may be physical locations, logos, building structures and decor, as well as processes, job assignments (and other displays of employee recognition), and how recognition and status are distributed. In student affairs organizations, these artifacts can be found in campus offices and where services are delivered, the logos and decor that offices use, the processes and policies that are designed and followed, how information is shared and what is shared, and how people and programs are recognized.

2. *The organization's heroes*

Heroes help define the organization's concept of success. These individuals represent what the organization stands for and reinforce the values of the organization through example. In student affairs, these individuals may be past or present staff members, professional leaders, and those who have generally been recognized for some attribute or contribution to the organization or unit.

3. *Organizational myths and stories*

Values and beliefs are not generally discussed directly, but they are often reflected in the stories and myths that are shared. They generally provide guidance about how things are done and what is valued by the organization. These stories or myths can be both positive and negative, and can explain what not to do or what to avoid.

4. *Behavioral norms and expectations: rituals, rights, and organizational taboos*

The way organizational members interact and the language and rituals they use demonstrate the values and norms of an organization. Everyday rituals such as department or unit meetings, informal social gatherings, more formal ceremonies such as awards ceremonies, training sessions, and so on, all portray the importance of organizational values and interactions within the organization. Organizational taboos convey the boundaries of what is acceptable behavior and are displayed through a variety of socialization processes.

5. *Shared values*

Shared values are at the core of effective organizational culture. What are the values that members across the organization share? Assessing what people say ought to be done can be compared with what is actually done. This comparison provides an understanding of what values are actually shared. (Bowditch, Buono, & Stewart, pp. 326–328)

Organizational Culture in Higher Education

Bergquist and Pawlak (2008) identified six cultures within the collegiate organization. Their goal was to both identify and define the cultures, and also to understand the interaction among those cultures within the collegiate organization. The following subsections summarize each of the six cultures.

Collegiate Culture

This culture is centered primarily in the disciplines represented by faculty. It values faculty research and scholarship and the shared governance processes of the faculty. It holds assumptions about the dominance of rationality in the institution, and it conceives of the institution's enterprise as the generation, interpretation, and dissemination of knowledge and as the development of specific values and qualities of character (Bergquist & Pawlak, 2008, p 15).

Managerial Culture

The managerial culture finds meaning primarily in the organization, implementation, and evaluation of work that is directed toward specified goals and purposes of the institution. This culture values fiscal responsibility and effective supervision, and it holds assumptions about the capacity of the institution to define and measure its goals and objectives clearly. It conceives of the institution's enterprise as the development of specific knowledge, skills, and attitudes in students so that they become successful and responsible citizens (Bergquist & Pawlak, 2008, p. 43).

Development Culture

The development culture finds meaning through the creation of programs and activities furthering the personal and professional growth of members of the higher education community. It values personal openness and service to others, as well as systematic institutional research and curricular planning. It holds assumptions about the inherent desire of all people to attain their own personal development and conceives of the institution's enterprise as the encouragement of potential for cognitive, affective, and behavioral development among all students, faculty members and administrators, and staff (Bergquist & Pawlak, 2008, p. 73).

Advocacy Culture

The advocacy culture finds purpose primarily in the establishment of equitable and egalitarian policies and procedures for the distribution of resources and benefits in the institution. It values confrontation and fair bargaining among constituencies, primarily management and faculty and staff members. It holds assumptions about the ultimate role of power and the need for outside mediation. It conceives of the institution's enterprise as either the undesirable continuation of existing social attitudes and structures, or the establishment of new and more liberal social attitudes and structures (Bergquist & Pawlak, 2008, p. 111).

Virtual Culture

The virtual culture finds meaning by addressing the knowledge-generation and -dissemination capacity of the postmodern world. It values the global perspective of open, shared, responsive education systems and holds assumptions about its ability to make sense of the ambiguity that exists in the world. It conceives of the institution's enterprise as linking educational resources to global and technological resources and broadening the global learning network (Bergquist & Pawlak, 2008, p. 147).

Tangible Culture

The tangible culture finds purpose in its roots, its community, and its spiritual grounding. It values the predictability of a value-based, face-to-face education in a physical space. It holds assumptions about the ability of old systems and technologies to instill the institution's values. It conceives of the institution's enterprise as honoring and integrating learning from a local perspective (Bergquist & Pawlak, 2008, p. 185).

It would seem that student affairs, even if it is composed of separate subunits or entities, is construed by the authors as part of some of the six academic cultures. In fact, the managerial, development, and advocacy cultures might be where one would expect to find elements of student affairs or at least their responsibilities. Surprisingly, student affairs entities appear to be overlooked, and the roles they play are not specifically mentioned in defining the six cultures. In fact, all of the cultures—except the managerial culture—are narrowly described from the perspective of faculty engagement and values, as though only faculty comprise the cultures of a collegiate organization. One can argue that student affairs could either reflect a seventh culture, whose subunits would display many of the attributes of all six of these cultural descriptions, or be blended within the values and framework of each of the six cultures. It is unfortunate that this work continues to portray the collegiate culture so narrowly. At the same time, it is an important descriptive work regarding culture in higher education.

Reflective Summary

1. What has been the historical development of the organization of your student affairs organization? How has the development of organizational studies influenced this development?
2. How do early theories of organizational behavior play a role in your understanding of organizations? Have any specific concepts or theories influenced your thinking?
3. How might you apply general systems theory to your view of your current student affairs organization?
4. How can social systems theory be used to explain the individual and environmental dimensions of student affairs organizations?
5. Create examples for yourself of each of the four frames from Bowman and Deal (2008) for your student affairs organization. How do they help you understand your student affairs organization?
6. Using Schein's concept of organizational culture, describe the culture within your student affairs organization. How does this description help you understand the interactions within your organization?

References

Argyris, C. (1957). *Personality and organizations: The conflict between the system and the Individual.* New York: Harper and Row.
Argyris, C. (1964). *Integrating the individual and the organization.* New York: Wiley.
Banning, J. H. (Ed.). (1978). *Campus ecology: A perspective for student affairs.* Cincinnati, OH: National Association of Student Personnel Monograph.

Barnard, C. (1938). *The functions of the executive.* Cambridge, MA: Harvard University Press.

Berger, P. L., & Lukmann, T. (1966). *The social construct of reality: A treatise in the sociology of knowledge.* Garden City, NY: Doubleday.

Bergquist, W. H., & Pawlak, K. (2008). *Engaging the six cultures of the academy.* San Francisco: Jossey Bass.

Berrien, F. K. (1980). Homeostasis in groups. In G. Chen, J. M. Jamieson, L. L. Schkade, & C. H. Smith (Eds.), *The general theory of systems applied to management and organizations* (vol. I, pp. 115–127). Seaside, CA: Intersystems.

Bertalanffy, L. von. (1968). *General systems theory.* New York: Braziller.

Bess, J. L., & Dee, J. R. (2008). *Understanding college and university organizations: Theories for effective policy and practice. Volume I, The state of the system.* Sterling, VA: Stylus.

Bolman, L. G., & Deal, T. E. (2008). *Reframing organizations: Artistry, choice and leadership* (4th ed.). San Francisco: Jossey Bass.

Boulding, K. (1956). General system theory—The skeleton of science. *Management Science, 2,* 197–208.

Bowditch, J. L., Buono, A. F., & Stewart, M. M. (2008). *A primer on organizational behavior.* Hoboken, NJ: Wiley.

Bowman, L. G., & Deal. (2008). *Reframing organizations: Artistry, choice and leadership* (4th ed). San Francisco: Jossey-Bass.

Buckley, W. (1967). *Sociology and modern systems theory.* Upper Saddle River, NJ: Prentice Hall.

Donaldson, L. (1985). *In defense of organizational theory.* Cambridge, U.K.: Cambridge University Press.

Durkheim, E. (1893/1894). *Division of labor in society* (W. D. Halls, Trans.). New York: Free Press.

Fayol, H. (1949). *General and industrial management.* London: Pitman (First published in 1919).

Follett, M. P. (1923). *The new state: Group organization and the solution of popular government.* New York: Longman.

Gresov, C., & Drazin, R. (1997). Equifinality: Functional equivalence in organizational design. *Academy of Management Review, 22*(2), 403–428.

Hatch, M. J., & Cunliffe A. L. (2006). *Organization theory* (2nd ed.). New York: Oxford University Press.

Herzberg, F. W., Mauser, B., & Snyderman, B. (1959). *The motivation to work.* New York: Wiley.

Jacques, E. (1952). *The changing culture of a factory.* New York: Dryden Press.

Katz, D., & Kahn, R. (1978). *The social psychology of organizations* (2nd ed.). New York: Wiley.

Lawrence, P. R., & Lorsch, J. W. (1969). *Organization and environment: Managing differentiation and integration.* Homewood, IL: Irwin.

Lewin, K. (1938). *The conceptual representation and measurement of psychological forces.* Durham, NC: Duke University Press.

March, J. G., & Simon, H. A. (1958). *Organizations.* New York:Wiley.

Maslow, A. H. (1954). *Motivation and personality.* New York: Harper and Row.

McClelland, D. A. (1965). Toward a theory of motive acquisition. *American Psychologist, 20,* 321–323.

McGregor, D. (1960). *The human side of the enterprise.* New York: McGraw-Hill.

Oshry, B. (1995). *Seeing systems: Unlocking the mysteries of organizational life.* San Francisco: Berrett-Koehler.

Schein, E. H. (1985). *Organizational culture and leadership.* San Francisco: Jossey-Bass.

Schein, E. H. (2004). *Organizational culture and leadership* (3rd ed.). San Francisco: Jossey-Bass.

Taylor, F. W. (1911). *The principles of scientific management.* New York: Harper.

Tosi, H. L., & Mero, N. P. (2003). *The fundamentals of organizational behavior.* London: Blackwell.

Tull, A., Hirt, J. B., & Saunders, S. A. (2009). *Becoming socialized in student affairs administration: A guide for new professionals and their supervisors.* Sterling, VA: Stylus.

Weber, M. (1947). *The theory of social and economic organization.* Glencoe, IL: Free Press. (First published in 1924.)

Weick, K. E. (1979). *The social psychology of organizing.* Reading, MA: Addison-Wesley.

Weick, K. E. (1995). *Sensemaking in organizations.* Thousand Oaks, CA: Sage.

Wheatley, M. J. (2006). *Leadership and the new science: Discovering order in a chaotic world* (3rd ed.). San Francisco: Berrett-Koehler.

3

THE ORGANIZATION

Environment Perspective

The leadership team for a student affairs division at a medium-size university was meeting to initiate a planning process that included revising their organizational plan to comply with the new institutional strategic plan, the development of strategies and initiatives to achieve the plan, and the assignment and possible reassignment of resources to carry out the plan. The vice president had called the group together to determine the key issues and goals that the new plan needed to address. The team was asked not only to be concerned with the issues and goals they wanted to address immediately, but also to consider the issues and challenges that would face them in the future and how were they going to address them. As the team discussed these topics, it became increasingly clear that both the external and internal organizational environments were of concern to them.

The external environment presented the biggest set of challenges because it consisted of issues over which the organization had little control. It also presented the first signals of what the future would hold. In recent decades, the realities of the external world had crept into campus life and were being displayed and acted out in the midst of the internal campus environment. Students brought their lives and social issues with them to college. The increased diversity among students added to both the excitement and the issues faced by the student affairs staff on a daily basis. Advances in technology were bringing the larger world to the campus; students previously sheltered on the college campus were now exposed to that world. Instantaneous communication with each other and with parents, family, and others throughout the world had broken down the walls of the campus and blurred boundaries. Social networking and texting, for example, had sparked new issues, both positive and negative, that the campus needed to address. Parents and other interest groups had become more engaged in the workings and expectations related to the learning and campus life experience.

Partnerships across campus and with the outside community had become the expected norms in relation to learning and student engagement. Change was occurring at an accelerated rate; even the concept of green environmentalism, which had just really caught on as a major campus cultural issue, was being viewed by many as passé. What was on the horizon was still uncertain, but both the external and the internal environments needed to be attended to in ways the organization had not dreamed of just a few years before.

T he environmental context is a critical consideration in ensuring organizational success. How the organization comes to understand the environment, how it positions its efforts to respond to changing environments, and how it understands the ethical implication of intentional environmental intervention are critical to the survival of student affairs organizations in the dynamic higher education environment.

Seeking an understanding of student affairs organizations from an organization–environment perspective includes a wide array of potential contributions from many distinctive views. Myriad theories, concepts, and unique terminology fall into an environmental context. It is beyond the scope of this book to decipher all the possible implications that these wide-ranging conceptions focusing on organizations and environments have for understanding student affairs organizations in higher education. There is much to gain, however, by trying to bring forward the important ideas and notions about organizations and their environments.

A number of distinctive organization–environment conceptions have potential for informing our understanding of student affairs organizations. An early and significant contributor to the understanding of the importance of the environment to human and organizational behavior was Kurt Lewin (1936). His work has had a major influence on the field of organizational behavior and change. His ecological formulation of behavior as a function of the person–environment transaction has also served the student affairs field by providing the basic foundation to the campus ecology movement (Banning, 1978). The early foundational work in understanding the organization–environment perspective must also include general systems theory (von Bertalanffy, 1968) as well as the social systems theorists like Bronfenbrenner (1979), who viewed human development in general from a systems/ecological perspective.

Of critical importance to understanding the organizational–environmental perspective, in addition to the foregoing foundational systems of ecologists von Bertalanffy and Bronfenbrenner, is the more recent development of organizational ecology. Within the organizational ecology literature are a variety of frameworks that link to the concept of organizational ecology, but they do not share a definition of the concept. For the purpose of introducing this chapter, two threads within the organizational ecology movement will be noted: the tradition focusing on the appreciation and use of the biological metaphor of ecology, and the tradition focusing on the importance of the physical environment within organizational ecology.

The first thread of organization–environment concept builds on the biological systems foundation and has tended to focus on the founding, adaptation, merger, and death of organizations (Hannan & Freeman, 1989). The role of the environment in these organizational issues has been viewed from various stances along a continuum of environmental determinism (Bess & Dee, 2008). Bess & Dee (2008) view population ecology (Hannan & Freeman, 1989) as embracing the most deterministic view of the environment with the others noted here moving toward the end of the continuum (with less emphasis on environmental determinism): institutional theory (DiMaggio & Powell, 1991), and resource dependency theory (Sherer & Lee, 2002). These formulations are seen as representing the positivistic paradigm. The paradigmatic views of constructivists and the chaos/complexity opponents are seen as rejecting the more traditional notion of the deterministic causation of the environment on organizations (Bess & Dee, 2008).

The second thread of organizational ecology focuses on the role of the physical environment. Steele (1986) highlights its importance in understanding organization behavior and change. The physical setting of the organization, the workplace, plays a critical role in the "dynamics of organizational life" (Steele, 1986, p. x.). In addition to the work of Lewin (1936) and Steele (1986), Barker's (1968) concept of behavioral setting, Wicker's (1979) theory of manning, and Moos's (1974) environmental dimensional framework also inform organizational behavior and change in ways that are useful to campus student affairs organizations.

In addition to the vast array of theories and conceptions associated with these two threads of the organization–environment perspective, each of these approaches in turn contains unique ideas and concepts. To bring this enormous and rich potential of viewpoints to bear on the understanding of the functioning of student affairs organizations is no small task, but the work of (Wittgenstein, 2001) provides a useful path. Willis (2007) points out the Wittgenstein's approach does not focus on trying to distinguish or compare large numbers of concepts across complex theories, but tries to find what

Wittgenstein calls "family resemblances." Willis further notes, "All members of a family may share a set of family characteristics but no single member of a family will have all these characteristics" (p. 185). This provides a path on which to proceed. Within all the theories and conceptions that fall under the umbrella of the organization–environment perspective and the associated organizational ecology theories, what can be deduced as the major family characteristics that have significant application for campus student affairs organizations? Answering this question is the focus of this chapter. The first step on this path is to explore the basic assumptions associated with the organization–environment perspective.

Major Assumptions of the Organization–Environment Perspective

Viewing the basic assumptions of the organization–environment perspective assists in developing a definition of the perspective that includes the major family resemblances. In the process of looking for key family resemblances, special attention was given to those with direct application to campus student affairs organizations. Morgan's (2006) discussion focused on the strengths of the "organismic metaphor" of ecology provides a place to start defining the major characteristics of the organizational ecology approach important to understanding organizations. From this discussion, a number of important characteristics were noted. First, a major characteristic was the emphasis placed on the transactions between and among organizations and environments, both from the intra- and interorganizational perspectives. Second, organizational function could be improved by attending to the "needs" of the environment. Third, organizations had a wide range of options to choose from when transacting with environments.

An extension of Magnusson and Endler's (1977) assumptions regarding the relationships between persons/environments and organizations/environments was also instructive in defining family characteristics. This extension or extrapolation supports the idea that organizational behavior is a function of a continuous process of multidirectional interactions and communications between organizations and the environment in which it functions. Organizations are intentional and active in their transaction with the environment. On the organizational side of the transaction, plans, goals, strategies, and tactics are important; on the environmental side, the conditions of the environment related to resources, opportunities, and threats are important.

Closer to the actual functional work of campus student affairs organizations is the set of assumptions behind the ecosystem design process associated with the campus ecology model (Banning, 1978; Western Interstate Commission for Higher Education [WICHE], 1973). These assumptions can also be extrapolated and reframed to focus on the organization–environment relationship. These assumptions include the following. The campus environment consists of all the stimuli that impinge on organizations, and these include physical and social stimuli. A transactional relationship exists between organizations and their campus environments; that is, the organization shapes the campus environment and is shaped by it. The shaping properties of the campus environment are important; however, organizations are still viewed as active agents who may resist, transform, or nullify environmental influences. Organizations attempt to cope with environmental conditions. Every campus organization has a design, even if the organization members are not consciously aware of it. Finally, successful organizational structure depends on intentional design and the participation of all campus members in the design process (see chapter 5).

From the foregoing assumptions, a definition for the organization–environment perspective for campus student affairs organizations can be developed. The definition includes the core family resemblances. The organization–environment perspective is a way to view the campus student affairs organization and the campus environment, where the following notions are important: understanding the nature of the environment, understanding the particular role of the physical environment, and the ethics of the intentional design of the organization–environment relationship.

Core Family Resemblances: The Importance of Understanding the Environment

It is important to present a sample of ways to understand and conceptualize the environment from a number of paradigmatic views. Conceptualizations of the environment are critically important to the understanding of the organization–environment model for student affairs organizations. This understanding needs to be developed sufficiently enough to give direction to organizational functions, yet historically the conceptualization of the campus environment has often been lacking. Possible reasons for this lack may include the fact that many of the members of the student affairs profession have counseling and/or student development as their primary background.

Although these areas are extremely valuable in providing important foundational skill sets to the work of student affairs, they both tend to focus individual and organizational attention and resources on individual student behavior, typically at the expense of a full appreciation and understanding of the role of the campus environment. Therefore, it is important to focus on the many potential ways to conceptualize the campus environment. The organization–environment model for student affairs organizations necessitates a full understanding of the environment. Bess and Dee (2008) suggest that environments can be looked at from a more typical positivist view, from a constructivist view, and from a postmodern view. A major post-positivist conceptualization of the campus environment can be found in Moos's (1974) environmental dimensional model. The constructivist view is framed within the concept of the "enacted environment" (Tierney, 2008) and Weick's (1995) concept of "sensemaking." The postmodern perspective of the organization–environment is viewed through the lens of complexity theories (Thorpe & Holt, 2008).

A Post-Positivist View of the Environment

An important positivist view of the environment that has been important to understanding student behavior is the framework presented by Moos's (1974) environmental dimensions model. The application of this model to the student environment and to the work of student affairs was presented by Banning and McKinley (1980). The model can also be useful in understanding both the internal and external environments associated with campus student affairs organizations.

Moos (1974) presents a conceptual framework for understanding human environments that encompasses six major dimensions: the ecological dimension, which includes a focus on geographical, meteorological, and physical design variables (campus architecture); the behavioral setting dimension; the dimension of organizational structure (see chapter 5); the dimension that includes the characteristics of the milieu inhabitants; the dimension of organizational climate; and the dimension of the reinforcement/reward structure of the environment (see chapter 4). As student affairs organizations think about their internal organizational environment as well as their relationship to the campus environment, these dimensions can provide useful insights into the organization–environment relationships.

The ecological dimension of geography, weather, and the physical environment has a major impact on the organizational functioning of student affairs organizations. At a regional level, geography, for example, can affect the very nature of student affairs organizational programmatic goals. Campuses abundant with outdoor recreational opportunities due to their geographic location most often have substantial programmatic efforts and resources devoted to providing students an opportunity to access, use, and remain safe within these outdoor adventure environments. On the other hand, the geographic placement of a college or university in a large inner-city location would probably include a student affairs organization that places emphasis and resources on the many and varied cultural opportunities afforded by the environment. When student affairs organizations look at themselves, the question, Where are we? within the notion of regional geography is a significant one.

Campus geography is also important to understanding the organization–environment perspective. What messages are given when the office for the chief student affairs officer is located outside the major administrative building and in a central location within a student service building? Geographical location of the organizational units of a student affairs division is also critical in terms of ease of communication and in staffing patterns.

Weather also affects student affairs organizations programmatically (midwinter at the University of Alaska—Fairbanks in contrast to midwinter at the University of California—San Diego), and it affects resource allocation to functions such as heating and air conditioning. Both the programmatic and ambient environmental conditions can affect student recruitment and student satisfaction. The physical environment, including the campus architecture, the design of student affairs buildings, and organizational interiors, also affect organizational functioning. The impact of this factor within Moos's ecological dimension will be addressed later in this chapter in great detail because it represents a major thread in the notion of organizational ecology. But the importance of this dimension can be noted just by asking a few simple questions: Are the student organizational units located in welcoming spaces? Is there adequate space for important intraorganizational functions? Are the units and programs of the student affairs organization accessible to the physically disabled?

Moos's dimension of behavioral setting draws attention to the work of ecological psychologists (Barker, 1968; Wicker, 1979). The basic notion of the behavioral setting is that the setting influences the behavior that occurs within it. Setting influences include history, rules, expectations, and physical structures of the setting (Murrell, 1973). For example, many student affairs organizations have a shared or sole responsibility for campus commencement exercises. Over the past few years, there has been an increasing concern expressed by the faculty and administration over the ever-increasing incidents of inappropriate behavior at commencement ceremonies. It is common to hear graduation referred to as the college circus. One institution asked a faculty committee to review the deterioration of student commencement behavior and to make recommendations for improvement. During one of the work sessions, one faculty member asked an interesting question: How does each new graduating class pick up on the previous student commencement behavior because few undergraduates attend a graduation prior to their own? The answer to this question, in part, is that the cues for the inappropriate behavior are part of a behavioral setting. The setting reminds the student of certain behavior.

The commencement exercises for this particular institution (as for most others) are held in the basketball field house. Students are seated, by colleges, on fold-out bleachers next to the court floor: the same seating as at basketball games. The physical setting (backboards and scoreboards are still visible) and the seating arrangement cues spectator-sport behavior, not graduation behavior. In fact, at one recent commencement ceremony, the students on the south side of the court yelled to their counterparts sitting on the north side: "We've got spirit, how about you?" The students on the north replied in a louder voice: "We've got spirit, HOW ABOUT YOU?" This back-and-forth volley continued with ever-increasing volume for several minutes. This behavior is appropriate for a sporting event, but not for a commencement exercise. However, the encoded messages of the "built environment" remind students of the yelling and cheering associated with competitive sporting events. In fact, by arranging students by colleges, each with their own banner, competition is formed to enhance the rowdiness called for by the field house environment. Institutions that are small enough to hold commencement in the college chapel probably do not have the severe rowdiness problem. The encoded messages in a chapel setting elicit behavior more compatible to the behavior that faculty and administrators are seeking for graduation ceremonies. This example provides the essence of the meaning of behavioral setting and its impact on organizational issues, as well as its direct impact on campus inhabitants.

The faculty committee recommended that students should not be seated in the bleachers but that chairs should be placed on the field house floor. They hoped such an arrangement would cue behaviors that are more chapel-like and not sporting-event-like. Obviously, many other factors go into student commencement behavior than just the physical setting and the seating arrangement. However, these built-environment factors may be far more important than previously thought.

Moos's dimension of organizational structure has a direct and obvious relationship to the purpose of this chapter. Both the intra- and interorganizational functioning of the student affairs organization is affected by the shape of the campus organizational structure, the location of the student affairs organization within this structure, and the reporting and communication lines within and outside the organization. In addition to structural location, the more dynamic structural issues of span of control, boundaries, available resources, and myriad other internal and external organizational structure issues affect the functioning of the student affairs organization. Details of the structural and dynamic organization–environment perspective are presented in chapter 5.

The organization–environment relationship is also affected by what Moos (1974) calls the characteristics of the inhabitants of the environment. The application of this dimension to both the external and internal environment of student affairs organizations is quite evident. The makeup of the student affairs staff in terms of age, gender, racial and ethnic background, sexual orientation, training, and experience all contribute to the very foundational nature of the organization. Different patterns of these and other characteristics help shape the organization–environment relationship. Staffing patterns are important aspects of all functioning organizations. The role of diversity in the student affairs organization–environment relationship is discussed later in this chapter and in chapter 9. In addition to looking at the characteristics of members of the student affairs organization, the external environment can also be viewed from this dimension. For example, the characteristics of the student body can also be an influence on student affairs organizations.

A campus curriculum devoted primarily to science and technology versus a curriculum focusing on the liberal and fine arts has a direct impact on student characteristics, organizational staffing, and programming. Likewise, the personal characteristics of other key administration members can also affect the campus student affairs organization. Reporting to a president with a chemistry background may influence the style of campus communication. In other words, the very makeup of key personnel within the environment defines the environment and affects organization–environment relationships.

A final but important Moos dimension is the reinforcement structure of the environment. This notion focuses on the simple question, On what does the environment pay off? Moos (1974) set up the mechanism for this dimension: "[P]eople learn what to do in different settings through usual learning processes, i.e., classical conditioning, instrumental conditioning, or trial and error learning, and observational learning or modeling" (p. 20).

Examples are abundant in the campus organization–environment. A student affairs organization that encourages, models, and rewards creativity is more likely to find a wider array of solutions to problems than an organization that does not reward these behaviors. Is teamwork rewarded by the organization? Is student input valued by all levels of the student affairs organization? Is crossing administrative boundaries rewarded or discouraged? Human resources dimensions of environments are discussed in more detail in chapter 4.

From the positivistic view of the nature of the environment within the organization–environment perspective, key dimensions have been identified: the ecological dimension, the dimension of the behavioral settings, the organizational structure, the nature of the inhabitants, the organizational climate, and the reinforcement dimension. Being sensitive to and understanding the role of these dimensions by student affairs organizational functions is critical to both current functioning and sustainability of the organization.

Conception of the Environment From a Constructivist View

The conception of the environment from a constructivist view focuses on how various dimensions and elements of the environment are viewed and constructed by the organization. The same weather, as part of the ecological dimension, for example, can be viewed and presented as positive or negative for enrollment depending on how it is viewed or framed. The weather patterns of the Midwest can be seen as having too much humidity or as refreshing because of the change of seasons.

The notion that the meaning of the environment is constructed rather than dictated by the environment itself has been a significant part of understanding the student campus environment transaction from the concept of environmental press (Pace & Stern, 1958). Pace and Stern defined environmental press as the nature of the environment as perceived by the inhabitants of that environment. This concept can help campus student affairs organizations understand how students view their environment and how different students view the same environment differently (Strange & Banning, 2001). The purpose of this section is to apply this same constructivist perspective to the campus student affairs organization. Two approaches assist in this translation: the "enacted environment" (Tierney, 2008) and "sensemaking" (Weick, 1995).

Within the enacted environment, ". . . participants develop interpretations about the nature of their organization from their social construction of the organization's culture based on historical traditions, current situational contexts, and individual perceptions" (Tierney, 2008, p. 11). Out of this construction, environments are viewed and understood. This view has direct application to the campus student affairs organization. For example, a large midwestern university did not make contraceptive interventions available for men or women until the mid-1970s. This delay was due to the constructed view, and from the policy that followed, that student sexual behavior was not an issue related to campus health services. Student sexual behavior was seen as the student's responsibility and therefore did not need a campus intervention. Upon the arrival of new leadership in the student affairs organization, this view was found unacceptable, and programs and services related to sexual behavior were initiated. The nature of the campus sexual environment had not changed, but the organizational view of this environment did. The array of health services was broadened because the "enacted" view of the environment had changed. As stated by Tierney (2008, p. 13), "[O]rganizations are less social fact and more ongoing social definition." To understand this ongoing social definition, the enacted environment, Tierney provides several recommendations that are directly applicable to campus student affairs organizations. He suggests that organizations focus on the multiple views of the organization–environment relationship. For example, they can ask simple questions, such as, Does our student affairs organization value innovation or do we value traditional ways of responding to issues? What are the ranges of views on this question and others like it? How do these various views affect decision making within the student affairs organization?

A second recommendation by Tierney (2008) is that an organization should look back to understand where it came from and what were important historical events in the organization's development. Each student affairs organization should try to understand its heritage and its traditions. For example, it would be reasonable to assume that a current student affairs organization that grew out of a practice called *deaning* and out of strong ties to the disciplinary responsibilities might be different in its view from an organization that grew out of an expanded counseling service. The history of one Rocky Mountain institution included the coming together of these two entities to form a more traditional student affairs organization: The two units were in the same building, but the students had to enter the dean's area through what they called the "bad door" and the one to the counseling center through what they called the "good door." These historical aspects of the campus environment affect how current issues are viewed. Finally, Tierney suggests the importance of institutional portraits. For the student affairs organization, an institutional portrait calls for more ethnographic self-studies. What is the culture of the organization? How have things been done historically, and how does this tradition influence decisions today?

This need for self-understanding is underlined by the work of Weick (1995) and his concept of sensemaking. This concept stresses the importance of an organization knowing how it makes sense of its environment. When a student affairs organization looks at an emerging issue, for example, the desire for greater involvement of many parents in the day-to-day campus life of their students, the sensemaking of the organization comes into play. Is a hovering parent to be programmatically embraced or is parental involvement to be discouraged? The answer to this question rests in part with how the organization makes sense of this new environmental challenge. If the sensemaking, as reflected in the student affairs mission, includes notions of university family, community connectiveness, and perhaps an interest in legacy enrollment programs, then embracing the involved parent "makes sense."

On the other hand, if the student affairs organization takes pride in seeing itself as a major player in assisting students to gain greater independence, greater autonomy, and the ability to negotiate the social world on their own terms, then it "makes sense" to develop policies and procedures that discourage parental involvement in matters such as room assignments, roommate issues, and academic curricular matters. Weick (1995) writes about the distinctive characteristics of sensemaking. Many of these characteristics, like Tierney's (2008) notions, have a direct application to student affairs organizational activity.

Student affairs organizations need to talk about and discuss their identity; in other words, what drives their sensemaking? Part of this discussion should address a look backward to historical events that played a role in sensemaking. Weick (1995) also raises the question, How is the organization producing the environment in which it is responding to by the "sense we make of it"? How is the campus academic organization's new career program to be viewed: Is it competitive boundary crossing or is it viewed as collaborative? The sense made of this change influences the unit's response. Weick also points out that much of sensemaking is influenced by the organizational socialization process. What are these processes within a student affairs organization? Are they serving the organization? Finally, Weick underscores the notion that sensemaking is not a static activity; it is ongoing. How can a student affairs organization build within its organization a monitoring system of sensemaking?

The constructionist view of the environment does not reject the objectivist view of the environmental dimensions presented by Moos (1974), but it adds another level of consideration and complexity: How are these environmental dimensions viewed by the student affairs organization and how does this affect the organization–environment relationships? The next section presents a postmodern look at the organization–environment relationship and considers chaos/complexity theory. In particular, we look at the lessons to be gained from this postmodern view of the student affairs organization.

Conceptions of the Environment From a Postmodern View

The postmodern view of the organization–environment relationship is most often captured by the notions of chaos and complexity. Numerous approaches fall within the postmodern notion, but Thorpe and Holt (2008) suggest that the term *complexity theories* serves as the umbrella label for the many varieties of approaches to understanding organizations from the postmodern point of view. A central tenet of a postmodern view is to question historical assumptions about the phenomenon of interest, in this case, the assumptions about how the organization–environment relationship has been viewed historically. For example, a postmodern view of the organization–environment relationship raises questions regarding the typical views of the objectivists and constructivists. Bess and Dee (2008, p. 158) note the following: "Postmodern theorists claim that the positivist emphasis on prediction and control and the social constructivist focus on sensemaking and image are based on problematic assumptions." Out of the vast literature associated with complexity theories and organization behavior and change, a few key concepts that apply to the campus student affairs organization will be highlighted: the nature of the organization–environment relationship, organizational change and complexity, and finally the need for organizations to appreciate and manage paradox.

From a complexity theories point of view, the traditional boundary between the organization and environment becomes blurred. The traditional view addresses how the organization needs to understand the dimensions of the environment and how to respond to environmental change. The view offered by the complexity theories is that there is a mutual adaptation and that change needs to be viewed, not from a reaction and adaptation view, but from a co-evolutionary view (Demers, 2007).

The campus student affairs organization participates as part of the environment, although it is typically seen as being distinct from the organization. In addition, complexity theories recognize the multiple systems of action that occur in the organization–environment relationship and that this complexity plus random events create chaotic conditions, but changes can occur unpredictably and be caused by small events in the system (Morgan, 2006). The impact of these conditions on organizations is outlined by Thorpe and Holt (2008): Organizations need to be able to respond with "greater democracy and power equalization" (p. 48) and to reexamine the role of hierarchy and control (Morgan, 2006). Under these conditions, more diverse responses become available for organizations. A second impact of complexity suggested by Thorpe and Holt (2008) is that organizational change works best when the changes are seen as larger than small incremental changes, yet smaller than radical changes. Finally, effective change is hindered by static long-range plans. The earlier example of programming for parent involvement can serve as an example. Given the sensemaking of a student affairs division that is devoted to the university family concept, plus the need to establish a legacy enrollment program, parent phone calls to the university are directed to the programmatic office of parental involvement. This activity gets rewarded; parents feel better about the university; and the president's office, knowing about this programmatic activity, feels better about the student affairs organization.

What appears to be a simple win-win response to an environmental challenge can become complex. First, the action by the student affairs program has changed parental expectations regarding the campus experience. A small event like a parent phone call to a professor to discuss a child's grade on an essay exam may be all that is needed to move the campus in the direction of chaos. The professor who received the phone call is taken aback by the fact that a parent of a student is now questioning her academic behavior. Perhaps at the same time, this professor becomes aware of the circumstances surrounding her last departmental hire where the candidate for the position brought his parents to the final interview to negotiate a startup package. These two random events combine in the professor's mind for the professor to ask, What are we doing at this university catering to parents in academic matters? She goes to faculty council and a faculty task force is developed to "securitize the parent involvement in the academic governance of the university" and "seek an explanation of student affairs policies regarding students' parents." The system is now in a state of chaos, and what was seen as a simple win-win outcome is now the center of a campus debate on the critical issues of academic freedom and governance. No president is eager to engage debates over these issues. What started this in the first place? The campus student affairs organization's programmatic efforts to engage involved parents?

The simple example illustrates the organization–environment perspective from the complexity theories. The boundary between the organization and the environment becomes blurred, and the student affairs organization ends up in a defensive position that it helped to create in the environment. Small random events can bring about dynamic situations that can create much complexity and/or chaos, taxing traditional hierarchies and control structures. This example underscores that, from a postmodern view, the environment is more than dimensions and more than how we view these dimensions. Given this view of organization–environment relationship, are there specific lessons to be found that will enable a campus student affairs organization to function in this state of complexity?

Two lessons emerge from the complexity theories that have practical merit for a student affairs organization. First, greater participation by a greater number of folks where notions of hierarchy and control are lessened (Morgan, 2006; Thorpe & Holt, 2008) contributes to organizational efficiency. For example, perhaps the student affairs division should have anticipated the campus cultural change they were about to promote with their program efforts, but including a wider range of campus offices, for example, representatives from the faculty senate, could have been helpful. Second, Johnson (1996) and Morgan (2006) both advocate organizations increasing their capacity for polarity management, or the ability to understand events, situations, and challenges not from an either-or perspective, but from a both-and perspective. Morgan (2006) noted that organizations in this postmodern environment "need to innovate, but avoid mistakes; think long term, but deliver results now; cut cost, but increase morale; be flexible, but respect the rules; collaborate, but compete; decentralize, but retain control; and lower costs, but keep high quality" (p. 282). If all these polarities were addressed by the student affairs division, would a parental involvement program have been established? Would it have been established differently? Would the establishment process have been different?

The family resemblance core of understanding the environment is of critical importance to student affairs organizations because they function within the campus and the larger environment. Their internal environment and the external environment that they participate in co-evolve. The discussion in this chapter outlined a number of ways in which this environment can be viewed: from a positivist view to the other end of the continuum, the postmodern view. Within all these views are a number of elements that lead to the second core resemblance: the importance of understanding the structural and dynamic components of the organization–environment relationship.

Core Family Resemblance: Importance of the Physical Environment

An important core resemblance within organizational ecology is the role of the physical setting. This is reflected in Steele's (1986) definition of organizational ecology: "[T]he pattern of reciprocal relationships and influences among organizational members and their *workplaces*" (p. ix) (emphasis added). It is important to point out the potential nature of the physical environment's influence. The major issue that must be addressed is the nature of the influence that the physical setting may have on organizational behavior. In the literature, the nature of the physical setting influence has been conceptualized by three positions (Bell, Fisher, Baum, & Greene, 1990; Porteus, 1977). First, environmental determinism suggests that there is a rather direct and causal link between the built setting and individual and organizational behavior. A second position, environmental possibilism, views the physical setting as one that offers opportunities and sets limits for organizational behavior. For example, if there is no meeting room large enough for the members of a student affairs organizational staff to meet, then this limits the possibility of many divisional activities. Finally, a third position is that of environmental probabilism, which assumes that certain behaviors have probabilistic links to the physical setting. The entrance to a student affairs organization can be built with varying degrees of welcome. A closed-door office with high counter-type desk arrangements within the office and no person to be seen has a very high probability of communicating an organizational message to outsiders that they are not welcome or expected. On the other hand, an office arrangement with an open door and a receptionist located within vision of the visitor signals a much more open and welcoming organization.

The nature of the influence of the physical setting on organizations also raises the question, How is this influence communicated? Why is an open door seen differently than a closed door? Rapoport (1982) provides an understanding of how the various degrees of influence are communicated. He suggests that, because physical environments and settings do not verbally speak, "it follows that they must represent a form of non-verbal communication" (p. 50). Rapoport refines this notion of nonverbal communication by suggesting that the physical setting "communicates, through a whole set of cues, the most appropriate choices to be made: the cues are meant to elicit appropriate emotions, interpretations, behaviors, and transactions" (pp. 80–81). These nonverbal communications can be sent by both the functional aspects of the physical setting as well as the symbolic aspects (Strange & Banning, 2001). For example, a midwestern campus located the office of their chief student affairs officer across the street from the main campus. This location made it more difficult for students to find and nearly impossible for students in wheelchairs to navigate. And the symbolism of the location suggested that it was not seen as a major or central player in campus organizational matters; "it was off to the side." The work of Steele (1973, 1986) and Becker and Steele (1995) can assist us with examining the role of the functional aspects of the physical setting on student affairs organizations, and Gagliardi (1990) and Vischer (2005) can assist us in understanding the role that symbolism can play in campus student affairs organizations.

Steele's (1973) approach focuses on the role that the dimensions of the physical setting play in organizations. Every physical setting can be viewed in terms of the relationship between and among the elements of the setting and the functions performed by the elements. Elements are those aspects of the physical setting that are likely to influence the functioning of individuals or groups in the setting. For example, an element could be a particular thing (a piece of furniture) or a pattern of things (the arrangement of furniture). Steele's taxonomy for the dimensions of the physical setting is as follows:

1. *Security and shelter* refer to protection from harmful or unwanted stimuli in one's surroundings.
2. *Social contact* refers to the arrangements of facilities and spaces that permit or promote social interaction.
3. *Symbolic identification* refers to the messages sent by settings, which tell someone what a person, group, or organization is like.
4. *Task instrumentality* refers to the facilities and layouts appropriate for carrying out tasks in a particular setting.

5. *Pleasure* refers to the pleasure or gratification the place gives to those who use it.
6. *Growth* refers to the stimulus for growth the setting gives the user. (Steele, 1973, p. 25)

Every student affairs organization is affected by these elements. What are the safety issues associated with organizational offices, including the ease of emergency services, campus parking, campus lighting, and so forth? Some organizational offices can become off limits due to safety concerns. How safe are programs that are offered at night? How safe is the accessibility to offices, particularly for those who are in wheelchairs? What are the organizational issues for the visually impaired? The arrangements of facilities and furniture can affect social contact. Where are the student affairs organizational buildings located? Do the locations afford or hinder contact with other campus personnel and students? Some campus admissions offices are located on a second or third floor in a building. This presents a functional hindrance when it comes to access for campus visitors and is in direct opposition to the function of the organization. The social contact element is also an important component of the interior spaces of the student affairs organization. For example, one vice president for student affairs used a round table rather than the traditional square one to support ease of communications with staff and students.

Symbolic elements of the physical setting are also important for the functioning of student affairs organizations. For example, the interiors of many offices within student affairs organizations communicate symbolically in many cases a lack of caring: no comfortable waiting areas, waiting areas populated by unhealthy plants and unattractive artwork, and no easy signals about how the reception area works. Tasks within an organizational setting are affected by the physical environment. Organizational performance is particularly affected by workspaces. Becker and Steele (1995) state, "[T]he form of buildings: the choice of furnishings; the arrangement of offices and work stations; the layout circulation; the number, location and character of conference and meeting rooms, stairwells, elevators, cafeterias, and break areas; choices about how and to whom space is allocated; and the nature of the processes to plan, design, and manage all of these workplace elements" (p. 11) affect the performance of the organization. Finally, the areas of pleasure and growth are affected by the physical setting. If the physical space or setting can engender a sense of place or emotional attachment (Taun, 1974), then notions of pleasure and growth become salient. For example, at the campus level, the sense of place related to campus planning has become associated with increased enrollment, student satisfaction, and increased alumni giving (Reeve & Kassabaum, 1997). The physical setting elements discussed here play a significant role in student affairs organizational functioning, but little effort appears to be spent in understanding this important relationship. The importance of this functional relationship between the physical settings and organizational behavior is further enhanced by looking at the symbolism that is communicated by these functional relationships.

Gagliardi (1990) addresses the symbolic nature of the organizational setting, particularly the physical setting and artifacts that are within organizations. He notes that "artifacts are the visual expression of a culture" (p. 3) and they communicate organizational values and identity. If the central student affairs organizational offices or key parts of the organizational structure are hidden in inconvenient basement locations, then the symbolism of this location is self-evident. The interior artifacts of an office can also communicate important messages. Physical arrangements, artwork, posters, and other cultural artifacts can communicate in powerful ways about complex topics (Banning, Middleton, & Deniston, 2008). For example, on one campus, a poster welcoming and celebrating the disabled worker was posted in front of the facilities office, which was inaccessible to wheelchair staff. The importance of the artifact's message was diminished, but it could also be construed as a lack of institutional sincerity about disabled staff. Campus student affairs organizations should understand the importance and power of the symbolic artifact messages and make the organizational artifact a central component to understanding the identity and values of the organization. As noted already in this chapter, sensemaking of an organization includes the symbolic values of its artifacts.

An additional effect of physical artifact communication focuses on the issue of status within an organization (Vischer, 2005). Vischer points out that people within an organization, their satisfaction, and their performance are affected by the status of office space location and size within the organization. The example of the central student affairs office located across the street from the main campus is a clear illustration of how organizational status is communicated. Understanding the communication of status is important. For example, Vischer points out the concept of status congruency, which focuses on how people within an organization look for congruency in their status relationships as communicated by organizational space. This is often viewed from an organizational hierarchy that suggests that the top officer of the organization have the largest office.

Even if the organization deliberately alters the hierarchal space relationship, with smaller space being occupied by the organizational head, an organizational communication message is delivered. For example, at a large midwestern campus, an academic provost moved his office to a metal building in the industrial/facilities section of the campus. Campus personnel were confused by this move. Was this a gesture to reduce status of ego and/or office, or was this just a symbol of odd behavior? Regardless of the intended or unintended message, it illustrates the importance of the physical setting to organizations. Campus student affairs organizations need to monitor the role that physical spaces and associated artifacts play in both understanding and communication of organizational behavior.

Core Family Resemblance: Intentional Design of the Organization–Environment Relationship

Explicit in all these views are the transactional or mutually shaping view of the organization–environment relationship and those members of organizations who take upon themselves the task of managing this relationship for the purposes of the organization. They deliberately intend to bring about change in the organization–environment relationship that benefits the organization.

The intentionality associated with bringing about change in the organization–environment relationship brings to the forefront the issue of ethics. At least three approaches can be utilized for judging the ethical behavior of organizations intending to make changes or not make changes in this relationship: (a) an ethical principles approach to aggregate from an individual decision-making level to an organizational level, (b) a fulfillment of community values approach, and (c) a community process approach.

The first criterion utilizes the ethical principles approach. What are the ethical principles that apply to decision making within the campus community? Kitchener (1985) offered a list of five principles that can be used to judge campus decisions: (a) respecting autonomy, (b) doing no harm, (c) benefiting others, (d) being just, and (e) being faithful. Caring can be added as a sixth principle to reflect the gender research on the importance of caring and fostering helpful relationships (Delworth & Seaman, 1984; Noddings, 1984).

A study conducted by the Council for the Advancement of Standards in Higher Education and reported by Dean (2006) identified seven ethical principles. These principles are listed by Dalton, Crosby, Valente & Eberhart (2009, p. 174) as: (a) *autonomy,* respecting freedom of choice; (b) *nonmalfeasance,* doing no harm; (c) *beneficence,* promoting the welfare of others, especially students; (d) *justice,* being fair and respectful to others; (e) *fidelity,* being faithful to our word and duty; (f) *veracity,* being truthful and accurate; and (g) *affiliation,* fostering community and public good. These principles are not absolutes. They give us guidelines, but they don't solve all the ethical issues. In real-life situations, some principles may be, and often are, in conflict with each other (Kitchener, 1985). To determine the level of ethical behavior for the campus community as a whole, each individual decision can be assessed by the ethical principles approach and the results aggregated to form a community-level assessment. This approach is not very practical or useful, but its discussion within a student affairs organization is instructive.

A second criterion in judging ethical behavior in the organization–environment relationship, the fulfillment of values approach, is derived from the work of Brown (1985). The campus as an organization and community has a set of values and goals usually reflected in a mission statement that guides its activities. For example, Brown (1985) suggests the following list of community-level values for higher education: (a) peace issues, (b) vocation as calling, (c) developmental progress for all, (d) theory and research, and (e) a humane learning environment. By adding the community/organizational values component, ethical behavior should be in concert with the ethical principles and also help fulfill the goals of the campus community.

To give guidance to the ethical issues associated with intentional design of the environment, the community process approach provides an important foundation. It suggests all those who are affected by the efforts to redesign the organization–environment relationship must have an opportunity for meaningful input into the process (Huebner & Banning, 1987). Kelman and Warwick (1978) suggest that questions like the following need to be asked when judging the ethical nature of the process to change environments: Who participated in the process? How were diverse interests represented? Who will benefit? Who will suffer? By what means will the decision be implemented, by coercion or by facilitation? Who is involved in the ongoing evaluation? The ecosystem design approach suggests that all who are to be affected by the decision must have an opportunity for meaningful input into the process (Huebner & Banning, 1987).

The following scenario illustrates that the choice of the ethical principles approach can lead to different conclusions regarding the ethics of an organization–environment intervention. A vice president for student services instructed the campus bookstore manager to remove *Playboy, Playgirl,* and *Penthouse* magazines from the shelves. It was a decision that the vice president made based on the knowledge of the relationship between pornography and violence against children, women, and men. From the ethical principles approach, the decision seemed correct. The decision also seemed ethical from the community fulfillment of values approach. The campus had a strong personal abuse policy, which stated: "Abusive treatment of individuals on a personal or stereotyped basis will be prohibited. . . ." So from both an ethical principles approach and a community value fulfillment approach, it appeared to be an ethical decision. The decision, however, failed to meet the criterion of the community process approach because no one was consulted. The issues were not discussed with students or with other members of the campus community. No outside input was sought. The decision was ethically flawed from the perspective of the community process approach for organization–environment change.

Reflective Summary

1. What are some examples of the organization–environment perspective that you have experienced in student affairs?
2. In your own experience, what are the ways in which the Moos dimensions have affected your work?
3. How has student affairs organizational sensemaking influenced how you think about your work?
4. Describe an event that gave you the opportunity to explore polarity management.
5. What are the student affairs organizational artifacts on your campus? Describe them.
6. Review a recent decision you made from the perspective of the ethical principles approach and the community process approach.

References

Banning, J. H. (Ed.). (1978). *Campus ecology: A perspective for student affairs.* Cincinnati, OH: NASPA Monograph.

Banning, J. H., & McKinley, D. (1980). Conceptions of the campus environment. In W. Morrill, J. Hurst, & E. Oetting (Eds.), *Dimensions of intervention for student development* (pp. 39–57). New York: Wiley.

Banning, J. H., Middleton, V., & Deniston, T. (2008). Using photographs to assess equity climate: A taxonomy. *Multicultural Perspectives, 10*(1), 1–6.

Barker, R. G. (1968). *Ecological psychology: Concepts and methods for studying the environment of human behavior.* Stanford, CA: Stanford University Press.

Becker, F., & Steele, F. (1995). *Workplace by design: Mapping the high-performance workscape.* San Francisco: Jossey-Bass.

Bell, P., Fisher, J., Baum, A., & Greene, T. (1990). *Environmental psychology.* Fort Worth, TX: Holt, Rinehart and Winston.

Bess, J. L., & Dee, J. R. (2008). *Understanding college and university organizations: Theories for effective policy and practice. Volume one.* Sterling, VA: Stylus.

Bertalanffy, L. von (1968). *General systems theory: Foundations, development applications.* New York: Braziller.

Bronfenbrenner, U. (1979). *The ecology of human development: Experiments by nature and design.* Cambridge, MA: Harvard University Press.

Brown, R. D. (1985). Creating an ethical community. In H. J. Canon & R. D. Brown (Eds.)., *Applied ethics in student services.* New directions for student services, no. 30 (pp. 67–79). San Francisco: Jossey-Bass.

Dalton, J. C., Crosby, P. C., Valente, A., & Eberhardt, D. (2009). Maintaining and modeling everyday ethics in student affairs. In G. S. McClellan & J. Stringer, (Eds.), *Handbook of student affairs administration* (pp. 166–186). San Francisco: John Wiley.

Dean, L. A. (Ed.). (2006). *CAS professional standards for higher education.* (6th ed.). Washington, D.C.: Council for the Advancement of Standards in Higher Education.

Delworth, U., & Seaman, D. (1984). The ethics of care: Implications of Gilligan for student services profession. *Journal of College Student Personnel, 25*(6), 489–492.

Demers, C. (2007). *Organizational change theory: A synthesis.* Los Angeles, CA: Sage Publications.

DiMaggio, P. J., & Powell, W. W. (1991). Introduction. In W. W. Powell & P. J. DiMaggio, (Eds.). *The new institutionalism in organizational analysis* (pp. 1–38). Chicago, IL: University of Chicago Press.

Gagliardi, P. (Ed.). (1990). *Symbols and artifacts: Views of the corporate landscape.* New York: Adline de Gruyter.

Hannan, M., & Freeman, J. (1989). *Organizational ecology.* Cambridge. MA: Harvard University Press.

Huebner, L., & Banning, J. H. (1987). Ethics of intentional campus design. *NASPA Journal, 25*(1), 28–37.

Johnson, B. (1996). *Polarity management: Identifying and managing unsolvable problems.* Amherst, MA: HRD Press.

Kelman, H., & Warwick, D. (1978). The ethics of social intervention: Goals, means, consequences. In G. Bermant, H. Kelman, & D. Warwick (Eds.), *The ethics of social intervention* (pp. 3–33). New York: Wiley.

Kitchner, K. (1985). Ethical principles and ethical decisions in student affairs. In H. J. Canon & R. D. Brown (Eds.), *Applied ethics in student services* (New Directions for Student Services No. 30, pp. 17–29). San Francisco: Jossey Bass.

Lewin, K. (1936). *Principles of topological psychology.* New York: McGraw-Hill.

Magnusson, D., & Endler, N. (Eds.). (1977). *Personality at the crossroads: Current issues in interactional psychology.* New York: Lawrence Erlbaum.

Moos, R. H. (1974). Systems for the assessment and classification of human environments: An overview. In R. H. Moos & P. M. Inset (Eds.), *Issues in Social Ecology* (pp. 5–28). Palo Alto, CA: National Press Books.

Morgan, G. (2006). *Images of organizations.* Thousand Oaks, CA: Sage.

Murrell, S. A. (1973). *Community psychology and social systems.* New York: Behavioral Publications.

Noddings, N. (1984). *Caring: A feminine approach to ethics and moral education.* Berkeley: University of California Press.

Pace, C. R., & Stern, G. G. (1958). An approach to the measurement of psychological characteristics of college environments. *Journal of Educational Psychology, 49,* 269–277.

Porteus, J. (1977). *Environment and behavior.* Reading, MA: Addison-Wesley.

Rapoport, A. (1982). *The meaning of the built environment: A nonverbal communication approach.* Beverly Hills, CA: Sage.

Reeve, J. R., & Kassabaum, D. G. (1997). A sense of place master plan: Linking mission and place. *APPA Proceedings,* 219–228.

Sherer, P., & Lee, K. (2002). Institutional change in large law firms: A resource dependency and intuitional perspective. *Academy of Management Journal, 45*(1), 102–119.

Steele, F. (1973). *Physical settings and organization development.* Reading, MA: Addison-Wesley.

Steele, F. (1986). *Making and managing high-quality workplaces: An organizational ecology.* New York: Teachers College Press.

Strange, C. C., & Banning, J. H. (2001). *Educating by design: Creating campus environments that work.* San Francisco: Jossey-Bass.

Taun, Y. E. (1974). *Topophilla.* Upper Saddle River, NJ: Prentice-Hall.

Thorpe, R., & Holt, R. (2008). *The Sage dictionary of qualitative management research.* Los Angeles: Sage.

Tierney, W. G. (2008). *The impact of culture on organizational decision making: Theory and practice in higher education.* Sterling, VA: Stylus

Vischer, J. C. (2005). *Space meets status: Designing workplace performance.* New York: Routledge.

Weick, K. E. (1995). *Sensemaking in organizations.* Thousand Oaks, CA: Sage.

Western Interstate Commission for Higher Education. (1973). *The ecosystem model: Designing campus environments.* Boulder, CO: Author.

Wicker, A. W. (1979). *An introduction to ecological psychology*. Monterey CA: Brooks/
  Cole.
Willis, J. W. (2007). *Foundations of qualitative research: Interpretative and critical
  approaches*. Thousand Oaks, CA: Sage.
Wittgenstein, L. (2001). *Philosophical investigations* (G.E.M. Anscombe, Trans.).
  Oxford, UK: Blackwell Publishers, Ltd.

4

INDIVIDUAL AND TEAM DIMENSIONS WITHIN STUDENT AFFAIRS ORGANIZATIONS

It was nearly 11:00 p.m. on a Thursday night and Jamie Perez was driving home from a long but exciting meeting with the student organization group that he advised. He was tired from a 14-hour day, but he was invigorated by the level of discussion and debate that had occurred at the meeting. The students had to make some tough decisions about how they were going to fund and staff a campuswide program on international global sustainability. The outcome of the discourse was secondary to the learning opportunity that had occurred during the heated and informative exchange. Jamie and his staff were pleased that so many of the students were assuming leadership roles on this important issue; at the same time, he was glad that it was nearing the end of the week. He longed for some quiet time with his family. He and his staff had been putting in a lot of night and weekend hours the past few weeks, and although this was common for this time of year, the end of the semester was in sight. He did not know what he would do if he did not have so many really dedicated staff who gave selflessly of their time to address what seemed to be endless demands and nearly impossible circumstances. Student needs seemed to be endless.

As Jamie turned into his driveway, his cell phone rang. It was the chief of police informing him that a large group of students were in the midst of a standoff outside one of the residence halls and that he and his staff were needed to help address the conflict. His immediate, almost programmed reaction was to begin dialing numbers to rally his staff to come and help. Once he completed his phone calls he turned his car around and headed back to campus. On the way, he called home to let them know that he was not sure when he would get there and that they should leave the light on for him. He said to himself: Such is life in student affairs.

S tudent affairs is a human-services-oriented profession. Most of the work in student affairs focuses on the human dimension of educating and developing students and providing them with services that can assist them in being successful. Somewhat ironically, attention to the organizational needs and human dynamics of staff members and their relationship to the greater organization are often ignored or at least not attended to as effectively as they could be. This neglect may be the result of a number of factors: high expectations on the part of organizational leadership, the lack of adequate resources to do anything different, a belief that intrinsic rewards associated with being part of the teaching and learning process are enough to maintain staff commitment, and/or a general misunderstanding of human relations theory and its importance to organizational effectiveness. No matter what the rationale or the resource reality in an organization, managing and caring for the human dimensions within student affairs should be the number 1 priority of the organization's leadership. Human resources and its related behavior will continue to be a significant issue within student affairs organizations, and how these issues are addressed has a significant influence on the organization's effectiveness.

Like Jamie Perez's situation in the chapter-opening vignette, working odd and late hours is not uncommon for many student affairs practitioners. Student affairs roles carry high expectations and demands, yet they also provide many intrinsic rewards. The demands of the job, handling emotional and physical crises, and the stress of being on call around the clock can take their toll on individuals and their lives outside work. The salary levels and benefits in most cases are adequate, but they do not always compare favorably with other professions, or even with other staff positions in other divisions within an institution. Rewards and recognition vary and are often determined by the attentiveness of institutional leadership and state and institutional rules and regulations. For example, bonuses or financial incentives are not common practices in higher educational organizations, and recognitions seldom carry any financial or resource incentives other than a kudo for doing a good job. At the same time, the personal rewards of being part of students' growth and development is very rewarding and individually stimulating.

Understanding the theory related to the human dimensions of organizational behavior, the interconnections among the individuals who make up an organization, the groups and teams within which they work, and how these units work as systems within the greater organization is essential to creating effective student affairs organizations. This chapter focuses on a variety of theories related to the individual dimensions of organizational behavior: individual attributes, such as perception, judgment, and attribution; motivation and human need; job enrichment; and other human relations theory. It also addresses issues of workgroups and teams, as well as the dynamics of individual differences and organizational learning, and their impact on organizational behavior.

Personality

All of us bring one fundamental attribute to our work: no matter what role we play in an organization, we bring our personalities to the job. Our personality is essentially who we are and forms what we conceptually label as identity. It orchestrates how we view as well as engage the world around us. A personality once formed appears to be somewhat stable and is unique to each of us. At the same time, researchers have uncovered some personality traits that seem to be common among various individuals. Five categories of such traits have been identified from an analysis of a large number of trait theories conducted over the years: (a) extroversion, (b) emotional stability, (c) agreeableness, (d) conscientiousness, and (e) openness to experience (Costa & McCrae, 1992).

There is no single theory of personality, and the extensive literature about personality includes research on traits, attitudes, perceptions, and drivers. Because we cannot do justice to the extensive research on personality in this book, we concentrate on some of the theory that relates to how personality interacts with organizations.

Personality–Organizational Theories

The attraction-selection-attrition cycle (Schneider, Goldstein, & Smith, 1995) explains how personality and organizations affect each other. People are attracted to and select the organizations they decide to enter and participate in. As similar people enter an organization and dissimilar people leave it, the organization becomes more homogeneous. The people who are part of the organization define the norms and create and maintain the culture of the organization.

Over time, this preponderance toward homogeneity may actually threaten the organization's survival. Homogeneity breeds like-thinking and a strong resistance to diverse ideas and change, and these traits, left unchecked, can lead to organizational decay. To alter this cycle, one must consciously change the composition of people in the organization. This is one reason that regularly bringing new blood into an organization at all levels of the hierarchy is healthy for an organization and can help maintain its vitality over time.

The organization personality orientation theory (Presthus, 1978) was designed to help explain how people accommodate themselves to work situations. This theory identified three organizational personality types. Organizationalists are oriented toward the place in which they work. Professionals are oriented toward the work they do. Indifferents are focused on things outside work; they work for pay so that they can focus on outside interests.

For example, in student affairs, the organizationalists are staff members who focus their loyalty and commitment to the institution. They seek to achieve the goals of the organization, and they seek rewards and upward mobility within the organization. They want to please the leadership because they seek advancement and recognition within the organization. Professionals are job- or responsibility-centered, and they are committed to their profession and professional goals. They focus on the job or their professional identity and not on the specific institution. They may see themselves as student affairs professionals who happen to work at a specific institution, but they could change jobs and institutions very easily if other opportunities are presented. Finally, indifferents do not really identify with their work or the organization and neither are a critical part of their individual identity. They work so they can be engaged in other activities and interests outside work, or they have become stagnant on the job and no longer have a commitment to the organization or their profession. They may do their job well, but they are not necessarily committed to the institution or their profession. They generally do not seek new opportunities to learn additional skills or to grow professionally.

Several personality characteristics have an impact on work environments. People have been found to be either positively or negatively affective toward work (Watson & Clark, 1984). Positive affectivity describes those who are positive, active, engaged, and strong. Negative affectivity can be described as negative; not very happy; and often distressed, fearful, and hostile. The two are not opposites of each other. People with high positive affectivity are seen as better leaders and managers, and are more satisfied with their work. They are also easier to deal with in the work environment.

Some evidence suggests that personality plays a larger role in organizations that are more loosely structured than in organizations that are more structured and controlled. In more structured organizations, personality traits are often confined, and socialization may be less frequent so that people conform to the organizational norms and authority imposed by management. In loosely structured organizations (a student affairs organization is an example), personality characteristics play a more dominant role in setting the norms and values within an organizational culture and have a greater social influence on peers.

Machiavellian or narcissistic personalities (Lipmen-Blumen, 2005; Lubit, 2004) have been found to be problematic in the work setting. They are individuals with high self-esteem and strong visible leadership skills, but they generally act in their own self-interests. They actually have little to no regard for others or for the organization other than what is in their personal interests. They are cool and calculating; may take advantage of others; and/or lie, deceive, or compromise morality with no guilt or remorse. They often use false or exaggerated praise to gain the favor of others and then turn on them to make personal gains. Their impact can be very destructive within organizations and devastating to individuals who are victimized by their behavior. Unfortunately, these personalities are not uncommon in today's society, and because of their manipulative skills, they can rise to high leadership roles in organizations, including higher education and student affairs.

Emotional Intelligence

Intelligence was initially conceived as being an attribute in the cognitive domain. More recently, a number of researchers have studied a different conception of intelligence know as emotional intelligence. This concept was adapted from the work of Harold Gardner (1983) and his work on multiple intelligences. The concept of emotional intelligence was popularized by Goleman (1995, 1998) and specifically applied to the workplace in his more recent work (Cherniss & Goleman, 2001). His work attempts to conceptualize the process by which individuals achieve emotional competence. It has evolved into a framework that includes four domains: (a) self-awareness, (b) self-management, (c) social awareness, and (d) relational management. Within these domains are 20 competencies that lead to mastery of emotional competence and that can enable one to be successful in managing one's work environment and one's life.

Myers-Briggs

One of the most widely used models for classifying personalities on the basis of how people perceive the world, what interactions they prefer, and the way they approach problems is the Myers-Briggs Type Indicator (Myers & Briggs, 1962). This model classifies people along a continuum of four dimensions, which in combination provide a type that reflects a variety of personality characteristics. The four dimensions include (a) introversion-extroversion, (b) sensing-intuition, (c) thinking-feeling, and (d) perceiving-judging. This model and the inventories developed to measure these dimensions have been researched extensively. The model has also been used within student affairs organizations with both students and staff members. It can be useful in helping individuals understand their own personality preferences, helping staff members understand the dimensional preferences of co-workers, and helping individuals and groups use the strengths found in each type to make their team efforts more effective.

Individual Decision Making and Attribution

In student affairs organizations, staff members at every level continuously make decisions. They make decisions about students, colleagues, how they will spend their time, with whom they will interact, how they will do their work, and so forth. These decisions result in behavior, and through the behavior of individuals, relationships are formed, services and programs are created, and the life of an organization unfolds. To understand organizational behavior, we must first understand some of the basic components of perception, judgment, and attribution that are at the core of human dynamics and behavior in organizations.

Perception

Perception is a fundamental attribute of each individual. It involves the process that individuals use to make sense out the world. It is the way we sort, organize, and attribute properties and characteristics, and attribute cause and effect to them (Tosi & Mero, 2003). Our perceptions define our reality and give meaning to the environment in which we exist. How we perceive and what we choose to perceive is learned. As we engage in the process of perception, we group specific perceived information into categories (schema) that make sense to us based on our past experiences. We tend to keep our interpretations of perceived information consistent with past experiences.

Our interpretations change when it is demonstrated that the past schema no longer works, and it needs to be expanded or is wrong. A number of conditions can affect our perceptions, including our physical and emotional state; the nature, intensity, and size of what is being perceived; and the context of the perceptual event. Although perception affects everything we do and every decision we make, the way we perceive others is exceptionally critical in organizational life.

What we focus on when we perceive has a great impact on how we assess or judge what is perceived. For example, if we perceive a staff member repeatedly coming to work late, looking distressed and disheveled, we can choose to focus on the perception of being late or we can focus on the way the individual looks, or on both the lateness and the looks together. Depending on our past experiences, especially those related to this employee, the focus of our perception may be on whatever appears to be in conflict with our previous perceptions of the person. If the staff member has generally been on time in the past and generally looks well groomed, we may pull the two perceptions together and draw a conclusion that something is going on outside work that is having a negative impact on the employee. If, however, the staff member has been late before or does not generally dress for success, then we are not likely to draw the same conclusion about our perceptions of what is happening.

What we focus on becomes our reality. If we focus on certain issues, they begin to shape our perceptions and frame our reality. Planning, for example, is likely to reflect the issues that we choose to focus on. Because these issues are part of our consciousness, we see them as important. This does not change the fact that other issues could be equally important. But they are not part of our conscious attention and therefore are not included in our planning and decision-making efforts.

Shared realities can be created within organizations and can influence the direction and focus of the organization. For example, there was a college president who would receive a single phone call or letter from a parent or a person outside the university voicing a concern. Without hesitation or further investigation, the college president would take this concern to a cabinet meeting for action. Before the meeting's conclusion, each of the vice presidents had marching orders to attend to this issue within their respective divisions. It did not matter that the issue had been a concern to only one person; the perception on the part of the president was that this particular issue was a great problem that had been brought to his attention and needed to be addressed. Over the years, countless hours were spent following up, changing policy, and personally attending to such complaints. Because of the perceptions of the president, these single-voiced concerns became part of his reality regarding the institution, and through his power, he created a shared reality among the other campus administrators. His perceived reality often changed the focus and sometimes the direction of the institution. Sometime this shared reality was positive and productive, and sometimes it served as a great distraction of energy and time from the stated goals of the institution.

Judgment

Judgments usually result from perceptions. These judgments cause us to act in specific ways. Judgments can be either positive or problematic to individuals and organizations. They can be problematic if the conclusions we draw from our perceptions are based on distortions or on misrepresentations of facts, or they are in complete disagreement with others' perceptions. A number of human tendencies can lead to inaccurate and problematic judgments, especially as they relate to others.

First impressions are very powerful and can have a lasting impact. These impressions are usually formed in a short span of time and are based on very limited information. They can be problematic when they outlast their usefulness and greatly influence future perceptions and judgments. Although there is increasing evidence that first impressions based on intuition (or the adaptive unconscious) can be an aid in perception and judgment, first impressions can also be wrong and misleading (Gladwell, 2005). Even when we have gained additional information, it is hard to change some of the first impressions we have about others.

Stereotyping is the process of attributing specific characteristics to a person on the basis of his or her membership in a specific group. This is based on the assumption that all people in a particular group have the same characteristics. To some extent, stereotyping occurs as a mechanism to reduce information-processing overload. Not all stereotyping is inaccurate or harmful, but it can be problematic with regard to the perceptions of the in-group as they relate to out-group members. Such perceptions, especially when they are applied to individuals, can be destructive to team relations, collaboration, and the overall work climate within organizations.

A halo effect is the process of allowing one characteristic of an individual to overshadow or reflect all other characteristics. This process can be skewed either positively or negatively (Tosi & Mero, 2003). For example, if an attractive, outgoing individual applies for a position and she or he appears to be enthusiastic and self-confident, one might assume that he or she can perform all of the aspects of a job, even though there is no evidence presented during the interview that this is the case. It is not unusual for those of us in student affairs organizations to decide to hire a person based on his or her interviewing skills, even though we have no evidence that these skills are sound demonstrations that the person can actually do the job.

Our expectations can have a lot to do with what we perceive or how we interpret what we see. Generally, we see what we want to see, and these perceptions affect our attitudes, beliefs, and behavior toward others. Projection is the process of placing blame for our own difficulties or feelings on someone else or projecting on others our own feelings or motives. It is also not uncommon for our perception of others to become reality. This process is referred to as a self-fulfilling prophecy, which results from our expectations leading to our behaving in a certain way, which in turn causes another person to act as we had expected. If I believe that a staff member is basically incompetent, I will generally treat him as though he is incompetent. I will not trust him with specific or important tasks or give him a lot of autonomy to do his job. I will see only those aspects of what is done that are not viewed as competent. Over time, my perceptions of the person will only reinforce what I see as incompetent and he is likely to start acting incompetent. Generally, selective perception, the process of paying attention to some information and filtering out other information, plays a role in this process. Once we have a perception, we generally cling to that perception. We see and hear what we need to make it consistent with our initial beliefs. Seeing things differently requires conscious and intentional awareness that our perceptions are limited and may be wrong. This is very difficult to do.

Attribution Theory

Attribution theory focuses on what is believed to be the reason or cause of behavior. How we view behavior and what we believe motivated or caused the behavior affects how we deal with the behavior. A number of factors help us determine why people act the way they do. Together, these factors are called attribution bias, and they are not always rational. These factors can be either a person's internal characteristics, such as intelligence, character, and/or personality, or they can be environmental factors, such as the nature of the job and/or the events that influenced certain responses to occur. What is important to us is not what really caused the behavior but what we perceive to be the reason for the behavior (Bowditch, Buono, & Stewart, 2008).

Individuals most commonly attribute favorable outcomes related to their own behavior to internal causes and unfavorable outcomes to environmental causes. This is known as self-serving bias (Bartunek, 1981). This type of bias is more frequently found in people with high self-esteem. People with low self-esteem are more likely to be self-deprecating and more willing to blame themselves for their mistakes or shortcomings.

Locus of control is the concept used to describe the way people view causation in their lives. Some individuals attribute the outcomes of their behavior to internal causes, such as their own effort or their intelligence, and as a result they feel that they are in control of their lives. Others see the outcomes of their behaviors as controlled by external sources, such as a boss that dislikes them or a job that is too demanding; as a result, their lives are controlled by forces outside themselves. Research has shown that the outcome of a situation is viewed differently for people who believe they are in control than it is for people who believe the outcome is controlled outside themselves. An internal locus of control has been found to correlate with higher levels of job satisfaction, and those who demonstrate it appear to be more comfortable with participative management (Rotter, 1966).

Individuals also more frequently attribute favorable outcomes that happen to others to environmental factors and negative outcomes to the individual's internal characteristics. Some theorists believe that much of the conflict that occurs between managers and subordinates is that managers often act on their own causal schemes rather than trying to understand those of the subordinates (Barron, 1996).

Motivation

Student affairs organizations are complex entities that are comprised of a variety of individuals with diverse needs, skills, perceptions, and expectations. They take on a variety of roles and responsibilities at different hierarchical levels within the organization. Each of these individuals brings their needs, expectations, dreams, and realities to their work. Leaders and supervisors within these organizations are charged with accomplishing the mission and goals of the organization, and they depend on the efforts of the student affairs staff to ensure that the organization's plans are carried out in the most effective and efficient way possible. Channeling and enhancing the motivation of individuals to achieve the goals and implement the strategies are a major responsibility of those in management roles. Understanding what motivates individuals and how motivation works is critical to leadership success.

Motivation has been defined as a force within a person that compels that person to act in a certain way (Atkinson, 1964; Bess & Dee, 2008; Goddard, Hoy, & Hoy, 2004). This force can be conscious or unconscious, and it can be stimulated by conditions outside (extrinsic) or inside (intrinsic) the individual. A number of theories and supporting research have attempted to address the issue of motivating behavior. Most of the research in this area peaked in the 1970s and 1980s and has not received much attention over the past 30 years. Yet it remains a critical area of understanding related to human behavior in organizations.

Abraham Maslow's (1954) theory of the hierarchy of needs is one of the most often referenced models of human motivation. His model states that human need, which underlies all human motivation, could be ordered into a hierarchy with five levels: (a) physiological needs, (b) security needs, (c) social needs, (d) ego or self-esteem needs, and (e) self-actualization needs. As needs are realized, the individual moves up the hierarchy (often depicted as a pyramid) to focus on the fulfillment of the next level of needs. The ultimate goal is to fulfill one's needs and then focus on fulfilling the needs of others through self-actualization. Although there is little research support for the idea of a needs hierarchy, the idea that employees have needs that motivate their performance, and that individuals have different needs and seek to fulfill them differently, is critical to understanding human performance and motivation in the student affairs workplace.

Alderfer (1972) provided evidence for only three of Maslow's original five levels of need. He labeled these needs ERG: (a) basic *e*xistence needs, (b) *r*elatedness needs, and (c) *g*rowth needs. He found that, at times, there was progress from one level to the next, that boundaries overlapped, and that people often went from one level to the next without fully satisfying the first level. This theory is more fully supported by research and is more empirically based than Maslow's theory.

McClelland (1965) identified three basic needs: (a) achievement, (b) power, and (c) affiliation. Even though all are found at any given time in most people, people develop a dominant orientation toward one of these needs based on one's socialization and life experiences. McClelland proposed that motivation is changeable and that people can be taught to increase motivation to achieve.

Within student affairs organizations, staff members are motivated by different needs, and they often seek to fulfill them in different ways. Some want to work directly with students and are motivated by the internal reward they receive from seeing students change and grow. Others are motivated by being able to use their abilities to organize and to shape practice and by knowing that they are responsible for making something happen. It is important that supervisors understand individual differences related to needs and how work helps to address those needs.

At the same time, it is important to understand that balance is a critical factor in supporting a healthy, well-balanced staff. Exploiting staff by having them work long hours and counting on their commitment to students and the needs that this type of work fulfills is problematic. Supervisors need to be very conscious of the trend within the field of student affairs to attract staff members who are overcommitted to their work. Although it is critical to have staff members who work hard, they also need to be coached to achieve a reasonable level of balance and to seek outside nonwork areas to help fulfill their needs. In recent years, several issues have arisen regarding the generation gap that has widened between young student affairs staff members who want balance and are unwilling to work long days and weekends, and the previous generation or supervisors who were socialized in the profession that the expectation of many long working hours is the norm.

Directing Motivation Theory

There has been considerable theory and research related to the issue of channeling or directing motives. McGregor (1960), through his Theory X and Theory Y, proposed that most managers make incorrect assumptions about the people they manage. Managers believe that employees are basically lazy, with personal values and behavior that run counter to the organization's goals. As a result, the managers believe that the employees have to be managed closely in order to be productive. McGregor argued that Theory Y was a more correct way to view workers' attitudes and behavior. From this perspective, workers are viewed as more trustworthy and self-motivated, and a rigid, controlling, centralized structure is unnecessary.

These ideas have influenced the organizational development of higher education generally and student affairs specifically, especially as they relate to faculty and professional personnel. Student affairs organizations are generally less controlling of day-to-day behavior, and staff members have great latitude in approaching their roles and responsibilities. Clearly there is more of a hierarchy related to decision making within student affairs organizations than in faculty departments, but few student affairs professional staff members punch a clock or keep precise track of their time or productivity.

At the same time, the level of expectations related to outcomes and productivity has been difficult to measure and account for within student affairs organizations. Simply expending energy and working long hours have not been sufficient evidence of work productivity. New efforts to measure student affairs staff productivity related to student achievement, learning, and/or success are making their way into student affairs organizational assessment and performance efforts. Second, although professional staff members have considerable latitude in how they spend their time, this is not always the case for support staff members who often have to keep time cards and have less latitude in carrying out their daily responsibilities.

Herzberg's motivator-hygiene theory (Herzberg, Mauser, & Snyderman, 1959) suggests that motivation is composed of two factors: those that prevent dissatisfaction but do not encourage people to grow and develop, and job-related dimensions that actually encourage growth. They labeled the former hygiene factors and the latter motivators. Thus, factors that provide job satisfaction are different than those that create job dissatisfaction. The research related to these ideas has produced mixed results, and questions related to intrinsic and extrinsic job factors and their relationship to job performance and satisfaction remain.

Although individual student affairs professional roles carry a lot of autonomy, they also carry a lot of responsibility and can result in high levels of stress and burnout. The work expectations are demanding and the level of compensation is not always competitive, especially for entry and midlevel positions. In the past, human services work has often fostered the idea that intrinsic motivators were more important than hygiene factors; student affairs roles were no exception. This resulted in a cover for supervisors not having to pay as much attention to these aspects of the staff reward structure. More recent research indicates that hygiene factors such as salaries and other work climate issues are important and do have an impact on motivation and job performance. These factors may require more attention if student affairs organizations wish to become more effective.

Process Theories of Motivation

Although content theories help us understand what types of factors stimulate and enhance human motivation, they do not effectively explain the process of motivation. A number of closely related theories fall into the process of motivation category. Process theories of motivation view human needs and drives as malleable in the course of interaction with the environment as perceived by the individual. Both the individual and the environment must be taken into account in understanding motivation (Bess & Dee, 2008, p. 306).

Expectancy Theory

Expectancy theory provides a framework for understanding how motivation operates. It assumes that motivation is the result of three components: (a) the expectation that increased effort will lead to good performance, (b) the expectation that certain performance will lead to certain outcomes and rewards, and (c) the value of the rewards or outcomes as viewed by the individual (Bowditch et al., 2008, p. 82).

This theory has a number of important implications for student affairs organizations. Rewards or other mechanisms used to motivate individuals must be desirable to the individuals. It is critical that supervisors find out what rewards and recognitions actually serve to motivate each individual, and not simply attribute their own needs and desires to others. As a result, reward systems should be created with a broad array of incentives and rewards recognizing the diverse motives of different staff members.

Second, differences in performance must actually result in differences in rewards. Too often in student affairs organizations, there is a belief that all staff members should receive a similar level of pay and recognition, and pay for performance compensation plans are frowned upon. The lack of differences in rewards eventually undermines high performance. Staff must perceive that their effort will result in good performance and a resulting assessment of good performance. Appropriate, specific expectations related to performance; proper training of supervisors regarding performance assessment and review; and sound and timely feedback regarding performance serve to enhance motivation to do good work and to achieve organizational goals. Student affairs organizations have not always attended to all of these aspects of sound performance review and feedback within their organizations.

Path–Goal Theory of Motivation

A process theory derived from expectancy theory is the path–goal model (House, 1971). According to this theory, individuals make choices based on the utility of the choice related to their desired outcomes. Individuals are motivated when they understand that their performance will be successful and will lead to desired rewards. Leadership efforts to motivate staff members should focus on clarifying each staff person's path to a desired goal or objective. In this case, the emphasis and actions of the supervisor should be on ensuring the correct amount of information to guide yet not overdirect the path to a goal. Feedback is critical, but overdirection can also be harmful. Setting shared personal performance goals on a regular basis and using them to evaluate staff performance are critical to enabling staff members to be motivated to achieve desired goals.

Goal-Setting Theory

A third closely related theory is the idea that setting goals can cause high performance. Considerable research has been conducted on the link between goal setting and performance (Locke, 1968). Specific goals appear to result in greater effort than do generalized goals. Goals that come from individual input and choice appear to result in higher performance, even if they are difficult. Unrealistic goals can be less effective than no goals at all.

Within student affairs organizations, it is critical that supervisors discuss with staff members ways to set clear and specific goals, make the goals challenging yet not impossible or unrealistic to achieve, and connect achievement of goals with valued rewards. What is even more important is that each staff member understands the relationship between his or her goals and the goals of the larger organization, and is engaged in formulating this connection. Regular feedback related to achievement of goals is essential for the effective assessment of performance.

Considerable research has focused on the power of self-set goals. This type of goal has been viewed as a more powerful goal related to both commitment and performance of the individual (Hinsz, Kalnback, & Lorentz, 1997). Bandura's (1977) work on the concept of self-efficacy is closely related to the issue of individual goal setting. Self-efficacy is defined as an individual's belief that he or she is capable of performing a specific task or achieving a specific goal. In general, people with high self-efficacy tend to set high performance goals, perform well, and succeed in achieving the goals they set (Sheldon & Turban, 2003; Locke & Latham, 1990).

Role of Punishment in Motivation

Much of the literature and supporting research related to performance stresses the importance of rewards and recognition and discourages the use of punishment in addressing behavioral issues in organizations. Punishment is considered unreliable as a source of motivation because it is very unpredictable, and it works only in limited and very controlled situations. Its use often results in undesirable side effects on the part of those being punished and may actually be counterproductive to the organization.

However, punishment, or at least the perceived threat of punishment, is often used in organizations for a number of reasons. For example, some behavior may require a punitive response. Second, the use of punishment is closely related to the level of power, or the frustration associated with not having the ability to reward. In these cases, punishment or the threat of punishment becomes an expedient and reinforcing mechanism for changing or directing behavior. Administrators who have considerable power and operate in the top-down style may use their power to create an environment that uses punishment, or the threat of punishment, to get things done quickly without questions and delays. This approach often appears to work quickly and does not require the time and patience that using shared, collaborative management approaches require. However, the long-term results are likely to be resentment and a lack of individual commitment to the processes and goals that the leaders want to achieve. Given all the evidence, punishment remains that least favored approach to dealing with motivation and performance issues. It should be used only in a very specific situation when a punitive response to behavior is the sole choice among management actions.

Social Comparison and Equity Theory

Another set of motivation theories focuses on the variables that surround the individual who is to be motivated. One approach within this set is the social comparison theory. This approach looks at how an individual's view of reality is based on her or his own experiences (Straw, 1977). It suggests that perceptions and attitudes about a particular job are constructed based on both the perception of the present job and the past experiences that are related to the present job. This approach helps to explain how individuals use both internal and external comparisons to determine what they perceive as appropriate behavior in the work environment. For example, although every work environment is unique and organizations have different expectations, requirements, and policies, individuals also use their past experiences to assess whether the current work environment is satisfactory. They actively compare work environment factors with those they have experienced and also with those they perceive as occurring in comparable work settings within and outside their work settings.

A model based on the social comparison approach is equity theory. This model holds that people compare their efforts and rewards with what they perceive as others' efforts and rewards. First, the individual determines those who, from their perspective, are equal comparisons, and then they create comparisons between themselves and those particular others. If the individual views these comparisons as unequal, an attempt is made to correct the perceived inequity through working more or less, or trying to obtain greater rewards. If the perceived equity cannot be achieved, dissatisfaction sets in and people may become disenfranchised or leave the organization.

This theory was originally applied to salary equity issues, but it has since been applied to other work conditions in organizations. The research on this theory has produced some very interesting finds as they apply to motivation. One of the findings suggests that people who perceive they are overrewarded tend to produce more and they may try to increase the productivity of others (Bowditch et al., 2008). One additional finding is that the perception of equity or inequity is based on the preference of the individual related to different outcomes (Bowditch et al., 2008). For example, one student affairs employee may be more focused on sharing, collaborating, and giving credit to others, while others may perceive that they are entitled to more than they may be actually due, or that their performance was greater than actually occurred. This theory helps us understand how we come to perceive what we judge to be fair and just and explains how these perceptions affect our motivation in our work environments.

Job Characteristic and Work Design Theory

Job enrichment and work design are relatively new areas of attention within organizational studies. These concepts have concentrated on the idea of building opportunities for growth and personal achievement into work itself and not just through rotating jobs or enlarging jobs. These areas of study focus on restructuring work to incorporate an understanding of the entire work process and to enable workers to take on some of the decision making previously entrusted only to supervisors and managers.

Job characteristic theory combines some aspects of both need and process theories related to motivation and work design. It was developed by Hackman and Oldham (1980) and modified by Griffin (1990). The theory suggests that there are three critical psychological states in individuals that influence the demonstration of different behavior. These states include (a) experienced meaningfulness of the work, (b) experienced responsibility for work outcomes, and (c) knowledge of results. These states, when activated by different characteristics of one's job, create different levels of motivation in individuals (Bess & Dee, 2008, pp. 302–303). The five core job characteristics include (a) job skill, the degree to which a job or role requires a variety of activities; (b) task identity, the degree to which the job completes work from start to finish; (c) task significance, the degree to which the job has a substantial impact on others; (d) autonomy, the degree to which the job provides freedom and independence in scheduling work and carrying it out; and (e) feedback, the degree to which the employee receives direct and clear information and assessment about the effectiveness of his or her performance (Hackman & Oldham, 1980). Research indicates that high levels of the three critical states result in high motivation, high-quality work performance, high levels of job satisfaction, and low absenteeism and turnover (Renn & Vandenberg, 1995).

This theory appears to have direct implication for student affairs work that can directly influence staff motivation. The way jobs are designed can have high levels of motivating potential if they are assessed as having a degree of each of the five job characteristics. Second, understanding the different levels of importance of psychological states of each staff member helps both the staff person and the supervisor understand how the various job characteristics affect performance motivation and, through effective job design, enhance the motivation of each staff member.

Student affairs professional roles, while containing a mix of these five attributes, do have a relatively high level of many of these characteristics. As a result, they are likely to foster high levels of motivation, high-quality work performance, job satisfaction, and low absenteeism. However, it becomes critical that supervisors effectively monitor the level of expectation and guard against not having the responsibilities become too burdensome, and that the feedback loop is checked on a regular basis. When roles contain high levels of autonomy, they are often difficult for supervisors to provide timely and critical feedback. Second, in times of budget stress, it is common to eliminate jobs and merge responsibilities to create larger roles, with considerable additional responsibility. Supervisors need to be attentive to job design principles, making certain that eagerness to advance and to be rewarded do not blind them to ensuring that staff roles are manageable and designed to attain effectiveness in performance and to maximize individual strengths. Attending to workload; the cycle of work demands; and the abilities of individuals to multitask, make appropriate decisions, and provide task-related leadership is critical to determining appropriate combinations of job responsibilities.

Feminist Theory and Motivation

In the last 30 years, new perspectives on motivation have emerged as a result of the influence of feminist scholarship. Glazer (1997) offers the perspective that motivation theory provides only a partial and limited view of human behavior in organizations. She and others argue that women tend to engender more empathy and connectedness with others as the basis of motivation, and these concepts have not been incorporated adequately in positivist approaches to studying motivation in organizations. The works of Gilligan (1982); Belenky, Clinchy, Goldberger, and Tarule (1986); and Kanter (1977) revealed different patterns of motivation and relationships with others that are gender-related. These authors have sparked new research in the areas of organizational behavior and administration. They suggest that there are gender-based differences in organizational culture and processes that could be improved if broader gender-inclusive perspectives were infused. This evidence calls for continued exploration of the similarities and differences of gender-related attributes in organizational culture and administrative practice within our organizations.

Group Dynamics in Organizations

Individuals exist within organizations as members of workgroups. These groups have a significant impact on the behavior of individuals, their work satisfaction and productivity, and the overall success and effectiveness of the organization. Workgroups are an essential part of the structure of student affairs organizations, and they play a central role in the work life of individuals within these organizations. To fully understand organizational behavior in student affairs organizations, one needs to develop an understanding and awareness of group dynamics and how to interact with workgroups and teams. When we consider groups in work settings, we are referring to two or more people who are aware of each other and who interact to achieve a common goal. The literature has made five basic distinctions about group characteristics: (a) primary and secondary, (b) formal and informal, (c) heterogeneous and homogeneous, (d) interacting and nominal, and (e) temporary and permanent (Bowditch et al., 2008).

There are also a number of ways in which individuals function and relate within a group. Status refers to the level or position an individual holds within a group; generally, an individual has either high or low status in a group. In most organizations, we expect *status congruence*, which indicates that the job title defines the individual's status in a workgroup. For example, a director of a unit would be higher than an assistant director and equal to another director in the organization in terms of status.

A role refers to the responsibilities assigned to or expected from an individual or group in a particular position in the organization. For example, one might be an adviser within a group of advisers in the career center. Role conflict occurs when the various roles that are assigned either within an organization or within one's life roles conflict with each other. At other times, individuals may experience role ambiguity because expectations assigned to a role may be unclear. Individuals can experience role overload when they do not have sufficient resources or time to perform the role (Bowditch et al., 2008).

These phenomena are common in student affairs organizations because many staff members have numerous roles that they play in their jobs. These roles can also conflict with roles they have outside work, such as being a parent or partner. Student affairs roles themselves are not always clearly defined, leaving a lot of gray area regarding expectations and performance outcomes. Recently, student affairs staff members have been asked to do more with less; quite often they do not have adequate resources and time to accomplish the goals and expectations they have been assigned.

All groups operate within a set of norms. Such standards or expectations relate to behavior, which can be written but more likely they are not. However, they are assumed to be commonly understood by group members. Group deviants emerge when staff members do not follow group norms. In serious cases, the group can ostracize those who violate their norms. Norms can take the form of dress codes, social expectations, and even thought and expression.

Conformity to group norms is generally associated with the desire to be accepted by the group. Status in the group can influence conformity. Generally, high-status members of groups have influence with regard to the various group norms and can dissent based on their status. Low-status staff members do not generally have this latitude and may conform because they believe that they have no choice, even though they may not be committed to the norms of the group. Expedient conformity (Smith, 1982) occurs when a member publicly engages in attitudes and behaviors that are acceptable to the group but privately holds beliefs that are at odds with the group. This type of conformity can occur at any level within an organization.

Cohesiveness refers to the level of closeness and desire to remain in the group by members and can have a powerful influence on group performance. These members generally share similar views, attitudes, performance expectations, and general behavior. Cohesive groups generally have strong norms and have harsher ways of dealing with deviant behavior. Cohesiveness that emerges from a shared ownership of organizational goals can enhance organizational effectiveness and productivity (Summers, Coffelt, & Horton, 1988). Cohesiveness, although generally viewed as a positive influence on groups within organizations, can lead to a pattern of behavior known as groupthink (Janis, 1972). This process can occur when either the cohesiveness of the group or the power of the leadership limits or excludes divergent or undesirable opinion and information from group consideration. This results in limited access to new ideas or critical information that can influence the life and effectiveness of the organization. Student affairs organizations have a tendency to establish strong cohesiveness; as a result, they need to be attentive to the devastating effects of groupthink.

Workgroups generally operate by focusing on both the task facing the group and also the process they use to complete the task or address the issue. Groups generally go through a number of developmental phases over time; these phases are often described as forming, storming, norming, performing, reforming, and adjourning (Tuckman, 1965). More recent research suggests that groups do not always follow this sequence of development and may skip or cycle back to prior stages during the development process (Chang, Bordia, & Duck, 2003). Groups take time to develop and tend to function at higher levels of development when they have been together for longer periods of time (Wheelan, Davidson, & Tilin, 2003).

The Role of Teams in Organizations

One of the realities of modern organizations is that few roles and work assignments are performed by a single individual alone. Teams are increasingly utilized as a fundamental work unit in all types of organizations, including student affairs. Work teams vary in the way they are structured and in the way they perform in various types of organizations. Their structure can range from a distinct formal structure to self-managed nonhierarchical teams, to virtual teams. According to the literature, workgroups and true teams display distinct differences. Teams share some of the characteristics of workgroups, but theoretically they are nonhierarchical entities that provide support and information sharing within an egalitarian environment. Leadership is not focused on a single individual and may be shared among members. Recognition and rewards focus on team achievement and individual contributions to team success (Hopkins, 1994; Katzenbach & Smith, 1993).

Research on the effective use of teams (Bechhard, 1960; Bensimon & Neumann, 1993) highlights the importance of providing teams with a clear set of goals and objectives, clear role expectations for members, and the procedures and processes for member interaction as well as interpersonal relationships and potential conflicts that develop among team members. Organizational leaders often make a number of mistakes in the attempts to utilize teams effectively. They often refer to a group as a team and then manage them as individuals, where performance is assessed on an individual basis rather than on group effort. Leaders also try to manage the processes and decision making within teams too closely, thus not permitting the team to self-manage. Finally, they engage teams in decision making where decisions have already been made, constraining the effectiveness of the team and its willingness to participate and collaborate with each other in the future (Bowditch et al., 2008, p. 181).

For teams to function effectively they must achieve a mutual level of trust. Trust within teams is not automatic and may take time and attention to development. Research has found that homogeneous groups develop functional performance more quickly than do diverse groups. With increasing diversity in the work environment, creating trust within a team is critical to organizational success. Within student affairs organizations, attention needs to be given to ensuring that individuals learn how to enable teams to build trust and to express diverse attitudes, perspectives, and emotions as well as explore shared values. Teams need to receive information and then entrusted with appropriate levels of self-management and reasonable, single-focused reporting relationships.

Teams can be created to serve a variety of functions within student affairs organizations, including task forces or project teams that have prescribed time frames, problem-solving teams that focus on a broader set of division-wide goals and issues, and self-management teams that fully control their work processes and resources. Task forces and project teams have been an essential part of student affairs operations for many years. In fact, most major process and procedural changes as well as problem-solving tasks are currently conducted through task forces or committees. At the same time, learning teams and self-managed teams are rarely found in most student affairs organizations, where hierarchy and centralized leadership control still dominate the work environment.

Group Norms and Work Climate

On the organizational level, the combination of existing norms together create a "prevailing collective of norms," which include attitudes and behaviors; together with the concept of morale, they form what is called the organizational climate, or work climate (Bess & Dee, 2008). This dimension can reflect a barometer of the perspectives and attitudes, including satisfaction and morale of the staff members, in an organization and is closely related to the concept of organizational culture. Organization or climate assessments are often used to assist leaders in improving the organization and addressing staff-related issues. Many student affairs organizations regularly engage in work climate surveys to gauge what is happening among the staff members within their division. These types of approaches have also been used to identify diversity-related work-climate issues and concerns.

Individual Differences in Organizations

All individuals bring their unique personalities and experiences to an organization, and these differences add important dimensions to an organization. At the same time, some roles and responsibilities are best served by certain skills and experiences. Not everyone can or is interested in performing every type of task or level of responsibility within an organization. Creating jobs that enhance individual strengths, thus permitting and encouraging individuals to grow and develop, is critical to organizational effectiveness. Creating opportunities for job changes and advancement that recognize individual growth and skill acquisition, and avoiding job stagnation, are also important to ensuring high motivation and vitality in staff performance.

Considering personality, ability, and experience as critical to performance success is also essential. Just because someone has performed well in one role, or at one level, does not mean she or he has the skills or experience to be able to perform well at another role or level within the organization. Too often individuals are promoted for reasons that have little to do with ability and experience and as a result, they may experience unnecessary failure in the role or not be able to advance the organization's goals effectively.

Creating a system for staff development and advancement that is transparent and open to all qualified individuals leads to greater commitment to the organization among staff members. Recognizing that everyone may not want to advance up the hierarchy but may want to try new roles and challenges by moving laterally within the organization is equally as valid to staff morale and perceived opportunities for advancement. Assessing individual skills and abilities among staff members on a regular basis and connecting this to performance assessment and staff development enable organizations to make the best use of individual skills and of diverse skills throughout the organization.

Staff Development

One of the most critical issues facing student affairs organizations is how to maintain appropriate levels of current competencies among a very diverse group of staff members, performing a very diverse set of functions and roles. Addressing staff development issues at all levels of the organization can be overwhelming and complex, and at times costly. For the most part, we should consider staff development needs in light of existing theory and foster opportunities for ongoing growth and development of people throughout their careers.

First, we must consider staff development as an ongoing process where education and skill development are obtained as one matures in the organization. Beginning with a sound orientation and through ongoing assessment, staff members can advance in their individual capability within the organization. Second, continuous education is required to address new and emerging knowledge and skills as the needs of the environment, students, and other constituents change. This type of development transcends the staff at all levels. It is important to stay abreast of emerging issues and trends to enable staff to be able to cope with the changing nature of the environmental demands.

Third, staff members often have a vision for their individual futures and seek the knowledge and skills needed for future opportunities both within the organization and elsewhere. Leaders within the organization should be mindful of these needs and attend to them in a fair and transparent way that projects a desire to help individuals achieve their personal goals. Fourth, institutions should be mindful of generating and fostering leadership skills throughout all levels of the organization. This development should include the advancement of both organization assessment and development skills as critical leadership attributes.

Finally, creating effective learning organizations that are open to continuous change and adaptive to changes in the environment can happen only if each staff person is competent in his or her roles and responsibilities and is committed to achieving organizational goals and fostering cooperation and collaboration among units. The necessary staff development within this area is ongoing and critical to the overall success of the organization. Organizational learning is discussed in more detail in chapter 5.

Reflective Summary

1. How do the concepts of personality, judgment, and attribution contribute to your understanding of individual behavior in your student affairs organization?
2. Think about how you use motivation theory to engage staff members in their work. Can you identify ways these ideas can improve the commitment and focus of staff members toward addressing the goals and improving the effectiveness of your organization?
3. From your perspective, how does social comparison and equity theory explain the observed behavior within your organization?
4. How are jobs and positions designed and redesigned in your organization? What criteria are used and to what extent is the process comprehensive and systemic? How can the existing process be improved?
5. How does the concept of individual differences influence how performance, promotions and/or opportunities, and staff development are addressed in your organization? Can the concept of individual differences offer suggestions about how these processes should be different?

References

Alderfer, C. (1972). *Existence, relatedness and growth: Human needs in organizational settings*. New York: Free Press.

Atkinson, J. W. (1964). *Introduction to motivation*. Princeton, NJ: Van Nostrand.

Bandura, A. (1977). *Social learning theory*. Upper Saddle River, NJ: Prentice Hall.

Barron, R. A. (1996). Interpersonal relationships in organizations. In K. R. Murphy (Ed.), *Individual differences and behavior in organizations* (pp. 334–370). San Francisco: Jossey-Bass.

Bartunek, J. (1981). Why did you do that? Attribution theory in organizations. *Business Horizons, 5*, 66–71.

Bechhard, R. (1960). Optimizing team-building efforts. *Journal of Contemporary Business, 1*(3), 23–32.

Belenky, M. F., Clinchy, B. M., Goldberger, N. R., & Tarule, J. M. (1986). *Women's ways of knowing.* New York: Basic Books.

Bensimon, E. M., & Neumann, A. (1993). *Redesigning collegiate leadership: Teams and teamwork in higher education.* Baltimore, MD: John Hopkins Press.

Bess, J. L., & Dee, J. R. (2008). *Understanding college and university organization: Theories for effective policy and practice. Volume I, The state of the system.* San Francisco: Jossey-Bass.

Bowditch, J. L., Buono, A. F., & Stewart, M. M. (2008). *A primer on organizational behavior* (7th ed). Hoboken, NJ: Wiley.

Chang, A., Bordia, P., & Duck, J. (2003). Punctuated equilibrium and linear progression: Toward a new understanding of group development. *Academy of Management Journal, 46*(1) 106–125.

Cherniss, C., & Goleman, D. (2001). *The emotionally intelligent workplace.* San Francisco: Jossey-Bass.

Costa, P. T., & McCrae, P. R. (1992). *Revised NEO Personality Inventory (NEO-PI-R) and NEO Five Factor Inventory* (NEO FFI). Odessa, FL: Psychological Assessment Resources.

Gardner, H. (1983). *Frames of mind: The theory of multiple intelligences.* New York: Basic Books.

Gilligan, C. (1982). *In a different voice: Psychological theory and women's development.* Cambridge, MA: Harvard University Press.

Gladwell, M. (2005). *Blink: The power of thinking without thinking.* New York: Little Brown.

Glazer, J. S. (1997). Beyond male theory: A feminist perspective on teaching motivation. In J. L. Bess (Ed.), *Teaching well and liking it: Motivating faculty to teach effectively* (pp. 37–55). Baltimore, MD: Johns Hopkins University Press.

Goddard, R. S., Hoy, W. K., & Hoy, A. W. (2004). Collective efficacy beliefs: Theoretical developments, empirical evidence, and future directions. *Educational Research, 33*(3), 3–13.

Goleman, D. (1995). *Emotional intelligence.* New York: Bantam.

Goleman, D. (1998). *Working with emotional intelligence.* New York: Bantam.

Griffin, R. W. (1990). Toward an integrated theory of task design. In B. M. Straw & L. L. Cummings (Eds.), *Work in organizations* (pp. 81–122). Greenwich, CT: JAI Press.

Hackman, J. R., & Oldham, G. R. (1980). *Work redesign.* Reading, MA: Addison-Wesley.

Herzberg, F., Mauser, B., & Snyderman, B. (1959). *The motivation to work.* New York: Wiley.

Hinsz, V. B., Kalnback, L. R., & Lorentz, N. R. (1997). Using judgment anchors to establish challenging self-set goals without jeopardizing commitment. *Organizational Behavior in Human Decision Processes, 17,* 287–308.

Hopkins, E. (1994). Camels of a different color. *Training and Development, 48*(12), 35–37.

House, R. J. (1971). A path-goal theory of leadership effectiveness. *Administrative Science Quarterly, 16*(3), 321–338.

Janis, I. (1972). *Victims of groupthink.* Boston: Houghton Mifflin.

Kanter, R. M. (1977). *Men and women of the corporation.* New York: Basic Books.

Katzenbach, J. R., & Smith, D. K. (1993). *The wisdom of teams: Creating the high performance organization.* Boston, MA: Harvard Business School Press.

Lipmen-Blumen, J. (2005). *The allure of the toxic leader.* New York: Oxford University Press.

Locke, E. A. (1968). Toward a theory of task motivation and incentives. *Organizational Behavior and Human Performance, 3,* 157–189.

Locke, E. A., & Latham, G. (1990). *A theory of goal setting and task performance.* Upper Saddle River, NJ: Prentice-Hall.

Lubit, R. (2004). *Coping with toxic managers, subordinates and other difficult people.* Upper Saddle River, NJ: Financial Times/Prentice Hall.

Maslow, A. H. (1954). *Motivation and personality.* New York: Harper and Row.

McClelland, D. (1965). Toward a theory of motive acquisition. *American Psychologist, 20,* 321–323.

McGregor, D. (1960). *The human side of the enterprise.* New York: McGraw-Hill.

Myers, I. B., & Briggs, K. C. (1962). *Myers-Briggs type indicators.* Princeton, NJ: Educational Testing Service.

Presthus, R. (1978). *The organizational society.* New York: St. Martin's Press.

Renn, R. W., & Vandenberg, R. J. (1995). The critical psychological states: An underrepresented component in job characteristics model research. *Journal of Management, 21*(2), 279–303.

Rotter, J. (1966). Generalized expectancies for internal vs. external control of reinforcement. *Psychological Monographs, 80,* 609.

Schneider, B., Goldstein, H. W., & Smith, D. B. (1995). The ASA Framework: An update. *Personnel Psychology, 48*(4), 747–773.

Sheldon, K. M., & Turban, D. B. (2003). Personality and the goals-striving process: Influence of achievement goal patterns, goal level and mental focus on performance and enjoyment. *Journal of Applied Psychology 88*(2), 256–265.

Smith, M. (1982). *Persuasion and human interaction: A review and critique of social influence theory.* Belmont, CA: Wadsworth.

Straw, B. M. (1977). Motivation in organizations: Toward synthesis and redirection. In B. M. Straw & G. R. Salancik (Eds.), *New directions in organizational behavior.* Chicago, IL: St. Clair.

Summers, I., Coffelt, T., & Horton, R. E. (1988). Work group cohesion, *Psychological Report, 63,* 627–639.

Tosi, H. L., & Mero, N. P. (2003). *The fundamentals of organizational behavior.* Malden, MA: Blackwell Publishing.

Tuckman, B. W. (1965). Developmental sequence in small groups. *Psychological Bulletin, 6*(3), 384–399.

Watson, D., & Clark, L. A. (1984). Negative affectivity: The disposition to experience aversive emotional states. *Psychological Bulletin, 96*(3), 465–490.

Wheelan, S. A., Davidson, B., & Tilin, F. (2003). Group development across time: Reality or illusion? *Small Group Research, 34*(2), 223–246.

5

STRUCTURE AND DESIGN OF STUDENT AFFAIRS ORGANIZATIONS

The telephone rang and Dr. Pat Harris, the vice president for student affairs, answered. The university president began the conversation by saying that he was calling to let her know that he had decided to restructure the university and that she would be reporting to the provost effective tomorrow. He continued by saying that, in his new role as president, he had determined that he needed to spend more time in external relations activities and could not devote as much time to having all five vice presidents reporting to him. He also believed that students would be better served if student affairs had a closer alliance with academic affairs and that this could be achieved by reporting directly to the provost. The president indicated that he intended to make some additional structural changes that would create a flatter organization and would also result in a more efficient and effective overall organization. He went on to state that he had asked the provost to study the matter and to make recommendations within the next two months about how to achieve this goal. He stated that it was not clear how these changes would affect the division of student affairs, but it was likely that they would have an impact on the division. The president then asked Dr. Harris to work with her staff to ensure that the transition would go smoothly and that the upcoming changes would be accepted with a strong commitment by everyone. He ended the conversation by stating that this information was likely to be in the morning paper and he did not want her to see it there for the first time. He assured her that he would continue to have contact with her and her staff, especially around issues that required his attention.

Tinkering with the organizational structure of collegiate institutions is very common, especially for new leaders. Dungy (2003) stated that organizational structures in higher education have changed more often and more frequently in the last three decades than in any other time in U.S. history. A number of experts in the area of organizational studies believe that we are in the midst of organizational change related to the design and structure of work-related organizations (Ashkenas, Ulrich, Jick, & Kerr, 2002; Bowditch, Buono, & Stewart, 2008; Galbraith, 2002; Goold & Campbell, 2002). Clearly, these changes will have an impact on student affairs and higher education organizations, too.

Now in the midst of serious economic constraints, increased accountability, and concern about organizational efficiency, higher education leaders are questioning their ability to sustain current organizational designs and support institutional programs and services. As changes in the external environment accumulate, existing organizational forms are less and less capable of addressing the issues and demands placed on collegiate organizations. New organizational forms will begin to emerge to address these external environmental challenges and opportunities. Organizational change within higher education is to be expected. However, simply tinkering with organizational structure by moving units and people around like pieces on a chessboard will not necessarily result in the goal of enhanced organizational effectiveness as desired by the president in the chapter-opening vignette. Although reporting relationships are an important element, they are only one factor to consider in an organization redesign process.

It is also true that organizational structure and design are not cookie-cutter processes whereby we mold organizations into a common form. Each organization is unique and requires a design that best meets its needs, challenges, and mission. As a result, fashioning effective organizational structure can be enhanced with an understanding of organizational behavior, structure, and design theory that can be applied to organizational design processes. Through the application of these ideas, organizations can be designed to meet their specific challenges and goals, as well as make them efficient and effective when dealing with a changing environment.

Organizational Structure Theory

The basic tenet of organizational structure theory is that an organizational structure should divide the work of the organization, and then differentiate, coordinate, and integrate the work at all levels within the organization to best meet the mission and goals of the organization. Organizational structure should be viewed as more than the physical or structural frame of the organization. It also defines the decision-making processes and connects the strategy and behaviors within the organizational cultures of the institution. It aligns resources and navigates them toward accomplishing the tasks and mission of the organization. In some cases, it is used to define the boundaries of the organization from the external environment and helps foster the organization's identity.

What has been rapidly changing with regard to organizational structure is the way in which the two principles of differentiation and integration are accomplished and how the interaction with the external environment occurs. Early organizational theory viewed organizations as mechanistic, hierarchical entities that had boundaries between the organization and the external environment. Hierarchy and functionality were the means for achieving organization success. Within higher education organizations, campus life and even the entire collegiate institution were viewed as being sheltered from the real world and conceptually were labeled as the ivory tower.

In today's organizations, the boundaries between the organization and the external environment are beginning to blur and in some cases merge. Dynamic changes in the external environment are forcing organizations to move away from controlling, hierarchical structures to those based on shared decision making and a focus on process, flexibility, and collaboration. As a result, organizations are starting to be seen more as open, organic systems that are in a constant state of change and require the ability to transform themselves continuously (Wheatley, 2006).

Organizational theories generally describe organizations as either mechanistic or organic in their structural design. Most student affairs organizations can actually be found somewhere on the continuum between these two concepts. Mechanistic organizations are highly structured, with centralized decision making and vertical information flow. They have clear definitions for jobs and standardized policies and procedures, and rewards come from adherence to instructions from supervisors.

Organic organizations are viewed as loosely structured and decentralized in their decision making, with lateral information flow. They are designed to be more flexible so that they can function within a rapidly changing environment. There is less emphasis on formalized job descriptions and specializations. In organic organizations, horizontal relationships across organizational units are just as important as vertical relationships with supervisors and subordinates. Rewards are made on the basis of sound decision making at all levels, as well as on collaboration and adaptability.

Research has found that four main factors influence decisions about how organizations are structured: (a) the environment, (b) the size of the organization, (c) its dominant technology, and (d) the organization's strategy (Bowditch et al., 2008; Galbraith, 2002; Goold & Campbell, 2002). The nature of the external environment and the challenges that it presents to the organization greatly influence how the organization is structured. The size of the organization and how it orchestrates its work has an effect on the need for differentiation and specialization of work.

Many theorists agree that strategy should drive structure (Galbraith, 2002; Goold & Campbell, 2002). However, this idea is complicated for organizations by the existence of different operating strategies at different levels within the organization. Within higher education organizations, the development and implementation of strategy is even more problematic because the creation of strategy is not generally systematic and well coordinated. Planning is often seen as a process independent of daily activity and takes long periods of time to create and implement. Various units set their own goals and implement them independent of other units. In other words, planning is not really integrated nor is it viewed as strategic. For example, many student affairs organizations do not have strategic plans, and few institutions actually use them to make daily decisions (Kuk & Banning, 2009). This organization phenomenon has led some theorists to suggest that senior leadership should spend less time crafting strategy and structure, and more time and energy developing the knowledge and competencies of their managers (Bartlett & Ghoshal, 1990). This is especially true if organizations are going to enable frontline staff members to have more direct decision-making authority and organizations are going to adapt to changing needs and issues within the environment.

As a singular structural form, the functional hierarchy is increasingly viewed as unable to address the challenges of modern organizations, and many new structural design alternatives are beginning to appear. The trend is toward less specialization and greater job rotation, except in areas with high skill tasks where the focus is on greater specialization in order to pursue greater depth. One example of this can be found in university legal counsel units, where legal issues are becoming more complex and thus require complex specialization.

Decision-making power is shifting to those with direct client contact, which creates flatter structures with more emphasis on lateral collaboration and fewer middle hierarchical layers. This in turn results in greater spans of supervision. Also there is a greater focus on eliminating fragmentation and more emphasis on end-to-end work responsibility. For student affairs organizations, this could be applied to creating structures that emphasize the use of more generalists, cross-training staff across units, having fewer middle managers in specialized functional areas, and working with the same students throughout the students' college experience.

Although the hierarchical, functional structure is still the dominant structure used in organization designs, this model is increasingly being combined with alternative structures, and new structural forms are also emerging. Examples of some of the new structural models offered by Galbraith (2002) include the product structure, market structure, matrix structure, hybrid structure, process structure, and geographical structure models. Each is described in the following subsections.

Product Structure Model

As a result of diversification, this model creates multiple functional organizations, each with its own product line. The college and academic department organizational structure within universities is an example of a product structure model currently used in higher education.

Market Structure Model

This type of model is rapidly increasing. It is based on the customer and her or his demand for individualized attention and products. This model makes use of outsourcing and scale of function to optimize the use of resources. It utilizes market segmentation to focus on specific markets. Banks and telecommunication have been leaders in the use of this model. Its current use in higher education is unknown, except possibly in a modified form within the admissions and alumni relations units of collegiate organizations.

Geographical Structure Model

This model is generally developed as organizations expand their offerings across territories and when the services need to be performed on location. This model is represented by multicampus institutions that have programs and services at branch campuses. These programs and services report to the local campus administrator and also to a central administration.

Process Structure Model

The process structure model is the newest generic structure and may take a number of different forms. Essentially it is based on the complete flow of work process. It is often referred to as a horizontal structure, where a single team is given end-to-end responsibility. This structure is demonstrating great application in terms of the redesign of processes leading to efficiencies and overall quality improvements. It is also very useful in assessing both product quality and performance. It may appear in modified form in higher education as assessment, program, and/or accreditation review teams that engage in self-assessment unit performance reviews, and also in advising and/or mentoring centers where advisers work with the same student for all of the student's undergraduate experience.

Hybrid Structure Model

Hybrid structure models are organizational structures that are designed by combining the principles and structural elements of two or more organizational models. They are also useful in designing subunits of organizations that may use one organization structural form and other subunits may use another. Choosing the most appropriate and effective structure should be decided by matching the organization's strategy with what is done best by the specific structure and its applications.

Matrix Structure Model

The matrix structure model is a specific type of hybrid organization that is designed by merging the functional structure with the process structure. It provides for functionality and also enhances cross-unit collaboration and communication. For example, this type of structure could consist of a student affairs marketing unit that serves the marketing needs of all the various units within the student affairs division. This model, applied in a number of variations, may be a sound approach for student affairs organizations to consider.

In some cases a basic functional structure can be augmented by adding a lateral structure. For others, creating a complete hybrid structure made up of components of the various structures can produce the most effective structure for an organization.

Current Organizational Designs in Student Affairs

The current organizational design of most student affairs organizations has evolved over many years and has emerged from adding new programs and services as stand-alone functional units when new demands and challenges occurred. For the most part, these organizations continue to operate as mechanistic, hierarchical structures that are based on the principles of providing functionally based programs and services to students. For example, student affairs organizations consist of a variety of functional units such as housing and residence life, student activities, counseling, student health services, and so on. Each of these units have their own programs and services and function independently of each other.

In some cases, they are being restructured to meet new challenges. These changes are appearing in the form of hybrid and matrix structures, and they are most evident in larger organizations where integration of functional units and sharing of divisionwide resources are needed (Kuk & Banning, 2009). For example, some divisions have adopted technology, student assessment, fundraising, and marketing units that span the entire division and serve all of the functional units' needs. The units that are served may even utilize shared funding.

Refocusing attention on the design of organizational structures could address some of the shortcomings of traditional hierarchical structures within student affairs organizations and help them address the challenges emerging from the external environment. Adding new dimensions to the structure could increase collaboration and foster greater efficiencies in the use of resources. Design and structure issues are critical to student affairs organizations (Kuk, 2009) and are likely to continue to be emerging issues as greater strain is placed on institutional resources.

Organizational Design

The basic idea behind organizational design is constructing and changing an organization's structure to achieve the organization's mission and goals more effectively. The theory behind organizational design is based on organizational behavior ideas and research. It has emerged as ideas, models, and processes that focus on the elements of organizational design and change. These ideas can be applied to student affairs organizations. A discussion of design theory follows; change theory and process are discussed in chapter 6.

Organizations of the past century focused on a variety of issues that were thought to promote organizational success, including (a) the size of the organization, (b) differentiation in roles and responsibilities, (c) increased specialization, (d) vertical chain of command, and (e) span of control (Ashkenas et al., 2002; Galbraith, 2002; Goold & Campbell, 2002; Wheatley, 2006). Institutional structure was used to help address organizational issues by creating boundaries, where levels of authority, definition of roles, and spans of control became critical issues for an organization. As a result, the organizational structure became a critical focal point related to organizational design. Over the years, higher education leaders have come to believe that systemic and organizational issues can be solved by changing the organizational structure and internal reporting lines. In most cases, however, changing reporting lines is not the sole answer to addressing current organizational issues.

In the past few decades, the factors important to organizational success have changed or have combined with existing factors to create very different ones. Emerging success factors for organizations include (a) speed and response time, (b) adaptability and flexibility to the external environment, (c) integration of work at all levels, and (d) ability to innovate (Ashkenas et al., 2002; Galbraith, 2002; Goold & Campbell, 2002; Wheatley, 2006). These new factors also require a new way of viewing organizational design and seeing structure as one component of effective design. Theorists have proposed a number of strategies for redesigning organizations to address current issues.

Some theorists (Ashkenas et al., 2002) address the issues related to organizational boundaries and propose changes that would confront and reshape four types of organizational boundaries: (a) vertical, (b) horizontal, (c) external, and (d) geographic. Such changes would result in organizations that are flatter, more cross-functional and lateral in focus, more engaged with the external environment, and more globally focused. All of these types of boundaries currently exist in student affairs organizations, and attending to each can provide guidance on areas that may require changes to current organizational design issues.

According to Gallos (2006), the design of an appropriate system for achieving an organizational mission and purpose requires that four ongoing tensions be addressed: (a) differentiation and integration (how to divide the tasks and work to be done and then coordinate the diverse efforts of individuals and groups), (b) centralization and decentralization (how to allocate authority and decision making across the organization), (c) tight boundaries and openness to the environment (how much to buffer and filter the flow of people and information in and out of the organization), and (d) bureaucracy and entrepreneurism (how to balance the requirements for consistency, predictability, and clarity with the need for autonomy, creativity, and flexibility) (Gallos, pp. 352–353).

Helgesen (1995) proposed creating a webbed organization as an alternative to hierarchical designs. This structure would disseminate through relationships and weblike communication channels that link everyone in the organization together. It would replace the pyramid structures that focused on vertical communication and leadership control. Instead, decision making and leadership would be transparent and would include everyone at all levels of the organization.

Galbraith's (2002) theory of organizational design focused on the components of organizational design and new and emerging structural models. In his model, strategy was the first component to be addressed in the five-point star model for designing organizations. These five points include the following:

> *Strategy*—Strategy is the basis for organizational success. Strategy is important because it establishes the criteria for determining among alternative organizational forms. Strategy dictates which organizational activities are most necessary and sets the stage for being able to make necessary tradeoffs in design.
>
> *Structure*—Structure determines the placement of power and authority in an organization. The structural arrangements include: specialization, shape, distribution of power and departmentalization. Specialization refers to the number and type of specialized jobs needed to perform the work. Shape includes the span of control (the size of reporting groups within a unit) at each level of the organization. Distribution of power has two dimensions. Vertically, it addresses the issue of centralization or decentralization related to decision making and control. Laterally, it deals with moving power to the unit dealing with the issue or situation. Departmentalization addresses the dimensions on which a department is formed within the organization.
>
> *Process*—Process addresses the functioning of the organization through vertical and lateral managerial activities. Vertical functioning deals with the allocation of resources and budgeting. Lateral processes address issues of workflow.
>
> *Rewards*—Rewards include aligning the goals of the employees with the goals of the organization. They provide the systematic approach to providing motivation and incentives for completion of the strategic direction. Rewards generally include salaries, promotions, recognitions, and enhancements to work or positions. Such systems must be congruent with strategy and structure to influence goals and direction.
>
> *People*—This area of design focuses on building and sustaining the organizational capacity to execute the strategic direction of the organization. It produces the talent needed by the organization through

hiring, training and development, and rotating human resources. Again, this area needs to be consistent with the strategy and structure of the organization to be effective.

Goold and Campbell (2002) view organizational design as being more comprehensive than focused on reporting relationships. They believe design should include a focus on the "skeleton" (structure) but also on the "connective tissues," which include the behaviors, the values, and the culture of the organization, for example, (a) a focus on the responsibilities allocated to units, (b) reporting and lateral relationships, (c) accountability within a unit, and (d) key reporting and coordinating processes. Goold and Campbell have fashioned a set of guiding principles that can be used to guide the assessment and design process.

Although each of these sets of ideas focuses on organizational design elements from a somewhat different perspective, they each offer ways of viewing organizational design–related issues and can be used to create an intentional and systematic assessment of current organizations. Essentially they provide strategies for pursuing a redesign process. The most important idea presented by all of these models is that design is a process that should be intentional and systematically engaged in by the organization's members. It is not simply moving the old ways of doing things into new reporting arrangements or creating new units to take on new responsibilities and attaching them to the current structure.

Another level of organizational design focuses on the level of work by looking at work-related responsibilities and workflow. Wiesbord (2006) focused on the concept of organizational design regarding the way work, specifically jobs, are constructed and structured in organizations. An effective way to enhance respect and value and to create community in a workplace is to involve people in redesigning their work. This can be done through the creation of design work teams that cut across organizational levels and functions. Teams can look at the whole organizational operation with the goal of optimizing both the technical and social systems. This can foster a form of social learning not found in traditional organizations, and it can change managerial approaches and the perceptions of the problem and the nature of the solutions. Work design needs to be an action research process and not a predetermined structure. For example, one approach to design might include the following scenario. A design team is created from the various units. It conducts three interacting analyses of the work system. One analysis creates a map of environmental demands; a second develops a flowchart of how the system(s) functions; and the third creates a social analysis, which looks at current jobs and focuses on making every job an effective one (Wiesbord, 2006). Based on these analyses new supervising, reward, and management systems can be created as the workflow and interaction is understood. All elements of this analysis are needed to understand and to make effective change in the current work system.

This type of overarching workflow analysis could be very helpful to student affairs organizations. In many cases, job responsibilities and work-flow are seldom analyzed in a uniform and comprehensive manner. Gener-ally, job responsibilities are assessed when vacancies occur or organizational responsibilities change. In these cases, the focus is on the roles being changed, not the entire unit or organizational system. Although it is impor-tant to conduct vacant-position analysis, position analysis is rarely done across a unit or organization and it rarely includes the factor of how work interacts with other parts of the system or with the external environment. These latter components of analysis could be helpful in identifying areas that can be redesigned to make work flow more effectively, streamline cross-unit collaboration, and affect the overall design of the student affairs organization.

Organizational Design From the Social Constructionist Perspective

A slightly different perspective of organizational design emerges from the social constructionist perspective, which holds that structures are created and re-created from the interaction of organizational members. Weick (1969) was among the first to argue that structure was enacted. This differs significantly from the positivist's view of structure as something tangible that the organi-zation possesses (signified by boxes on an organizational chart). Enactment theory claims that "structure is something that the organization does" (Orton & Weick, 1990). From this perspective, structure exists in the minds of organizational members. It is a cognitive map that preserves previous actions, sorts and arranges current experiences, and produces expectations of future actions (Bess & Dee, 2008; Weick, 1988). These cognitive maps become social structures through ongoing communication among colleagues in the organization. Thus, organizational structures may actually be the result of individual perceptions, shared by colleagues within the organization and reflecting the social relationships among members, rather than a struc-ture prescribed by the organization's leadership.

Within this concept, student affairs organizations would actually be the result of the interactions that occur among staff members and can be changed by changing the cognitive maps that staff members create about how they interact within their organization. This could be done by changing the language and ideas related to organizational structure, and discussing the values and expectations associated with more lateral and collaborative organizational designs. It can also be done by rewarding and recognizing these types of behaviors among staff members. Eventually, the actual design of the interactions within the organization would change to conform to the new cognitive maps that staff members create as individuals and among their collective understandings. This approach to redesign appears to be more realistic than simply redesigning an organizational chart and expecting that everyone will easily conform to the new diagram in terms of day-to-day behavior.

Coupling (Weick, 1976), either tight or loose, is a concept that explains the relationship and interconnection of units within an organization to each other. Loosely coupled organizations are not held together through management control but rather through the interactions that members construct together. There can be both tight and loose coupling within the organization. When units are not responsive or connected to each other, the system is decoupled or loosely coupled. Tight coupling occurs when units are essentially controlled and given little autonomy in determining their own direction and actions. Higher education is considered to be a very loosely coupled structure with various systems or organizational units operating fairly independently of each other (Bess & Dee, 2008; Birbaum, 1988).

Structuration theory (Giddens, 1984) provides another way of thinking about organizational design. It suggests that both individuals and groups are active agents who create the structures in which they work, but they are also constrained by the previous structures that they created. Although they create structure through daily actions, individuals and workgroups also exist in the context of the current structures they have created before. Thus, organizational structure becomes fairly stable and resistant to change. If change is to occur, the behavioral pattern that created the structure in the first place must change. As a result, organizational change must not only provide a sound organizational model to adopt, it must also disrupt the daily behavior that created the current structure and enhance behaviors that support the new design.

In accord with this theory, design changes within a student affairs organization must not only offer a new model of change, they must also alter the behavior and cognitive processes that created the current structure. This could occur by providing rewards and recognition for engaging in new cross-unit collaborative behavior and for engaging in new cross-training activities, as well as by discouraging reliance on the old ways of interacting and utilizing resources.

Student Affairs Organizational Design

There has not been a lot of research and attention given to understanding organizational design and behavior within student affairs organizations. Although early references to student personnel services were descriptive of the type of services and programs that should be provided, these efforts did not clearly discuss what organizational structures or reporting lines should be used to organize and provide these programs and services. More recent efforts in student affairs literature have offered several general models and guiding principles related to structure and design, but they have not applied existing organizational theory extensively to student affairs organizations. The following discussion is a general summary and discussion of the organizational theory and research that has been published related to student affairs organizations.

Kuh (1989) identified four conventional models for examining different organizations. These models included (a) the rational model, (b) the bureaucratic model, (c) the collegiate model, and (d) the political model. This model and the work of Ambler (1993; 2000) were among the few early discussions of student affairs organizations.

In 1992, Ambler conducted a survey of more than one hundred student affairs divisions and found a wide variety of unique and different organizational structures. Just prior to his 2000 publication, Ambler repeated the distribution of the survey to the same sample of student affairs programs and found that many had experienced institutional changes that affected the divisions' structure. Some of these changes include the adoption of the provost reporting model, establishment of an executive officer for enrollment management, increased use of technology within the division, and the privatization of some services. He found that, despite these changes, the four basic models of management structures previously indentified for student affairs organizations remained in the institutions he surveyed (Ambler, 2000).

Revenue Source Model

This model was based on the fact that auxiliary units in public universities were often required, by law, to cover all the costs associated with their operations from their revenue sources. Similarly, excess revenue and reserve funds generated by auxiliary units may not be used for other functions within the institution. The impact of this model on organizational design depended on the number of auxiliary units, the financial restrictions and requirements of each auxiliary unit, the amount of funds involved, and the extent of other student affairs functions that were funded by general or state-appropriated funds.

Affinity of Services Model

In this model, services were clustered by the nature or similarity of their purpose, usually along the lines of some standard classification system that described the nature of the services. This model was generally used in student affairs divisions where the programs and services were quite numerous and diverse.

Staff Associates Model

This model was viewed as a compromise between a bureaucratic and a flat organizational model. It permits the senior student affairs officer to provide general direct leadership to the range of units within the division while controlling the technical and administrative tasks through staff assistants. These staff assistants did not usually have any line authority and were responsible for an overarching area of the division's administration, such as the budget, technology, and human resources.

Direct Supervision Model

Within this model, all student services units reported directly to the senior student affairs officer. This model was more likely to occur in relatively smaller student affairs divisions (Ambler, 2000).

Ambler (2000) offered a number of guiding principles to use for considering organizational structure: (a) the origin of organizational structure, (b) the role of the chief student affairs officer, (c) organizational symmetry, (d) stability, (e) autonomy, (f) staff involvement, (g) titles, and (h) organizational communication. Kuk and Banning (2009) found that the basic components reported in Ambler's studies were still in place, although some modest changes were beginning to occur.

Allen and Cherrey (2000) in their work *Systemic Leadership,* applied the ideas of systems and learning organizations to student affairs organizations, leadership, structures, and student affairs practice. They discussed the idea of fragmentation and its application to traditional hierarchical organizations.

They offered the ideas of connectivity and networking as a more systems-focused view of how student affairs organizations could become more effective. Allen and Cherrey discussed a vision for student affairs organizations based on new ways of relating, influencing change, learning, and leading and on what needed to change in student affairs practitioners' thinking to integrate these new dimensions of organizing and implementing student affairs practice.

Strange and Banning (2001) created a comprehensive model for student-friendly and learning–supportive environments. They focus on the dimensions of organizational environments, their structural anatomy, dynamics, and the relationship of these environmental dimensions to creating effective learning environments within college campuses. This model was not directed, however, at the actual structure or design of student affairs organizations.

In their work on rethinking student affairs practice, Love and Estanek (2004) used organizational development theory and new science ideas to challenge student affairs practitioners to think differently about their work and student affairs structures and processes, and to adopt new models for change. They provided four conceptual lenses (valuing dualism, transcending paradigms, recognizing connectedness, and embracing paradox) as a way of thinking differently about student affairs practice. This work was process-focused and provided a useful tool for engaging practitioners in thinking and acting differently, but it did not specifically address issues related to organizational structure and design.

Manning, Kinzie, and Schuh (2006), in *One Size Does Not Fit All*, discussed the organization of student affairs. Their discussion is based on a study of 20 high-performing colleges and universities. This work highlighted the history of student affairs organizations, as well as contemporary issues that affect organizational structures within student affairs. They suggested that three approaches to student affairs work influenced the organization of student affairs: student services, student development, and student learning. They built a strong case for asserting that the structure of student affairs should be closely shaped to align with the mission of the institution. From analysis of the interviews and their review of student affairs literature, Manning et al. (2006) created 11 student affairs organizational models. Six of the traditional models were developed through an analysis of the student affairs literature, and five new innovative models grew out of the DEEP research study they conducted. Each of the models are discussed in the following subsections.

Extracurricular Model

The extracurricular model is organized to provide predominantly student life and social student development programs and services in and out of the classroom environment. This model assumes that the mission of student affairs is entirely separate from academic units.

Functional Silos Model

The functional silos model organizes functions, services, and programs from a management and leadership approach rather than student development. Units perform their functions and services as discrete entities, and integration and communication is achieved through loose coordination.

Student Services Model

The student services model organizes functions, services, and programs from a management and leadership approach rather than student development. Functions and services often cluster together, with the focus on providing quality programs and services and with close coordination of similar units. There is minimal if any integration of programs and services with academic units.

Competitive/Adversarial Model

The competitive/adversarial model assumes that both student affairs and academic units are concerned with what students learn and how they grow, but there is little acknowledgment of the contribution of the other. Student affairs units operate independently of academic units.

Co-curricular Model

The co-curricular model assumes that both student affairs and academic units are concerned with student learning and how they grow. Student affairs and academic affairs have complementary but different missions, but they acknowledge the contributions of the other to student learning.

Seamless Learning Model

Student learning experiences are conceived as integrated and continuously happening across all aspects of the student experience and campus life, in and outside the classroom. The mission of the institution and those of student affairs and of academic affairs units are dedicated to the total student learning experience. This model assumes that every member of the institution and the student affairs organization can contribute to learning.

Student-Centered, Ethic-of-Care Model

This model centers on care and relationships, with a fundamental basis in addressing what students need to be successful. It is geared toward the goal of facilitating student success; integrating services; and providing policies, programs, and practices centered on the ethic of care. This model focuses on students who have the most need of support.

Student-Driven Model

The student-driven model assumes that student learning is enhanced by greater student involvement and engagement and that identification with the institution contributes to student persistence and success. Student involvement and leadership serve as core operating principles, and valuing students as integral members of the community is a strong component in governing the organization. Students drive campus activities and make decisions about campus life.

Student Agency Model

The student agency model assumes that students have the primary role and responsibility for their education. It also assumes that students are completely responsible for student life, and they perform as full and equal partners with faculty and staff in these efforts. Students assume as much responsibility as possible in the development of their learning experiences by managing campus life and helping to design curriculum. Students serve as workers in providing a wide range of student services and programs.

Academic/Student Affairs Collaboration Model

The academic/student affairs collaboration model assumes that both student affairs and academic affairs units place student learning at the center of their goals and activities and that they create institutional coherence about student success. Student affairs and academic affairs emphasize mutual territory and combine efforts to engender student engagement and success. The work between academic affairs and student affairs is supported with tightly coupled student affairs structures and philosophies that support student learning and success. This model assumes seamless collaboration between student affairs and academic affairs units on a routine basis.

Academic-Centered Model

This model assumes both student affairs and academic units place student learning at the center of their members' goals and activities. This model is organized around the academic core and promotes the academic experience over co-curricular activities. The student affairs department serves as a support to the academic focus of the institution and is almost invisible in the academic focus. Both student affairs and academic affairs units share responsibility for student success (Manning et al., 2006).

Manning, Kinzie, and Schuh's work provides a sound framework for linking student affairs organizational design to the educational focus and strategic mission and goals of student affairs organizations. However, it does not provide any guidance or models on how to restructure organizations to ensure the creation of this link, nor does it introduce organizational design theory into the process of utilizing these models.

Hirt (2006) focused on understanding the professional life of student affairs practitioners at six different types of higher education institutions. This portrait depicted the distinctive differences in how student affairs work is carried out at different institutions and what differing skills and understanding are needed to be effective practitioners. Although her work does not directly address issues of organizational structure, it makes a strong case for viewing institutional type and the context of student affairs work as critical factors in creating unique organizational designs and structures that are strongly aligned with the institution's mission and goals.

Kuk (2009) and Kuk and Banning (2009), building on the work of Hirt (2006) and Ambler (1993), researched current student affairs organizational structures and found that the most common models of organizational structure were those based on institutional type. The following summaries of existing types of structures, taken from the *Handbook of Student Affairs Administration* (Kuk, 2009) includes baccalaureate colleges, master's degree colleges and universities, research and doctoral degree universities, and associate's degree colleges.

Baccalaureate Colleges

The student affairs organizational structure of most baccalaureate and liberal arts colleges are modest in scope and hierarchical depth. These organizations have a few professional staff members who serve a primarily small-scale, resident student body. They are usually led by a dean of students or vice president for student affairs, with assistants and associates who both manage functional units and serve in a general capacity. Although the assistants and associates may have functional responsibility for a particular area such as housing, student activities, or counseling, the levels within the organization are not very deep, and staff members often cross various student affairs service areas. For example, a residence hall director may be responsible for a residence hall and also advise student groups or provide advising and/or counseling to the general student population. These student affairs organizations may have closer formal and informal ties with the academic units within the college. In some cases, student affairs may report through a dean of the college or an academic dean to the president, or they may report directly to the president and be part of the college's executive management team.

Master's Degree Colleges and Universities

These institutions are generally larger and have more complex student affairs organizations than do baccalaureate colleges, with more defined hierarchical and functional units. They may still retain a level of general responsibilities within functional units. These organizational structures are usually not very hierarchical or deep with regard to numbers of staff members in each unit. As a result, the staff members within these functional units may have a broad array of responsibilities, and they may serve a more general role that covers many responsibilities within the unit. For example, residence life personnel may serve as residence hall directors and housing assignment personnel, and they may handle student conduct or other administrative or student development functions within their operation. Student activities personnel may work with student organizations, advise the campus programming board, and conduct student leadership activities.

These organizations, although functional in structure, are often served by centralized budgeting and human resources operations, and they may receive resources services from other institutional units such as facilities, maintenance, and security units. If auxiliary units do exist, they are likely to report, wholly or in part, to the finance or administrative division and to collaborate with student affairs where the two divisions overlap, such as in the administration of housing or college union operations. The number of specific functional units within student affairs organizations is likely to vary among institutions, with public institutions more frequently including enrollment service areas and private institutions having a separate enrollment management unit or division. Student affairs organization leaders in these types of institutions often report directly to the president and serve as members of the cabinet or as executive teams of the institution.

Research and Doctoral Degree Universities

Student affairs organizations at research and doctoral degree institutions are generally the most complex among higher education institutions. Serving large numbers of students, these organizations are more hierarchical and specialized within their functional units than are other types of organizations. Staff responsibilities are likely to be very specialized. For example, an individual staff member's exclusive role may be to provide training for residence hall staff, or to advise the university programming board.

A vice president for student affairs or an associate provost generally leads these organizations. In addition, there may be associate or assistant vice presidents and/or provosts managing the day-to-day responsibilities of several functional units. This added layer is seldom found in other types of student affairs organizations. The breadth and complexity of these organizations require a number of layers; they may, at times, have other matrix organizational structure overlays, such as division committees or budgeting and technology units that provide organizational coordination and division-wide services to all functional units.

These organizations are also more likely to have auxiliary and fee-funded units that operate decentralized financial systems and thus generate revenue and expend resources within their own units. The organizational structure of these units is often influenced by state and/or institutional financial laws and regulations that govern the use and accounting of auxiliary operational funds. Because of their nature, the complexity of these organizations is often increased; they may include accounting, maintenance, custodial, service, and commercial sales and marketing and security personnel that are not generally found in student affairs organizations at other types of institutions. Although these student affairs organizations have more decentralized control of their programs and services at the unit level, the complexity, multiple organizational layers, and specialization often provide for less financial flexibility and staff mobility within the student affairs organization as a whole. In recent years, student affairs organizations at research institutions have increasingly been shifted to report to the provost and/or senior academic officer or senior vice president of the institution and not directly to the president. In most cases, the student affairs leader retains a voice on the executive team or cabinet but does not meet directly on a regular basis with the president.

Associate's Degree Colleges

Student affairs at associate degree colleges, also known in the public sector as community colleges, is a relatively new organizational entity than at other types of institutions. Student affairs at most community colleges consist of providing student services and academic support services focused on enhancing student success. These organizations may include enrollment service units, counseling, academic advising, transfer services, and student activities, as well as other student engagement and leadership-related campus services and programs.

Community colleges generally serve local and/or regional student populations; as a result, they have not traditionally provided student services, such as residence halls, health centers, and recreation centers, for campus residential students, and they have not had these types of functional units as part of the student affairs organizational portfolio. Because these institutions are not residentially focused, they may provide services for students who take evening classes, but because students leave campus at the end of their day, these student affairs organizations are not required to organize their programs and services to cover an around-the-clock operation like residential collegiate institutions do.

However, some community colleges are building residence halls and recreation centers and essentially becoming residential colleges. With the addition of these facilities and service units to the student affairs portfolios, the mission and organizational focus of student affairs units will probably change. International students are also having an increased presence on community college campuses, and this growing population will require additional support services. These programs and services generally fall within the responsibilities of student affairs organizations to provide.

At community colleges, the student affairs departments may report to a vice president or a dean responsible for both academic and student affairs, or they may report directly to the campus president or campus chief executive officer (CEO). In either case, student affairs is more closely tied to academic units within the institution and is not generally viewed as being separate and distinct, as may be the case in other institutional types (Kuk, 2009).

These emerging typology-based structural designs may be influenced by a variety of larger organizational changes, including the increased use of institutional bench marketing practices. The specific elements and units within these structures are influenced by size, history of the institution, the preferences of leadership, and the challenges presented by the external environment. Although they are not identical, they do possess some similarities in the way they are organized (Kuk, 2009; Kuk & Banning, 2009).

Organizational Learning Theory

The learning organization as a concept is closely aligned with the concepts of systems, organizational structure, and organizational design. It is generally used to describe certain types of activities that occur at any one of several levels of organizational analysis: (a) the individual, (b) the team or group, and (c) the organization as a whole. A number of theorists, including March (1991) and Senge (1990, 2005), generally define organizational learning as the organization's ability to adapt to change. Other ideas included in this concept are improving performance and increasing effectiveness within the organization. The concept of organizational change is addressed more specifically in chapter 6.

How organizations learn is an issue that is paramount in today's fast-paced, constantly changing environment. According to Dibella and Nevis (1998), there are actually three different perspectives on learning-related questions. The normative perspective is that organizational learning takes place only under a unique set of conditions. The developmental perspective is that the learning organization represents a late stage of organizational development. The capability perspective presumes that learning is innate to all organizations and that there is no one best way for all organizations to learn (p. 4).

The theory of single-looped learning and double-looped learning (Argyris & Schon, 1978) differentiates two distinctive types of learning that occur in organizations. Single-looped learning occurs as part of the feedback loop that is generated from examining the effects of ongoing behavior and organizational processes. This type of learning is used to modify and correct operational errors that keep the organization running smoothly. Double-looped learning goes a step further in the learning process and attempts to go beyond correcting behavior to actually assessing if the goals and processes are correct and then makes the appropriate changes to these goals and processes. Thus, questioning the organization's basic assumptions and beliefs is needed to transform the organization and create real learning within it.

James March (1991) proposed that organizations must constantly balance their need for efficiency with their need for flexibility. He differentiated between two modes of learning: exploitation, the use of existing knowledge and resources to achieve value from what is already known, and exploration, which is the redevelopment of knowledge and understandings to create new ways of understanding, through seeking new options, experimenting, and doing research. This process of exploration challenges organizational change theory and introduces the notion of learning organizations to alter how we think about change.

According to Senge (1990, 2005), superior performance depends on superior learning. The need to understand how organizations learn is critical to their survival. The old model of organizational behavior embedded in most organizations, which espouses the notion that the top managers think, and the middle managers and bottom staff members act, must give way to integrating thinking and acting at all levels. Learning organizations must focus on generative learning and the creation and expansion of learning, and not just adaptive learning, which is about coping. Today's learning organization seeks to meet the latent need of the customer and focus on what customers might truly value, even if they have not experienced this and would never think to ask. Generative learning, unlike adaptive learning, requires new ways of viewing the world. It requires the ability to see and understand the organizational system and its relationship to the external environment.

In learning organizations, the leader's role focuses on being organizational designers, instructors, and coaches. Leaders are responsible for building organizations where people are continually expanding their capabilities to shape their future. Leaders are responsible for designing and building a foundation of purpose, focus, and core values. Second, they design, with input from organizational members, the policies, strategies, and structures that translate guiding ideas into decisions and actions. Third, leaders create effective learning processes whereby the organization's strategies, processes, and structures are continually improved by the organization's members. Leadership in organizations is discussed in greater detail in chapter 8.

Senge (1990) stresses the importance of organizational learning as the process of expanding the organization's capacity to meet its goals, and particularly the capacity to make organizational changes and adjustments. Within this organizational learning approach, systems thinking (Senge, 2005), including the concepts of circles of causality and the importance of feedback and reinforcement, is emphasized.

Student affairs organizations have begun to embrace the conceptual ideas associated with learning organizations. They have started to apply elements of the principles associated with these ideas to segments of their organizations; however, adoption of these concepts on a large scale, throughout student affairs organizations, has not been widely implemented.

One of our goals is to assist in making connections among traditional organizational concepts, models like learning organizations, and the work and literature of the student affairs profession. An instructive link between

Senge's organizational learning and how the concept can be of practical value in student affairs organizational functioning is Blocher's (1974, 1978) ecological learning model.

Blocher's model focuses on the student learning–environment relationship, but the model is also applicable to the learning processes associated with organizations and their members, like the campus student affairs organization. Blocher's (1974) organization of learning environments model is an open systems model that includes three subsystems: opportunity, support, and reward. These three subsystems organize seven critical conditions for growth and development: (a) involvement, (b) challenge, (c) integration, (d) support, (e) structure, (f) feedback, and (g) application. In this case, these conditions are needed within a student affairs organization to be a learning organization that creates "the acquisition and maintenance of new patterns of thinking that are qualitatively different from preceding patterns" (Blocher, 1974, p. 19).

The opportunity subsystem provides the available tasks or opportunities to an organization for new learning. This component of the model leads to some very practical questions for the campus student affairs organization. What learning opportunities are being provided by the organization? How important are the staff development activities of the organization? What levels of resources are provided for professional growth activities, like conference and workshop attendance?

The new learning associated with these organizational efforts is increased according to the Blocher model by the conditions of involvement, challenge, and integration. Involvement calls for personal engagement in the learning task that puts at risk significant personal values, like letting go of past thinking to engage new ways of thinking about organizational issues. Student affairs development and training programs that incorporate active debate about campus issues may produce more involvement than an informational meeting about the issue. For example, the pros and cons within an active debate focusing on changing the campus drinking age may produce more involvement and new thinking than a meeting to review current policy.

The second critical condition for learning within the opportunity structure is challenge. Are the opportunities presented by the campus student affairs organization challenging? Blocher suggests that, in order to increase the challenge of a learning opportunity, the variables of novelty, complexity, abstractness, ambiguity, and intensity need to be present. Typical staff development programs often do not reflect these variables.

Finally, in addition to tasks needing to be involving and challenging, they also need to provide the condition of integration. How can new learning be integrated with past experiences? For example, staff discussion could focus on the question, Does changing the campus drinking age bring about a change in goals or just strategies for the maintenance of a healthy learning environment? What organizational changes need to be made given the outcome of the discussion? Can the new learning associated with these questions lead to an integration of old and new ways of proceeding?

Once the organization provides itself with tasks, programs, or opportunities that create involvement, challenge, and integration, the organization also needs to give attention to Blocher's second subsystem, the support subsystem. The support subsystem contains two additional critical learning conditions: structure and support. According to Blocher, structure "provides a new and higher level way of processing and organizing information about some phenomenon" (Blocher, 1974, p. 21). For example, if a student affairs organization, in its discussion of its first-year student orientation program, could elevate the discussion from the nuts and bolts of the current program to viewing student orientation from an "ecological transitions" (Bronfenbrenner, 1974) framework, where the focus is on change in role and place, new learning might occur for the organization. A second learning condition associated with the support subsystem is the concept of support. Blocher defines support as the "need to provide a relationship network that communicates empathy, caring, and honesty" (p. 21) so that members of the organization are not fearful to engage new ideas and models. Particularly important for organizational learning is the creation of an organizational climate that is perceived and experienced as a safe place for new thinking, new models, and new relationships.

Finally, the third Blocher subsystem is the reward subsystem. It is critical in bringing about two important conditions of the learning organization: feedback and application. Blocher defines feedback as "a condition that gives . . . continuous, accurate, and unambiguous information" (p. 21). The obvious practical question is, What are and how do the student affairs organizational feedback systems work? Are new ideas tossed into the organizational mix recognized and given an organizational response? Like many organizations, the campus student affairs organization may have its version of the black hole when it comes to new ideas. The second critical condition of the reward subsystem is application. New learning is enhanced if it has applicability. What can organizations find in their learning opportunities that can serve as new lessons for continuing issues?

Student affairs organizations can become the learning organization (Senge, 1990). The Blocher model (1974), with its roots in student affairs work, can help provide one path to organizational learning by giving attention to the subsystems of opportunities, support, and reward and the seven conditions for learning associated with these systems.

DiBella and Nevis (1998) also focused on how learning actually occurs in organizations. Their model, the organizational learning cycle, consists of three processes: (a) knowledge creation or acquisition, (b) knowledge dissemination, and (c) knowledge use. All three processes are critical for organizational learning. If student affairs organizations are going to design their organizations to be learning organizations, they should be conscious of these three processes and ensure that they are intentionally embedded in the day-to-day operations of the organization at all levels.

Reflective Summary

1. Where do you view your student affairs organization on the continuum between mechanistic and organic organizations? Why do you view it the way you do?

2. If you could restructure your current student affairs organization in a new form, what do you envision it would look like? What organizational form would you use as a model and why would you use it?

3. How would you orchestrate an organization redesign process for your student affairs organization?

4. What variables and organizational concepts would you focus on in the redesign process?

5. How would you use the concepts of tight and loose coupling and structural cognitive maps to influence the redesign efforts in your student affairs organization?

6. How would you adopt the principles of organizational learning to promote greater organizational effectiveness in your organizational design?

References

Allen, K. E., & Cherrey, C. (2000). *Systemic leadership: Enriching the meaning of our work.* Lanham, MD: American College Personnel Association and the National Association for Campus Activities.

Ambler, D. A. (1993). Developing internal management structures. In M. J. Barr (Ed.), *The handbook of student affairs administration* (pp. 107–120). San Francisco: Jossey-Bass.

Ambler, D. (2000). Organizational and administrative models. In M. J. Barr & M. K. Desler (Eds.), *The handbook of student affairs administration* (2nd ed.) (pp. 121–134). San Francisco: Jossey-Bass.

Argyris, C., & Schon, D. (1978). *Organizational learning: A theory of action perspective.* Reading, MA: Addison-Wesley.

Ashkenas, R., Ulrich, D., Jick, T., & Kerr, S. (2002). *The boundaryless organization: Breaking the chains of organizational structure.* San Francisco: Jossey-Bass.

Bartlett, C. A., & Ghoshal, S. (1990). Matrix management: Not a structure, a frame of mind. *Harvard Business Review, 68*(4), 138–145.

Bess, J. L., & Dee, J. R. (2008). *Understanding college and university organization: Theories for effective policy and practice. Volume 1: The State of the System.* Sterling, VA: Stylus.

Birnbaum, R. (1988). *How colleges work.* San Francisco: Jossey-Bass.

Blocher, D. H. (1974). Toward an ecology of student development. *Personnel and Guidance Journal, 52*(6), 360–365.

Blocher, D. H. (1978). Campus learning environments and the ecology of student development. In J. H. Banning (Ed.), *Campus ecology: A perspective for student affairs* (pp. 17–23). Cincinnati, OH: National Association of Student Personnel Administrators.

Bowditch, J. L., Buono, A. F., & Stewart, M. M. (2008). *A primer on organizational behavior* (7th ed.). Hoboken, NJ: Wiley.

Bronfenbrenner, U. (1974). *The ecology of human development.* Cambridge, MA: Harvard University Press.

Dibella, A. J., & Nevis, E. C. (1998). *How organizations learn.* San Francisco: Jossey-Bass.

Dungy, G. J. (2003). Organization and function in student affairs. In S. R. Komives & D. B. Woodward (Eds.), *Student services: A handbook for the profession* (pp. 339–357). San Francisco: Jossey-Bass.

Galbraith, J. R. (2002). *Designing organizations: An executive guide to strategy, structure and process.* San Francisco: Jossey-Bass.

Gallos, J. (2006). Reframing complexity: A four-dimensional approach to organizational diagnosis, development and change. In J. Gallos (Ed.), *Organization development: A Jossey-Bass Reader* (pp. 344–362). San Francisco: Jossey-Bass.

Giddens, A. (1984). *The constitution of society.* Berkeley: University of California Press.

Goold, M., & Campbell, M. (2002). *Designing effective organizations.* San Francisco: Jossey-Bass.

Helgesen, S. (1995). *The web of inclusion: A new architecture for building great organizations.* New York: Doubleday/Currency.

Hirt, J. B. (2006). *Where you work matters.* Lanham, MD: University Press of America.

Kuh, G. D. (1989). Organizational concepts and influences. In U. Delworth & G. R. Hanson (Eds.), *Student services: A handbook for the profession* (2nd ed.) (pp. 209–242). San Francisco: Jossey-Bass.

Kuk, L. (2009). The dynamics of organizational models within student affairs. In G. S. McClellan & J. Stringer (Eds.). *The handbook of student affairs administration* (3rd ed.) (pp. 313–332). San Francisco: Jossey-Bass.

Kuk, L., & Banning, J. H. (2009). Designing student affairs organizational structures: Perceptions of senior student affairs officers. *NASPA Journal, 46*(1), 94–117.

Love, P. G., & Estanek, S. M. (2004). *Rethinking student affairs practice.* San Francisco: Jossey-Bass.

Manning, K., Kinzie, J., & Schuh, J. (2006). *One size does not fit all: Traditional and innovative models of student affairs practice.* New York: Routledge, Taylor, and Francis Group.

March, J. G. (1991). Exploration and exploitation in organizational learning. *Organization Science, 2,* 71–87.

Orton, J. D., & Weick, K. (1990). Loosely coupled systems: A reconceptualization. *Academy of Management Review, 15,* 203–223.

Senge, P. M. (1990). *The fifth discipline: The art and practice of learning organizations.* New York: Currency/Doubleday.

Senge, P. M. (2005). The fifth discipline: A shift of mind. In J. M. Shafritz, J. S. Ott, & Y. S. Tang (Eds.), *Classics of organizational theory* (6th ed., pp. 441–449). Boston, MA: Thomson/Wadsworth.

Strange, C. C., & Banning, J. H. (2001). *Educating by design: Creating campus learning environments that work.* San Francisco: Jossey-Bass.

Weick, K. (1969). *The social psychology of organizing.* Reading, MA: Addison-Wesley.

Weick, K. (1976). Educational organizations as loosely coupled systems. *Administrative Science Quarterly, 21*(1), 1–19.

Weick, K. (1988). Enacting sensemaking in crisis situations. *Journal of Management Studies, 25*(4), 305–317.

Wheatley, M. J. (2006). *Leadership & the new science: Discovering order in a chaotic world* (3rd ed.). San Francisco: Berrett-Koehler.

Wiesbord, M. (2006). Designing work: Structure and process for learning and self-control. In J. Gallos (Ed.), *Organization development: A Jossey-Bass reader* (pp. 583–601). San Francisco: Jossey-Bass.

6

ORGANIZATIONAL PROCESS
AND CHANGE THEORY

Dr. Pat Harris sat at her desk contemplating her plan for orchestrating the organizational changes presented to her by the president and provost of her institution. She knew that the changes were to take place, some starting immediately, and that others would occur over the next few months. This schedule did not provide a lot of time, and she was concerned about how to fully engage her staff members and still meet the prescribed deadline for implementation.

The president shared that the reporting relationship of the division of student affairs would change immediately and would henceforth report to the provost; Pat would consult with the provost to make additional changes to create greater efficiency, reduce costs, and enable greater collaboration with academic units within the institution. The president indicated that he had asked the provost to provide him with more specifics and gave him a two-month window to develop the plan. Pat Harris knew that if she wanted to have some input into what would happen regarding the organizational change, she had to develop some alternative plans that she could present to the provost for consideration. If she did not act quickly, the student affairs division would be left with the changes proposed by the provost. Pat had already discussed some ideas with the provost, and he had agreed that she could have a month to develop a set of plans and processes that he would consider as part of the plan to be proposed to the president. The provost also indicated that any proposed plans would be subject to the scrutiny of the other vice presidents who were also affected by the organizational changes requested by the president.

Pat Harris felt that it was critical to engage her staff fully at all levels in this discussion and provide them with the opportunity to help create the change process. She also was aware of the sensitive nature of these discussions; she realized that positions and responsibilities would change, that the division's organizational structure and processes would probably change, and that some positions would be eliminated, all of which would place considerable stress on the staff members.

Pat now wrestled with crafting a change plan that would meet the president's goals and still adhere to the values of the student affairs division; she debated about which change model and components of a change process to utilize. Pat's objectives were to engage her entire staff and at the same time provide some structure, goals, desired outcomes, and a focus to ensure that the process was constructive and would be completed in the time allotted. She wanted to create a process for input and assessment that was inclusive, creative, and realistic. She wanted to discourage territorial and protective thinking and to ensure that members of the division would feel free to propose and consider a wide variety of ideas and strategies, especially those that challenged the status quo. Pat wanted the process to be transparent but also to minimize stress and overreaction to proposed issues that might be considered. She also knew that both the redesign and the process had to be well orchestrated and well crafted so that it supported the division's interests as well as the larger institution's needs. Past experience had shown her that any change would not be supported by either her staff or the greater organization without careful consideration.

L ike most organizations, student affairs units need sound decision making and the ability to deal with political situations and human conflict within their organizations. However, student affairs practitioners, largely as a result of their training and their human relations/helping orientation, often try to avoid conflict and political situations (Moore, L.V., 2000). As a result, they risk making poor decisions and may not address ongoing concerns and issues. As new forms of organizations emerge with a greater focus on flatter, boundaryless structures, issues related to process and change take on a new role and context in organizations. This chapter focuses on the positive and necessary elements of these aspects of organizational behavior in an effort to improve their use in the student affairs organizational context and to minimize negative perceptions.

To conceptualize organizational change, it is important to understand the concepts of power, politics, conflict, decision making, and communication as they relate to organizational functioning in general and to student affairs units more specifically. Because these concepts drive most other institutional processes in one way or another, they are foundations for moving toward a discussion of organizational change. The concept of change, although frequently referenced in its use with students, is not widely understood and applied within student affairs organizations. Research indicates that most student affairs units do not engage easily in change processes nor are they structured to respond to the changing demands of their environments. Understanding this cultural norm, its origins, and how leaders around the student affairs division might capitalize on strategies for change and transition is important to sustaining momentum.

Power, Politics, and Conflict

Higher education is challenged by multiple and conflicting agendas and priorities, changing markets and resources, continued demands for accountability and efficiency from its multiple constituents, and a growing need to articulate why higher education matters to the greater good (Duderstadt, 2000). This is not entirely unique to higher education, but it is complicated by the long-standing belief that somehow, higher education is the pathway to personal and societal benefit. The organizational reality is that postsecondary institutions continue to become more complex and less singularly focused (that is, if they ever were singularly focused), leading to perceived increases in politics, uneven power distribution and exertion, and conflict. The purpose here is not to debate the practical reality of these claims, to eradicate conflict from our colleges and universities, or to suggest politics will not exist if we all get along; rather, the intent is to lay out how a better understanding of these concepts is beneficial as they connect to best practice in student affairs, perhaps moving toward productive politics and real organizational change.

P. Moore (2000) suggests that politics may be the "most employed and least understood concept among the words we use to describe important aspects of our work" (p. 178). He defines politics as those processes that influence the direction of the institution and the allocation of resources. Power contributes to how one might affect politics, and it is often considered the key organizational resource (Bolman & Deal, 2003). Yet it is important to remember that power comes from multiples sources, including those power bases that are organizational (e.g., positional power or authority attributed to a position, control of rewards and sanctions, networks and alliances), and personally derived (knowledge, expertise, charisma, communication skills). Effective change agents realize that these multiple forms and sources of power become most useful depending on the issue and circumstance (Bolman & Deal, 2003; Morgan, 1999). This perspective also reminds us that student affairs professionals throughout the division, and not just those at the top, have opportunity to exercise power and influence on the organization, its decision making, direction, and so forth. Wergin (2007) calls this leading from within because the ability to affect change in the system is far more broad than we often realize or want to accept.

This also means that we have to accept, at least to some degree, the presence of conflict, defined as a situation between two or more parties whose perspectives are deemed incompatible (Moore, L. V., 2000). The tensions of growth and decline, the struggles over competing agendas and variable resources, the challenges associated with simultaneously being effective and efficient in providing meaningful experiences and learning environments for students causes some conflict within the organization, within the division, and among student affairs professionals. Although many in student affairs shy away from conflict, the ability to address and manage conflict is an important skill for leaders and change agents (Moore, L. V., 2000). Avoiding conflict, remaining nonresponsive, or reacting across a limited spectrum of responses typically is unproductive, leading to missed opportunities for creativity and change, as well as recurring interpersonal dilemmas, polarizing issues, and marginalization of ideas and people (Moore, L. V., 2000). Student affairs professionals have conversations about conflict with students regularly; they just have to see the corollary in their own practice.

Culture

Thinking about organizational processes and change is more beneficial when you realize that, in student affairs, we often characterize our units and divisions through imagery that represents a set of core professional values we hold in theory, if not always in practice. The family metaphor is frequently used to describe the profession and those within it. We often speak of the lofty goal of being student-centered, having rich traditions of the larger academy (e.g., commencement with full regalia, residence hall openings, welcome week, football weekends, and Final Four basketball tournaments), and many other stereotypic images of colleges and universities (Bergquist & Pawlak, 2007; Birnbaum, 1988) that feed into a similar perception of collegiality and higher-order purpose of our work—a type of professional calling on behalf of students. Although we aspire to remain collegial at least in terms of being friendly campuses, most academic institutions are no longer characterized according to the organizational definition of collegial: small in size, shared goals, lots of face-to-face interaction, consensus decision making, and minimal status differentials (Birnbaum, 1988). Institutional decline or growth, continued academic diversification, increased online instruction and technological advancement, entrepreneurial spirit, cultural diversification, internationalization, off-site branch campuses in other domestic and international locations are just some of the factors that can affect the collegial atmosphere and change the way that the college functions, makes decisions, and approaches change (Amey, Jessup-Anger, & Tingson-Gatuz, 2009).

P. Moore (2000) suggests that politics may be the "most employed and least understood concept among the words we use to describe important aspects of our work" (p. 178). He defines politics as those processes that influence the direction of the institution and the allocation of resources. At the same time, organizational theorists and most experienced administrators acknowledge that all colleges and universities are political organizations; how susceptible they are to political behavior, and therefore how much student affairs professionals might be affected, varies (Hirt, 2006). Even liberal arts colleges, long considered the model of less political if not nonpolitical institutions (Birnbaum, 1988), are becoming arenas for competing goals, coalition building, win-lose decision making leading to uneven power distribution, and the potential for decreased collaboration across areas of the college that directly affect student affairs work.

Amey, Jessup-Anger, and Tingson-Gatuz (2009); Bolman and Deal (2003); Hirt (2006); P. Moore (2000); and others make the argument that, although the idea of politics and political organizations tend to evoke negative connotations, there is nothing inherently negative about politics or conflict, or their role in decision making and organizational behavior. Just as we know that challenge is as necessary as support in student development, conflict often manifested as organizational politics is necessary for a college to grow and change. The greater complication comes in not understanding how the organization works so that one can be a proactive member rather than being negatively affected by institutional politics, power, conflict, decision making, communication patterns, and other normal aspects of organizational functioning. Kuh, Siegel, and Thomas (2001) call this being a culturally competent student affairs practitioner or good organizational analyst (Amey et al., 2009) and see this as key to survival and effective practice.

Understanding culture not only provides administrators with a way to assess their institutions and departments but also a way to identify tasks and appropriate roles for themselves, thereby reducing some of the dissonance created by role conflict, role ambiguity, and other aspects of work in student affairs. As Whitt (1993) suggests, "[T]he potential reward [of discovering the culture of an organization] is greater understanding of both the visible and the tacit elements—the furniture, scripts, and invisible props . . ." (p. 93). This includes most aspects of organizational functioning, including change. At the same time, organizational analysis is not the answer for all the difficulties facing professionals in student affairs. Making sense of things; being aware of ideologies, rituals, and symbols that motivate and alienate members; identifying key supporters and networks; and reconceptualizing leadership as embodying these ideals is an important component of navigating institutional decision making, having the politics work with you rather than against you, negotiating conflict and effectively using communication channels and networks. It also becomes a critical feature of leading change (Amey et al., 2009).

Decision Making

Many student affairs professionals, especially those new to the field, believe that most decisions are straightforward and typically top-down, that the designated leader has the final say-so, and that their own authority is very limited. Others sought or were hired by an institution that touted a team or participative approach to management, where everyone would be involved in decisions and discussions of mission, goal setting, and evaluation. Still others believed they were hired into one of the two approaches just described and found reality to be very different. It is important to recognize the difference between what we say and what we do in decision making and between espoused theory and theory in use (Argyris & Schon, 1977), and to become quickly aware of the way things actually get done in your unit or institution. For example, it is unlikely that decisions are made with all the necessary information in hand, all the alternatives identified and considered, and the best decision determined. Rather, throughout all of higher education, including student affairs, it is far more likely that decisions are made by well-meaning administrators reflecting their best judgment with the information available at the time. Often, these decisions mirror past successes, or at least not past failures, and as a result may lead to maintenance of a sense of status quo. This sense of decision satisficing (Birnbaum, 1988) exists because colleges and universities are very complex, information is filtered and distorted by the perspectives of those who transmit it, interactions are intricate and loosely coupled, and outcomes are often uncertain. The reality of working with students often demands in-time decision making rather than carefully gathering all the data and weighing each option before action is required.

Being familiar with the subtle and obvious ways in which decisions are made—who is involved and at what level, and the penalties for ineffective decisions and the rewards for effective ones—is part of understanding your unit (Amey et al., 2009). These things are often learned by trial and error, by observing others, and by asking some basic questions such as the following: Does the director sign off on everything before anyone is allowed to move ahead? Are symbols and symbolic meaning (including something as simple as event T-shirts and staff nameplates) common and effectively used throughout the office? Is everything, from what to do for the administrative assistant's birthday to next year's proposed budget, discussed at department meetings? How much latitude do you have about attending an upcoming event casually mentioned in passing by your supervisor? Does an invitation to be creative and innovative and to take the lead mean only if you come up with decisions that do not require anything to really change or within limits that are not very well stated? Understanding proper procedures, cliques, active countercultures, and informal networks common in every organization helps student affairs professionals work more effectively and efficiently, build supportive connections, capitalize on opportunities, and succeed more consistently on behalf of students (Amey et al., 2009).

Everyone sometimes feels as if they do not have enough information or the right facts to make decisions and take action. Yet the better we understand the department, division, and institution in which we work, the more we can see what is enough and not feel like we are being excluded or left to our own devices. How the institution makes decisions and enacts them (so how things really happen in your workplace) is what Tierney (1991) calls organizational strategy. Student affairs professionals need to realize that, in addition to being purposeful in developing good contacts and networks, they need to pursue additional sources rather than believing someone is intentionally withholding things if they do not receive the information they seek. Asking questions, listening carefully, seeking perspective outside one's office, and building a strong informal network helps new professionals see how to gather and broker information more effectively.

Communication

In colleges and universities, even in highly structured ones where memos, written records, handbooks, and standard operating procedures are the norm

(Birnbaum, 1988; Bolman & Deal, 2003), information rarely flows only hierarchically, from the top down. This would apply also to divisions of student affairs, often characterized as traditional organizational structures (Fenske, 1990), with vertical orientations (Keeling, Underhile, & Wall, 2007) and pyramid personnel charts. In practice, listservs, instant messaging, online resources, and email communication enhance the speed and volume of information flow, often making instantly accessible what information gatekeepers traditionally had discretion to provide. Personal networks are also very integral to the socialization of student affairs professionals and provide another communication web on which to draw. At the same time, the communication explosion does not always mean information accuracy (Amey et al., 2009). Effective practitioners must be skilled at gathering information from multiple sources and in multiple forms, including beyond the student affairs unit in which they work. Learning who to ask for what, who is a reliable information source, and the organizational cycles for which information is most important help increase effectiveness and efficiency. Knowing whom to call for the best answer is not always a function of a person's position on the organizational chart.

Organizational Change

The concept of change, although frequently mentioned in reference to students, is not widely understood and applied within student affairs organizations. Research indicates that most student affairs organizations do not engage easily in change processes, nor are they structured to respond effectively to the changing demands of their environments. Although much is written about organizational change, especially in the management literature, the topic is less prevalent in higher education research, and infrequent when focused on student affairs organizations within colleges and universities. Because these units or divisions are found within larger academic institutions, change is best understood as a multilayered process. It happens within student affairs organization and occurs in, or at least is affected by, the broader institutional culture of the college or university in which the student affairs unit is located. As demands on higher education institutions shift and the role of student affairs evolves, many divisions may have to adapt their mission, priorities, structure, and practices if they are to continue to align with the central academic mission of their institution (American College Personnel Association [ACPA] & National Association of Student

Personnel Administrators [NASPA], 2004; Jessup-Anger, 2009). Diamond (2002) noted, "The number one issue facing higher education today is this: Effectively initiating, implementing, and managing intentional, meaningful, planned change" (p. 481). This translates into similar circumstances and demands facing student affairs.

It is also important to understand that there is no one way to think about or enact change in student affairs (or in other formal organizations) any more than there is one model or theory that is appropriate for understanding college students' development. Multiple approaches and models of change exist. Fullan (2001) even advises leaders to avoid the checklist approach because change is such a fluid and a messy endeavor, and it should embrace the complexity of the process instead. How to know what will work in your unit is tied to understanding the culture, norms, beliefs, ways of communicating, models of decision making, who has what kind of power, and other features of overall organizational culture (Bergquist, 1992; Tierney, 2008; Woodard, Love, & Komives, 2000). In the 1980s, during what was also a period of significant institutional turbulence, Creamer and Creamer (1989) suggested, "Studies of organizational development and of planned change are not abundant in student affairs, yet insight into the interaction of institutional factors is imperative to ensure successful program implementation" (p. 29) and other forms of restructuring and change.

Any change involves a stimulus, which can come from within the unit or from outside it. Beliefs about best practices for students often drive change in student affairs, as do the need to find a work–life balance and time for self-development for individual staff members (Blanchard, 2009). In student affairs, external forces come in many forms related to the changes occurring in the larger academic institution, including university mandates to cut budgets in times of recession; external program reviews that reflect overall student experiences in and out of the classroom; expanding and diversifying student populations; and adopting new data management systems for financial aid, admissions, and registrar functions. The catalysts for change may also come from outside the institution, such as innovative practices learned through professional development and conference participation; reports and funding initiatives generated by external agencies such as *Learning Reconsidered* or *Achieving the Dream*; or even through the agendas of a newly hired director or vice president within the division.

The change itself comes from embracing the tensions and conflict inherently provoked by the stimulus and making decisions about what to institutionalize and what to let go. In a way, this is a form of unfreezing (Bridges &

Bridges, 2000), which helps members of organizations let go of their assumptions about how things *have* to work, how they matter within the institution (including reference to a second-class-citizen mentality often prevalent among student affairs professionals), and who can create change. This unfreezing then allows members to refreeze new beliefs, actions, models of change, and ways of being effective in achieving goals on behalf of students.

Even though the higher education change literature does not often focus on student affairs per se, it is still possible to identify some key tenets and considerations of organizational change and to discuss how these foundations may apply to student affairs as a professional practice. Some emergent factors that are important to consider as one begins to adapt and change in student affairs are senior administrative support; distributed leadership and ownership; transparent, inclusive processes built on the value of collaboration; a climate of planning and strategy development; organizational culture; and sufficient training, development, and institutional resources.

As noted in chapter 1 of this book, institutional structures are not permanent, and current organizational theories have moved toward beliefs that they are fluid, adaptive, and boundaryless. Though we argue against hierarchy as the best way to organize and to create systemic change, there remain embedded assumptions that bureaucracies drive decision making, power, leadership, communication channels, and change processes. If it does not come from the top, then it is not going to happen or be supported. Although we know intuitively and empirically that change occurs as often from the bottom up (e.g., Spears, 2002; Wergin, 2007), we revert quickly to reliance on senior-level leaders to state the charge, deal with the conflict or problems, and think things through for us. Although their perspectives may have some advantages given their location in the organization, student affairs divisions (even at small schools) have become complex enough that overreliance on a single leader for creating change is flawed. Leadership theorists have moved away from this top-down, singular leader idea (e.g., Bensimon & Neumann, 1994; Helgeson, 1995; Spears, 2002), yet those in student affairs often look up for guidance and change (as well as offering criticism and concern) before they look horizontally to peers and those in other units at the same organizational level, or even before they look within.

At the same time, researchers have consistently identified support from senior administration as key to organizational change (e.g., Creamer & Creamer, 1989; Eckel & Kezar, 2003; Furst-Bowe & Bauer, 2007; Hunter, 2006; Kezar, 2003; Manning, Kinzie, & Schuh, 2006; Sandeen, 2001). This almost sounds like it contradicts the arguments just made about the multidirectional sources of leadership and change, and the need for student affairs professionals to see themselves as change agents regardless of their location within the institution. The point is that, although senior leaders may not be instigators of the change or even directly involved, their affirmation, communication, commitment, and willingness to allocate resources are regularly found to be central to successful efforts. Although his research extended beyond higher education, Collins (2005) is clear that organizational greatness was achieved through the leadership of "Level 5 Leaders" who were first and foremost focused on the cause, the organization, and the work, rather than themselves. "A Level 5 leader displays a paradoxical blend of personal humility and professional will" (Collins, 2005, p. 32). Collins seems to typify the way in which many student affairs professionals approach their work, and the level of commitment, drive, and passion that has long exemplified the profession.

Dynamic leadership is insufficient to achieve real change (Fullan, 2001), as those who have worked tirelessly in student affairs are well aware. This is especially true when a single champion leads the charge (Amey, 2005) and does not have a broader base of support and investment. Bensimon and Neumann (1994) found that team-based leadership was generally more effective, and Helgeson (1995) speaks of a leadership web as a source of creative energy and change. Eckel and Kezar (2003) concluded that change best occurs when "leaders at multiple levels work compatibly" (p. 87). These authors and others (Bringle & Hatch, 1996; Creamer & Creamer, 1989; Handy, 2002; Seifter, 2001) advocate involving others and engendering broad ownership for initiatives both for the cognitive insights and talents that can be brought to bear, and for the ability to sustain change as it becomes a part of institutional life.

Building on the need for greater involvement and multiple champions, Woodard, Love, and Komives (2000) urged a deep commitment to inclusivity and civility in any change endeavor. Those in student affairs more readily commit to change efforts initiated with them rather than those that are done *to* them (Jessup-Anger, 2009), as is true for most human resources organizations such as colleges and universities (Morgan, 1999). Developing effective coalitions and alliances requires open communication, transparent processes, and a keen awareness of organizational politics (Collins, 2005; Eckel & Kezar, 2003; Fullan, 2001; Kuh, 1996). In the same way that student affairs professionals need to understand the complexities that affect decision making and the way things get done in their units and institutions, change agents need to be aware of preexisting conflicts, competing motivations, and historical power struggles (Kezar, 2001) that may work against the good idea that is the focus of their change efforts.

Change agents may make the most of the high levels of commitment of their staff members by ensuring that they simultaneously create a strategic (related to the direction of the division) and contextual (taking the broader environment) planning environment (Dooris, Kelley, & Trainer, 2004). Student affairs leaders can create significant change by "pursuing priorities in a planned way, thinking and acting strategically to implement plans, and making adjustments based on changing conditions" (Woodard et al., 2000, p. 69). This provides the space for listening to the needs, concerns, and ideas of constituents; different perspectives to see alternatives and opportunities; the context for strategic decision making; and the capacity to build a shared mission and direction.

Contextual planning, by definition, takes organizational environments and cultures into account (Peterson, 1997) and is beneficial in creating sustainable change, which is important in student affairs. The embedded assumption that everyone in higher education has students' best interests as the foundation of their work is often part of the professional stance of those who choose careers in student affairs. Colleges and universities are often much more complex, however, which returns us to a theme in this book that understanding the institution's and division's cultures are really key to effective practice and sustainable change (Claar & Cuyjet, 2000; Kezar & Eckel, 2002; Kuh, 1996; Reisser & Roper, 1999; Tierney, 2008). The strength of the interrelationships of the shared assumptions, beliefs, and values, and the behaviors of the members of any unit that constitute its culture, including those in a student affairs division, is part of why Diamond (2002) identified organizational culture as one of four primary barriers to achieving change in higher education. At the same time, capitalizing on culture through symbolic leadership (Tierney, 1991) can make this a strength and key change strategy (Kotter, 1996). If the culture and the various subcultures of an organization are ignored when using change strategies, the effort is unlikely to succeed (Kezar & Eckel, 2002).

Something often overlooked when implementing change are the level of staff preparedness to engage in this work and the support they need throughout the change process. Appropriate training and feedback, professional development opportunities, and organizational resources (human, financial, structural) are all critical success factors to consider (Claar & Cuyjet, 2000; Diamond, 2002; Eckel & Kezar, 2003; Kezar, 2003; Sandeen, 2001). This may be especially important in student affairs organizations when many staff are younger, new(er) professionals with limited experience and high turnover, and where there are also more senior staff members whose longevity with the institution belies limited different organizational strategies and perspective. As Sandeen (2001) observes, change agents must carefully consider the professional background, values, knowledge, and abilities of their staff members when beginning a change process.

It is not surprising that new roles and responsibilities are resisted if staff members feel unprepared to assume them, so appropriate training in advance and professional development along the way are essential. In his study of organizational change in three divisions of student affairs, Jessup-Anger (2009) found that in units whose staff members were involved in professional development activities and therefore aware of national trends, current literature, and innovations occurring at other universities, and who had a general individual priority of lifelong learning, change was implemented more easily. Sufficiently prepared staff members and financial resources are key foundations of successful change endeavors, although *sufficient* remains a term best defined in context. Certainly, in sustaining change efforts, student affairs organizations need to commit resources appropriately and creatively to support change (Ausiello & Wells, 1997; Claar & Cuyjet, 2000; Sandeen, 2001).

As noted earlier, research on organizational change in higher education comes in waves and is not uniformly available; the research in student affairs specifically is equally limited, if not more so (Kezar, 2003). Early writing was often anecdotal or applied management change theories to student affairs without consideration of the very factors identified as critical in that same research. Although early literature provided ample viewpoints on how change and implementation efforts were expected to occur, there was still no empirically derived student affairs change model available to guide practitioner decision making. In the mid-1980s, after studying senior student affairs officers who had managed change efforts in their institutions, Creamer and Creamer (1989) developed the probability of adoption change (PAC) model. The authors continued to test and revise their model, applying it to myriad case studies of student affairs and student affairs/academic affairs collaborations (Creamer & Creamer, 1989; Creamer, Creamer, & Ford, 1991). They concluded that nine factors most influenced the likelihood that change would be adopted: "the circumstances under which the change took place, value compatibility, idea comprehensibility, practicality, leadership of the change, championship, advantage probability, strategies, and the amount of opposition to planned change" (as cited in Jessup-Anger, 2009, p. 46). Because Creamer and colleagues' research focused on the perspectives of senior student affairs officers, it lacked the understandings held by mid-level or entry-level professionals, who are more likely responsible for actually implementing change initiatives. Unfortunately, this is often the case in the extant research, as it is in the planning for change in practice (Ausiello & Wells, 1997; Kotter, 1996; Sandeen, 2001). Jessup-Anger's (2009) recent study and others like it are needed to understand more fully whether organizational change principles are perceived similarly throughout the student affairs organizations compared to the perspectives of those in positions of greater authority.

More recently, scholars have broadened their research to include the perspectives of participants throughout an organization during periods of change. Ward and Warner (1996) believed that change had to be considered as a cognitive and affective process, positing that fears held by individuals contributed to failed change initiatives in student affairs organizations. When change agents proceed too rationally (Morgan, 1999), they look past the effects of the process and how the aspects of change are understood by those enacting and being affected by the change itself (Ward & Warner, 1996). As an example, one-stop support centers were popular in community colleges in the early 1990s and were deemed a very student-centered change initiative that gathered various support services together in one location, presumably increasing coordination, integration, and convenience for students. Relocation anxiety, cross-training needs and subsequent time allocated for the training, loss of professional identity, and changes in reporting structures and evaluation systems were just some of the costs involved with these innovations that were minimized in the minds of senior leaders but were felt deeply by student affairs professionals in the trenches. When the staff members' perspectives and concerns were not adequately accounted for and addressed, these strategies failed, even though the initial goal of better service for students was a shared priority. If initiatives were successful, it is probable that student affairs leaders were following the tenets articulated in Ward and Warner's research: support an individual's change, manage meaning making, communicate with transparency and consistency, break down artificial and perceived organizational barriers, and empower staff members to participate actively in the change process. Manning's (2001) research on the importance of managing meaning and Dalton and Gardner's (2002) work on evaluating and negotiating collective attitude during change build on Ward and Warner's early work to reinforce that, just because change seems necessary or obvious at the level of senior staff members does not mean it will be embraced readily or adopted easily even by the most experienced staff elsewhere in the student affairs organization.

Scholarship since the mid-1990s has continued to increase our understanding of change in student affairs. Some of the work is based on empirical data, and other models of change are postulated from reviews of the literature in different disciplines (Allen & Cherrey, 2003; Doyle, 2004; Hunter, 2006; Keeling et al., 2007; Kezar, 2003; Kuh, 1996; Smith & Rodgers, 2005; Woodard et al., 2000). Kuh's (1996) six key change principles for creating seamless learning environments is perhaps cited the most often, in part because he took into account the nature and culture of student affairs divisions: (a) generate enthusiasm for institutional renewal, (b) create a common vision for learning, (c) develop a common language, (d) foster collaboration and cross-functional dialogue, (e) examine the influence of student cultures on student learning, and (f) focus on systemic change. Kezar (2003) included these change principles along with the concepts of restructuring and planned change in her work with Eckel (Kezar & Eckel, 2002) examining collaborations between academic and student affairs units. Although her findings often mirror Kuh's, of importance to the person instituting change in students affairs is Kezar's conclusion that institutions using more than one strategy were more successful in the change process than those that employed only one. Extrapolating this finding to the level of individuals, we can argue that change agents throughout the division of student affairs are more likely to meet with success if they integrate frames (Bolman & Deal, 2003) or multiframe processes (Amey & Brown, 2004) than if they use only a single approach.

Transition

It is also important for those facilitating change to realize that transition is a critical part of every evolutionary process. According to Bridges and Bridges (2000), transition is the state that change puts people into. Change is external, while transitions are internal to the individual, referring to the reorientation that has to transpire before change can really work. Transition consists of several phases, the first of which is saying goodbye or letting go of the way things used to be, including the lived experiences and past identities of individuals. For example, when two student affairs units are merged in times of budget cuts, as logical as the change may be, the transition means that staff members may no longer work with friends they worked with for many years or report to people whose priorities they understood (Bridges & Bridges, 2000). In Jessup-Anger's study (2009), the change in work responsibilities and positions that was a by-product of preparing to adopt a new institutional initiative was resisted by many members of the student affairs division, sometimes to the surprise of senior administrators. This resistance to job change and the need for adequate training are more examples of transition often overlooked in change efforts.

The second stage of transition is shifting into neutral (Bridges & Bridges, 2000), which captures that phase where individuals have let go of past practice and identities but have not yet been able to adopt fully new ways of being and move forward with the change. This time of great uncertainty and ambiguity is uncomfortable and often lasts a long time. As a result, staff members may rush into the new circumstances without fully understanding what it means or how it will affect their practice, or they become quite resistant as a way of slowing down the change process. In reality, staff members cannot do what is expected of them if they do not understand and accept it. Yet senior administrators often do not see how their logical ideas and directives proposed in the vice president's cabinet may not translate into the organization, and they may wonder why change does not occur more readily. The final stage of transition is moving forward (Bridges & Bridges, 2000) when members begin behaving in new ways. This can be particularly challenging in student affairs divisions that have historically punished risk taking and independent thinking. In these arenas, members may be more inclined to wait to see how changes play out rather than be willing to act as early adapters of the new direction.

Thinking about change in more complex terms and using multiple strategies and frames in the process allow for "real change" (Woodard et al., 2000) or "deep change" (Fullan, 2001; Quinn, 1996). This involves examining basic assumptions, beliefs, priorities, and behaviors, and either affirming or modifying them so that policies and practices can be aligned with the core values and principles of the organization (Woodard et al., 2000). Achieving this alignment, or at least moving toward it, is what leads to significant behavioral change, the possibility of institutional transformation, and the opportunity for organizational learning because members have addressed their individual transitions.

Organizational Learning

Organizational learning can occur when practice is genuinely questioned (Senge, 1990), when there is rigorous assessment that guides decision making

(Furst-Bowe & Bauer, 2007; Keller, 2004), when team-based leadership (Bensimon & Neumann, 1994) and flattened organizational (Helgeson, 1995) approaches are embraced along with inclusive and collaborative decision-making strategies (Collins, 2005; Kotter, 1996; Seifter, 2001), and when risk taking is supported (Kezar, 2001). It requires effective communication within and beyond the division of student affairs (Amey et al., 2009), and a willingness to share and develop best practices (Diamond, 2002; Hunter, 2006). It also demands a different kind of leadership not only from senior staff members but also from those throughout the organization if they see leadership as learning and if they model learning-focused behaviors, critical reflection, and constructive feedback (Amey, 2005). Wheatley (1999) found that organizational systems need to learn about themselves if change is really to unfold. This requires that members are aware of what others are doing and are willing to examine their own practice regularly, which is not always easy or part of the culture of student affairs organizations. As Collins (2005) observes, educational organizations, often characterized by a culture of niceness, are frequently limited in their ability to express candor and constructive criticism and to share brutal facts, and thus make the difficult dialogues and honest conversations necessary to promote change a significant challenge. In this way, they often diminish the ability to learn as an organization or as members within that structure.

Scholars agree that leaders should work to increase learning capacity throughout the organization in support of change and implementation efforts (Heifetz, 1994; Senge, 1990, 1998). They also acknowledge that organizational learning occurs in many ways according to an institution's history, culture, constituents, and current circumstances. They are often less clear, however, on exactly how this all takes place. Research on teams and academic institutions involved in promoting learning-change efforts makes clear that this is a very time-consuming enterprise that does not always lead to fail-safe strategies for organizing that best serve students (Amey & Brown, 2004; Manning et al., 2006; Moore et al., 2000). In fact, Amey (2005) says that research more often suggests that organizational learning is an ongoing negotiation between innovative (challenge) and traditional (support) thinking. This approach to organizational functioning belies "right strategies" advocated by those who wield greatest expert or positional power (Senge, 1998) and that often permeate staff meetings and other group discussions. For example, traditional staff training organized around expert thinking reinforced the need to express "right" answers to demonstrate your intellectual

standing in the group, preparation for practice, and readiness for taking on advanced tasks (Amey & Brown, 2004).

Although there remain codes of conduct, legal guidelines, and institutional regulations to which practitioners must adhere, future work in student affairs demands the latitude to question past practice and advance new ways of thinking about the way we serve students if we are to do this work effectively in the midst of changing student needs. Moving toward strategic thinking and organizational learning requires transitions in how members approach and think about their work, and how they engage with each other (Kezar, 2003; Peterson, 1997; Rowley, Lujan, & Dolence, 1997; Senge, 1990). There is good reason to move from staking claims of expertise to collaborating, where multiple perspectives are drawn on and deeper ownership of collective ideas is the norm. Strategic thinking that drives organizational learning reaps richer rewards, and the challenges facing student affairs professionals demand this kind of second-order, adaptive thinking that is not satisfied with "the way we've always done things" (Amey, 2005; Argyris & Schon, 1977; Heifetz, 1994).

As important as this kind of organizational learning is, it is not easy. Because it takes time to cultivate and develop a learning culture, organizational learning often falls outside the traditional staff evaluation cycle and standard performance indicators. The need to produce and measure outputs often truncates organizational learning in deference to quick fixes and traditionally acceptable unit products, for example, how many students were seen in one day's counseling sessions instead of how well the student's concerns were addressed. Although organizational learning results in deep change, it requires changed structures, flattened hierarchies, cross-unit collaborations, willingness to challenge and be challenged, risk taking, and a core commitment to reflective practice. Organizational learning occurs if student affairs professionals invent new strategies that circumvent institutional obstacles, conduct tradeoff analyses where compromise is achieved through inquiry into the probabilities and values associated with specific actions, and get beneath preconceived ideas of alternatives and consequences (Morgan, 1999; Senge, 1990). A unique synergy should be apparent: Organizational learning is fostered through an institution that is flexible and adaptive (Lawler & Worley, 2006); to be flexible and adaptive, members of the student affairs divisions have to be engaged in organizational learning. (See chapter 5 for a discussion on organizational learning.)

Summary

Organizational learning in student affairs means adopting the art of managing and changing the contexts of practice and seeing these as fundamental responsibilities of each person in the division. It means moving toward the place where staff members are willing to reconsider the organization's viability so that new forms of practice can evolve (Morgan, 1999), such as networks of similar services (Ambler, 2000) and decentralized structures that locate student services within the academic units of the institution (Morgan, 1999). It means being willing to ask the difficult questions of our practice, as professionals and as members of the institutions in which we conduct our practice. And it means we have to be willing to live with a degree of ambiguity while we look for the kinds of organizational change that lead to more effective work on behalf of students.

Reflective Summary

1. What assumptions do you have about the leadership needs of your organization?
2. In what ways are the members of your organization encouraged to assume leadership responsibilities, or to be "leaders from anywhere"? How can you encourage others do be leaders?
3. How do you describe the leadership in your organization? Do definitions differ depending where one is in your organization (e.g., entry level, midlevel, senior-level professional)?
4. Consider someone you think is an effective leader and one who is not. What are the differences?
5. Think about a challenge your organization has faced. Regardless of how it turned out in the end, how would you describe the challenge in terms of leadership?
6. Why is it important to know what you believe in as a leader? In what ways have your beliefs been put to the test in your organization?
7. Think about your experiences and identity. How do you think these factors affect you as a leader and your leadership?
8. What activities do you engage in as part of your leadership development plan?

References

Allen, K. E., & Cherrey, C. (2003). Student affairs as change agents. *NASPA Journal,* *40*(2), 29–42.

Ambler, D. A. (2000). Organizational and administrative models. In M. J. Barr, M. K. Desler, & Associates (Eds.), *The handbook of student affairs administration* (pp. 121–134). San Francisco: Jossey-Bass.

American College Personnel Association/National Association of Student Personnel Administrators. (2004). *Learning reconsidered: A campus-wide focus on the student experience.* Washington, DC: Author.

Amey, M. J. (2005). Leadership as learning: Conceptualizing the process. *Community College Journal of Research and Practice, 29,* 689–704.

Amey, M. J., & Brown, D. F. (2004). *Breaking out of the box: Interdisicplinary collaboration and faculty work.* Charlotte, NC: Greenwood Press/Information Age Publishing.

Amey, M. J., Jessup-Anger, E., & Tingson-Gatuz, C. R. (2009). Unwritten rules: Organizational and political realities of the job. In M. J. Amey & L. Reesor (Eds.), *Beginning your journey: A guide for new professionals in student affairs* (3rd ed., pp. 15–38). Washington, DC: NASPA.

Argyris, C., & Schon, D. A. (1977). *Organizational learning: A theory of action perspective.* Reading, MA: Addison-Wesley.

Ausiello, K., & Wells, B. (1997). Information technology and student affairs: Planning for the 21st century. In C. McHugh Engstrom & K. W. Kruger (Eds.), *Using technology to promote student learning* (New Directions for Student Services No. 78, pp. 71–81). San Francisco: Jossey-Bass.

Bensimon, E. M., & Neumann, A. (1994). *Redesigning collegiate leadership: Teams and teamwork in higher education.* Baltimore, MD: Johns Hopkins University Press.

Bergquist, W. H. (1992). *The four cultures of the academy.* San Francisco: Jossey-Bass.

Bergquist, W. H., & Pawlak, K. (2007). *Engaging the six cultures of the academy: Revised and expanded edition of the Four Cultures of the Academy.* San Francisco: Jossey-Bass.

Birnbaum, R. (1988). *How colleges work.* San Francisco: Jossey-Bass.

Blanchard, J. (2009). Reconciling life and work for the new student affairs professional. In M. J. Amey & L. Reesor (Eds.), *Beginning your journey: A guide for new professionals in student affairs* (3rd ed., pp. 133–146). Washington, DC: NASPA.

Bolman, L. G., & Deal, T. E. (2003). *Reframing organizations: Artistry, choice, and leadership.* San Francisco: Jossey-Bass.

Bridges, W., & Bridges, S. M. (2000). Leading transition: A new model for change. *Leader to Leader, 16,* 30–36.

Bringle, R. G., & Hatch, J. A. (1996). Implementing service-learning in higher education. *Journal of Higher Education, 67*(2), 221–239.

Claar, J., & Cuyjet, M. (2000). Program planning and implementation. In M. J. Barr, M. K. Desler, & Associates (Eds.), *The handbook of student affairs administration* (pp. 311–326). San Francisco: Jossey-Bass.

Collins, J. (2005). *Good to great and the social sectors: A monograph to accompany good to great.* Boulder, CO: Author.

Creamer, E. G., & Creamer, D. G. (1989). Testing a model of planned change across student affairs and curriculum reform projects. *Journal of College Student Development, 30,* 27–34.

Creamer, E. G., Creamer, D. G., & Ford, R. H. (1991). Construct reliability of the probability of change (PAC) model. *Journal of College Student Development, 32*(1), 31–38.

Dalton, J. C., & Gardner, D. I. (2002). *Managing change in student affairs leadership roles* (New Directions for Student Services No. 98) (pp. 37–48). San Francisco: Wiley Periodicals.

Diamond, R. M. (2002). Some final observations. In R. M. Diamond (Ed.), *Field guide to academic leadership* (pp. 471–490). San Francisco: Jossey-Bass.

Dooris, M., Kelley, J., & Trainer, J. F. (2004). *Successful strategic planning* (New Directions for Institutional Research No. 123) (pp. 5–11). San Francisco: Jossey-Bass.

Doyle, J. (2004). Student affairs division's integration of student learning principles. *NASPA Journal, 41*(2), 375–394.

Duderstadt, J. J. (2000). *A university for the 21st century.* Ann Arbor: University of Michigan Press.

Eckel, P. D., & Kezar, A. (2003). *Taking the reigns: Institutional transformation in higher education.* Westport, CT: Praeger.

Fenske, R. H. (1990). Evolution of the student services profession. In U. Delworth, G. R. Hanson, & Associates (Eds.), *Student services: A handbook for the profession* (pp. 25–56). San Francisco: Jossey-Bass.

Fullan, M. (2001). *Leading in a culture of change.* San Francisco: Jossey-Bass.

Furst-Bowe, J. A., & Bauer, R. A. (2007). Application of the Baldridge model for innovation in higher education. In T. S. Glickman & S. C. White (Eds.), *Managing for innovation* (New Directions for Higher Education No. 137, pp. 5–14). San Francisco: Jossey-Bass.

Handy, C. (2002). Elephants and fleas: Is your organization prepared for change? *Leader to Leader, 24,* 1–5.

Heifetz, R. (1994). *Leadership without easy answers.* Boston: Belknap.

Helgeson, S. (1995). *The web of inclusion.* New York: Doubleday Books.

Hirt, J. B. (2006). *Where you work matters: Student affairs administrators at different types of institutions.* Lanham, MD: University Press of America.

Hunter, M. S. (2006). Lessons learning: Achieving institutional change in support of students in transition. In F. S. Laanan (Ed.), *Students in transition: Trends and issues* (New Directions for Student Services No. 114, pp. 7–15). San Francisco: Jossey-Bass.

Jessup-Anger, E. R. (2009). *Implementing innovative ideas: A multisite case study of putting* Learning Reconsidered *into practice.* Unpublished dissertation. Michigan State University East Lansing.

Keeling, R. P., Underhile, R., & Wall, A. F. (2007, Fall). Horizontal and vertical structures: The dynamics of organization in higher education. *Liberal Education, 93*(4), 22–31.

Keller, G. (2004). *Transforming a college: The story of a little-known college's strategic climb to national distinction.* Baltimore, MD: Johns Hopkins University Press.

Kezar, A. (2001). Understanding and facilitating change in the 21st century: Research and conceptualizations. *ASHE-ERIC Higher Education Report, 28*(4). San Francisco: Jossey-Bass.

Kezar, A. (2003). Enhancing innovative partnerships: Creating a change model for academic and student affairs collaboration. *Innovative Higher Education, 28*(2), 137–156.

Kezar, A. J., & Eckel, P. D. (2002). The effect of institutional culture on change in higher education: Universal principles or culturally responsive concepts? *The Journal of Higher Education, 73*(4), 435–460.

Kotter, J. P. (1996). *Leading change.* Boston: Harvard Business School Press.

Kuh, G. D. (1996). Guiding principles for creating seamless learning environments for undergraduates. *Journal of College Student Development, 37*(2), 135–148.

Kuh, G. D., Siegel, M. J., & Thomas, A. D. (2001). Higher education: Values and culture. In R. B. Winston Jr., D. G. Creamer, T. K. Miller, & Associates (Eds.), *The professional student affairs administrator: Educator, leader, and manager* (pp. 39–64). New York: Brunner-Routledge.

Lawler, E. E., & Worley, C. G. (2006). *Built to change: How to achieve sustained organizational effectiveness.* San Francisco: Jossey-Bass.

Manning, K. (2001). Infusing soul into student affairs: Organizational theory and models. In M. A. Jablonski (Ed.), *The implications of student spirituality for student affairs practice* (New Directions for Student Services No. 95, pp. 27–35). San Francisco: Wiley.

Manning, K., Kinzie, J., & Schuh, J. (2006). *One size does not fit all: Traditional and innovative models of student affairs practice.* New York: Routledge.

Moore, K. M., Fairweather, J. S., Amey, M. J., Ortiz, A., Mabokela, R., & Ruterbusch, M. (2000). *Best practices for reform in undergraduate education in science, math, engineering, and technology: A knowledge framework.* A Report to the National Science Foundation and SRI International. East Lansing, MI: Center for the Study of Advanced Learning Systems, Michigan State University.

Moore, L. V. (2000). Managing conflict constructively. In M. J. Barr, M. K. Desler, & Associates (Eds.), *The handbook of student affairs administration* (pp. 393–409). San Francisco: Jossey-Bass.

Moore, P. (2000). The political dimensions of decision making. In M. J. Barr, M. K. Desler, & Associates (Eds.), *The handbook of student affairs administration* (pp. 178–196). San Francisco: Jossey-Bass.

Morgan, G. (1999). *Images of organizations* (2nd ed.). Beverly Hills, CA: Sage.

Peterson, M. W. (1997). Contextual planning to transform institutions. In M. W. Peterson, D. D. Dill, L. A. Mets, & Associates (Eds.), *Planning and management for a changing environment: A handbook on redesigning postsecondary institutions* (pp. 127–157). San Francisco: Jossey-Bass.

Quinn, R. E. (1996). *Deep change: Discovering the leader within.* San Francisco: Jossey-Bass.

Reisser, L., & Roper, L. D. (1999). Using resources to achieve institutional missions and goals. In G. S. Blimling, E. J. Whitt, & Associates (Eds.), *Good practice in student affairs: Principles to foster student learning* (pp. 113–132). San Francisco: Jossey-Bass.

Rowley, D. J., Lujan, H. D., & Dolence, M. G. (1997). *Strategic change in colleges and universities: Planning to prosper and survive.* San Francisco: Jossey-Bass.

Sandeen, A. (2001). Organizing student affairs divisions. In R. B. Winston Jr., D. G. Creamer, T. K. Miller, & Associates (Eds.), *The professional student affairs administrator* (pp. 181–209). New York: Routledge.

Seifter, H. (2001). The conductor-less orchestra. *Leader to Leader 21*, 38–44.

Senge, P. M. (1990). *The fifth discipline: The art and practice of the learning organization.* New York: Doubleday.

Senge, P. (1998). Leading learning organizations. In W. E. Rosenbach and R. L. Taylor (Eds.), *Contemporary issues in leadership* (4th ed., pp. 174–178). Boulder, CO: Westview Press.

Smith, S. F., & Rodgers, R. F. (2005). Student learning community of practice: Making meaning of the student learning imperative and principles of good practice in student affairs. *Journal of College Student Development, 46*(5), 472–486.

Spears, L. C. (2002). Tracing the past, present and future of servant-leadership. In L. C. Spears & M. Lawrence (Eds.), *Focus on leadership: Servant-leadership for the twenty-first century* (pp. 1–18). New York: Wiley.

Tierney, W. G. (1991). Organizational culture in higher education: Defining the essentials. In M. Peterson (Ed.), *ASHE reader in organization and governance in higher education* (pp. 126–139). Lexington, MA: Ginn Press.

Tierney, W. G. (2008). *The impact of culture on organizational decision making: Theory and practice in higher education.* Sterling, VA: Stylus.

Ward, L., & Warner, M. (1996, March). *Creating environments for change: Strategies for transcending fear.* Paper presented at the annual meeting of the American College Personnel Association, Baltimore, MD.

Wergin, J. F. (2007). Why we need leadership in place. In J. F. Wergin (Ed.), *Leadership in place: How academic professionals can find their leadership voice* (pp. 1–20). San Francisco: Jossey-Bass.

Wheatley, M. J. (1999). *Leadership and the new science: Discovering order in a chaotic world* (2nd ed.). San Francisco: Berrett-Koehler.

Whitt, E. J. (1993). Making the familiar strange: Discovering culture. In G. D. Kuh (Ed.), *Cultural perspectives in student affairs work* (pp. 81–94). Lanham, MD: American College Personnel Association/University Press of America.

Woodard, D. B., Love, P., & Komives, S. R. (2000). *Leadership and management issues for a new century* (New Directions for Student Services No. 92). San Francisco: Jossey-Bass.

7

ECOLOGICAL SCANNING

An Approach to Student Affairs Organizational Assessment

John Carton has been vice president for student affairs for nearly 10 years and had the experiences of adjusting to a new president about 7 years ago; he is now going through the process again. The campus has just hired a new president and unlike any prior president, this one was hired from a financial corporation where he served as chief executive officer (CEO) for nearly 15 years. This is the first time the university has stepped outside the traditional practice of hiring an academic leader to be president. John is a bit anxious about the new relationship; he is not sure what to expect from leadership that comes from outside the academy. His anxiety was heightened a bit after his first presidential cabinet meeting. At the meeting, the new president asked the members of the cabinet to come back in two weeks to share their past, current, and future plans regarding organizational assessment. The president assured the group that his request did *not* suggest that he devalued traditional student learning outcomes assessment, but he did want to have a clear picture of how the current organization was working and how effectively each of the units were managing their resources and addressing the institution's goals.

John immediately called a meeting of his division's leadership team. Over the next day, he pored over materials that described organizational assessment and various models and processes that could be used to assess his organization. Although his division members had been engaged in student-focused outcome and satisfaction assessment for some time, they had never really addressed the issue of assessing their organization. John knew that he needed to be honest about where they were with this approach to assessment and that he would need to help his staff members understand why this type of assessment was important to add to the assessments they were already using. He decided to approach the immediate request from the president by asking his team members to address three key questions. Once they had tackled these questions, he would develop a strategy for both organizing the information requested by the president and also develop a comprehensive plan for engaging in this type of assessment in the future. John's first question focused on what the division leaders knew about the external environment that they were engaged with and how they knew it. Second, how effective had their units been in addressing the needs and challenges that the environment presented to them, and how did they know they had been successful? What challenges would they need to address in the not-too-distant future and how were they planning to organize and deploy their resources to address these challenges?

M uch has been written about assessment in higher education (Banta, Lund, Black, & Oblander, 1996) with a primary focus on student learning (Walvoord, 2004). However, in her book *Assessing Organizational Performance in Higher Education,* Miller (2007) calls for an additional focus, "assessors in higher education must go beyond assessment of student learning outcomes and institutional effectiveness and into assessment of performance of whole organizations, programs, and processes" (pp. xv–xvi). This broader focus falls under the concept of organizational assessment. Harrison (1987) citing the work of Lawler, Nadler, and Cammann (1980) describes organizational assessment as the "gathering of useful data about organizations through social science research techniques" (p. 11).

Examples of useful organizational data (Lusthaus, Adrien, Anderson, Carden, & Montalvan, 2002) include stakeholder information; observations of facilities; observations of the dynamics among people; formal organizational rules, norms, and values; organizational capacity, including leadership, financial management, organizational structures, inter- and intraorganizational linkages; organizational performance and motivation; and environmental issues, including legal, political, sociocultural, and physical. The purpose of this chapter is to present the concept of ecological scanning as a framework for organizational assessment activities related to student affairs organizations. After the introduction of the concept of ecological scanning, implementation strategies and two nontraditional scanning methods will be presented with examples.

Ecological Scanning

Ecological scanning is not a term that is found in the assessment literature, but an important theme in this book has been to understand a variety of theoretical applications to student affairs organizations. To do this, one needs to address the characteristics of personnel, the inter- and intraorganizational environment in which the student affairs division resides, and the transactional relationship between personnel/leadership and the environment. This is the essence of understanding all ecological models related to organizations; therefore, the concept of ecological scanning as a framework for student affairs organizational assessment is relevant. The assumption of this notion is that assessment processes are used to gather information regarding organization functioning that help the organization build strategies to address its current and future goals.

Like all organizations, the campus student affairs organization functions and makes decisions based on its organizational strategy. The concept of strategy in the organizational literature is difficult to define. Chaffee (1991) suggests three models of strategy. She defines these as linear strategy, which focuses on planning to reach organizational goals; adaptive strategy, which emphasizes the organization's need to adapt and change in relationship to the environment; and interpretive strategy, which focuses on the organization's ability to understand and promote organizational metaphors that give meaning to environmental and interorganizational challenges.

More recently, Bess and Dee (2008) presented an expanded framework on strategy building based on the early work of Chaffee (1985). The Bess and Dee framework is similar because it includes the linear and adaptive models, but it expands the interpretive model to include the emergent model. This component of the model calls for assessments of historical organizational strategies in order to understand current organizational functioning. In addition, the Bess and Dee framework includes a symbolic model that emphasizes the importance of sensemaking and organizational culture in the development of strategy. Finally, the Bess and Dee framework includes a postmodern perspective on organizational strategy that underscores the role of politics and power in shaping how an organization functions. Whichever definitions or model of strategy one chooses to embrace, a critical notion to all definitions is gathering information on which to plan and develop strategies. Chaffee (1991) noted, "A basic premise of thinking about strategy concerns the inseparability of organization and environment . . ." (p. 225). This notion of inseparability is the key element in the concept of ecological scanning. There are two major practical foundational structures within the concept of ecological scanning: environmental scanning and ecological interventions.

The first major practical foundational work related to the concept of ecological scanning is the more familiar term *environmental scanning*. The concept of environmental scanning has its roots in the strategic planning literature and in the linear model of strategy development (Bess & Dee, 2008). Aguilar (1967) is credited with the introduction and development of the concept of environmental scanning in relation to organizational behavior. The concept of environmental scanning as introduced by Aguilar refers to the systematic collection of information external to the organization. This collection process serves two purposes for the organization. One purpose is to organize the information flowing into the organization and the second is to provide the organization with early information about changing environmental conditions that could affect the behavior of the organization. His emphasis was on the environment external to the organization and the purpose was a reactive one: to seek information to inform the organization reactions.

Morrison's (1985, 1987, 1993) work has been instrumental in the efforts to bring the process of environmental scanning to higher education and outlines environmental scanning as a ". . . structure to identify and evaluate trends, events, and emerging issues of import to the institution" (Morrison, 1987, p. 9). Banning (1995) later translated Morrison's structure to the campus housing organization.

Stoffels (1988) expands on the Morrison definition, suggesting that "[e]nvironmental scanning is a methodology for coping with external social, economic and technical issues that may be difficult to observe or predict but that cannot be ignored and will not go away . . ." (p. 5). This definition emphasizes not only the importance of the concept, but its dynamic quality as well. The early importance of environmental scanning for strategic and futuristic organizational processes is noted by Brown and Weiner (1985), Hayden (1986), and Lieshoff (1993).

More recently, this aspect of environmental scanning has been highlighted by Anderson (2010), who sees environmental scanning as "an organizational adaptive behavior" (p. 27). Particularly, the role environmental scanning plays in strategic planning have been noted. Moen (2003) states that environmental scanning makes planning possible, and Mafrica (2003) speaks of the importance of scanning to the management of change. The transition from scanning to planning is often built on the notion of "scenario writing." Scenarios are stories built on scanning and organizational information that pose alternatives for the organization strategies (Anderson, 2010; Bryson, 1988; Chermack & Lynham, 2002; Whiteley, Porter, & Morrison,

1989). In summary, environmental scanning is a process that looks at a variety of information sources, but primarily at environmental information external to the organization, to try to determine the trends, events, and emerging issues that could help develop possible scenarios and strategies for the future.

Ecological scanning embraces the foregoing notions of environmental scanning, but it shifts the focus from the external environment to the major components of an ecological perspective: persons, environments (both external and internal), and the transactional relationship among these components. This shift in focus is important. Hough and White (2004), citing the work of Bluedorn, Johnson, Cartwright, and Barringer (1994), stated, "The scanning literature is . . . limited by an almost exclusive focus on scanning the external environment" (p. 781). They concluded that this restricted focus of traditional scanning "ignores the fact that top managers must gather operational information from within to assess firm strengths and weaknesses and match those with external opportunities and threats" (p. 790). Ecological scanning addresses both the internal and external environment and the many human and behavioral transactions among these complex systems. Ecological scanning provides an answer to Hough and White's call for the need for "scanning behaviors . . . to account for the external environment of the organization and internal environment, in particular the functional responsibilities of the individual manager" (p. 790).

The second practical foundational element of ecological scanning is the ecological intervention model of Felner and Felner (1989). The ecological perspective on interventions (Felner & Felner, 1989) can provide a conceptual framework from which to view, organize, and evaluate assessment activities. The assumption is that organizational assessment activities are implemented to evaluate the organization's strategies and positions relative to the degree of need for change. Organizational change embraces the notion of organizational interventions. The ecological interventions perspective presents a framework that gives a practical guide upon which to direct and focus the process of ecological scanning on traditional ecological components: person, transactions, and environments (Banning & Kuk, 2005).

The first component of the Felner and Felner (1989) model is the person-focused interventions designed to focus on issues within an organization (leadership, personnel capacity, staff skills, etc.) as well as the personalities associated with external environments and organizations. Internally, this component is most often addressed by personnel changes and training. An ecological scanning activity is directed toward these person/personnel issues.

The second component noted by Felner and Felner (1989) is transactional-focused interventions. The ecological scanning activity would focus on the issues coming from person variables combining with environmental conditions such as leadership style in relation to the changing environment, organizational structure in relation to new challenges and personnel capacity, and so on. For example, a western state university operated for many years with a capped enrollment. As a result, the university's admission outreach efforts were primarily based on finding the top students to attract to the university, rather than a broad strategy of introducing the university to a wide audience. The latter strategy resulted in many good students and their tax-paying families being told that there was no room at the university for them. This resulted in poor public relations for the institution and made many more enemies in the state than friends. When the enrollment cap policy was eliminated by the state and the university decided on a new rapid growth strategy, personnel/environment transaction issues emerged. Could an admissions staff trained to seek only the best in an almost secretive mode make a change to a set of skills calling for a more open and inclusive outreach program? This necessitated a classic transactional-focused examination and intervention. A transactional intervention works on both sides of the environment–person focus; it includes both sides of the person–environment equation. In our example, the leadership and personnel of the admissions function could be given time for retraining, and the university's aggressive growth plans could also be scaled back to a more manageable level.

Finally, the third Felner and Felner (1989) component, environmentally focused interventions, addresses issues within the physical and social environment (resource levels, physical facilities of the organization, etc.). For example, at the student affairs organizational level, office location often plays an important role. When an admissions office is located on the second floor of a building, it is seen as far less welcoming than one located on the first floor. Organizational communications, the employment of teams, and other cooperative efforts can be enhanced by making a change in office location and arrangement.

In summary, ecological scanning has its roots in environmental scanning and ecological interventions. The former gives a structure to the process of scanning; the latter gives directional targets for the scanning.

Implementation of Ecological Scanning

The implementation of the ecological scanning framework for student affairs organizational assessment activities is guided by several important implementation questions. What information does a campus student affairs organization seek in an ecological scan? What methods of information gathering are available to campus student affairs organizations for ecological scanning? And finally, how do student affairs organizations construct the ecological scanning function?

What Information Does a Campus Student Affairs Organization Seek in an Ecological Scan?

Deciding what information to scan is the first step in implementation. The campus student affairs organizations would scan information sources related to the mission, goals, and strategies of the organization. These activities of the organization give direction about where to look for information. Morrison's (1987) classification scheme is helpful in answering questions concerning types of information. He suggests that the person doing the scanning look for trends, events, and emerging issues.

A trend is defined as a series of social, technological, economic, or political characteristics that can be measured or estimated over time (Morrison, 1987). Stoffels (1988) suggests a similar definition and notes scanning trends related to demographics, social issues, regulatory changes, and economics. A student affairs organization would be interested, for example, in student enrollment trends and student living preferences.

An event is defined by Morrison (1987) as a discrete, confirmable occurrence that makes the future different from the past. Again, Stoffels (1988) suggests a similar category called events/breakthroughs. These are often either political (e.g., passing of new state regulations regarding admissions standards) or technological (e.g., new form of electronic billing system for the institution). An example for a campus student affairs organization is the approval of a state policy that would make early retirement attractive. This event could affect staffing as well as cause an immediate drain on institutional capacity.

Morrison's (1987) final category is an emerging issue. An emerging issue is defined as a potential issue that arises out of a trend or event that may require some form of response from the organization. For example, an emerging issue might be the availability of entry-level staff. Perhaps student affairs preparation programs are noting that many of their graduates are opting for positions in the human relations functions of businesses and non-profit organizations, which may result in a shortage of new professionals' willingness to accept jobs in student affairs.

The ecological scan looks at information that might be related to the student affairs organization, seeking the trends, events/breakthroughs, and emerging issues that could affect the functioning and future of the organization. A number of scanning methods are available to guide this process.

What Methods of Information Gathering Are Available to Campus Student Affairs Organizations for Ecological Scanning?

Stoffels (1988) suggests four different scanning methods. First, scanning can be implemented at an informal observational level. A student affairs staff member could scan at a very informal level; for example, he or she could observe during a walk across campus how the campus might have an impact on the student affairs organization. Informal observations could also be information obtained from a student affairs conference or an item in a journal or newspaper related to the mission of the campus student affairs organization.

At the second level, conditioned observation, an ecological scan might take an issue that emerged during the informal scanning process and begin to seek more in-depth information regarding the issue (Stoffels, 1988). For example, an informal observation by a staff member that suggests that the student affairs profession is becoming less attractive would be pursed in greater depth. Under conditioned observation, the student affairs ecological scanning activity might wish to pursue other sources of information that would confirm the extent of the trend that emerged from the more informal ecological scanning. These conditioned observational activities can focus both within and external to the organization.

If this trend was confirmed or if the probability appeared high that this trend could affect the campus student affairs organization, then Stoffels (1988) suggests a third level of scanning called informal search. During an informal search, the ecological scanning process seeks specific information related to the possible trend. An informal survey of student affairs preparation programs regarding the employment locations of their graduates would be a likely approach for the example we have been using to illustrate these points.

The final method suggested by Stoffels (1988) is the formal search method. This method calls for establishing a formal methodology for searching for specific information. A frequently used methodology in this type of ecological scanning is the survey approach. It is beyond the scope of this chapter and this book to provide all the surveys available to assist campus student affairs organizations in the ecological scanning process. However, significant and helpful resources for this information are available in the following works: Banta, Lund, Black, and Oblander (1996); Miller (2007); Walvoord (2004); and Wergin and Swingen (2000).

When invoking an ecological model, the method of assessment calls for one that can address myriad interactional and transactional variables addressed in an ecological perspective. Attention needs to be focused on person and environmental variables, and particularly the transactions among these variables. Although complex and sophisticated quantitative designs are capable of addressing this interactional complexity, the why and how of ecological relationships is often addressed from a qualitative research perspective. This section of the chapter concludes by presenting two methodologies within the qualitative paradigm that could be especially helpful to ecological scanning, but have not been associated historically with the student affairs assessment activities. These two methodologies are qualitative meta-analysis and visual ethnography. Both hold promise for serving campus student affairs organizations in their assessment activities.

Qualitative Meta-Analysis

Since the work of Glass (1976), quantitative meta-analysis has become an important strategy in research synthesis efforts. Now joining this synthesis effort is qualitative meta-analysis (Schreiber, Crooks, & Stern, 1997), first introduced into the literature by Stern and Harris (1985). They used the term to refer to the process of synthesizing a group of qualitative research findings. Other terms have also emerged in the literature, for example, meta-ethnography (Noblit & Hare, 1988), aggregating findings (Estabrooks, Field, & Morse, 1994), and meta-synthesis (Jensen & Allen, 1996); all of these focus on a similar process of synthesizing qualitative findings. Schreiber, Crooks, and Stern (1997) proposed the qualitative meta-analysis as the preferred term and defined it as follows: "Qualitative meta-analysis is the aggregating of a group of studies for the purpose of discovering the essential elements and translating the results into an end product that transforms the original results into a new conceptualization" (p. 314).

Qualitative meta-analysis involves pooling research findings from qualitative studies for the purpose of aggregating and analyzing the findings to produce greater understanding regarding a phenomenon of interest. (See Paterson, Thorne, Canam, and Jillings, 2001, for a practical guide to qualitative meta-synthesis.) Conceptualized this way, qualitative meta-analysis can serve a primary role in the synthesis of ecological scanning information obtained from literature relevant to student affairs organizations. The procedural steps taken during this type of ecological scanning are perhaps best outlined in the work of Paterson and colleagues (2001). These steps are similar to those used in more traditional quantitative meta-analysis: formulating a research or scanning question, seeking and selecting the appropriate body of research, performing analysis to answer the research question, and finally developing the synthesis and disseminating the findings of the scan. This approach is a qualitative content analysis that examines documents that allows for the "communication of meaning" (Altheide, 1987, p. 68) rather than the strict deductive coding typical to classical content analysis (Krippendorff, 2004).

Banning and Kuk (2009) used this method in scanning doctoral dissertations to answer the question: What can we learn from the examination/scan of recent doctoral dissertations on the topic of organizational issues associated with student affairs organizations? This study used a bounded qualitative meta-study framework that diverged from the typical qualitative meta-analysis in two ways: The study is bounded by a search of a specific research "genre" (the doctoral dissertation), and not all research publications focused on student affairs organizations. The method included a scanning of the Proquest Digital Database for dissertations within the past five years using the search terms *student services* or *student affairs* and produced a list of 451 titles. This list was reduced to 144 by eliminating the dissertations that were not focused on student affairs or student services specific to higher education. Finally, the criteria of *specific to organizational issues* reduced the number of dissertations to 32. The criteria of *specific to organization issues* did not include the topics of staff development, leadership characteristics, or job satisfaction unless addressed from an organizational perspective.

A thematic analysis of the scanned material in the Banning and Kuk (2009) study provided a number of interpretations. First, student affairs organizations, as they move forward with restructuring, are driven by the concept of learning and therefore closer collaborative styles and structures with academic affairs. Second, student affairs organizations continue to be complex entities, and studies regarding organizational and management functioning addressed this notion. Third, student affairs organizations, like many other types of structures both within and outside higher education, recognize the importance of organizational culture. And finally, student affairs organizations continue to be responsive to multiple groups. A major scanning outcome or scenario for the future of student affairs organizations obtained through the meta-analysis (scanning) was that, as student affairs organizational restructuring occurs in the future, these efforts will be influenced by the traditional learning/academic side of the institution.

Visual Ethnography: Behavioral/Physical Trace Observational Method

The second ecological scanning methodology to be highlighted stems from the field of visual ethnography, specifically the method of behavioral/physical trace methodology (Ziesel, 1975, 1981). Students, faculty members, staff members, and visitors use the campus environment in a variety of ways. It is impossible to observe or scan all campus behavior at the time it is occurring, but behavior leaves "traces" (Bechtel & Zeisel, 1987). These behavioral traces can be reconstructed to produce increased awareness of the person–environment interactions, and they can be used as an ecological scanning method to increase the overall understanding of the campus environment and to assist campus student affairs organizations in their planning and strategy efforts.

Environmental psychologists and campus ecologists are not the first groups to infer behavior from traces. Archaeology, as a science, is built on this methodology. As Bechtel and Zeisel state, "Few give a thought . . . to the fact the fossils of tomorrow are the garbage dumps of today" (Bechtel & Zeisel, 1987, p. 32). Zeisel (1981) presents a number of ways to read traces that can be useful in gaining a greater understanding of how people use the campus environment. With these results, the strategies of a campus student affairs organization can be informed. Zeisel's methods are (a) by-products of use, (b) adaptation of use, (c) displays of self, and (d) public messages.

By-products are produced by people interacting with the environment. These by-products of behavior can be further defined by the concepts of erosion, leftovers, and missing traces (Bechtel & Zeisel, 1987). An example of erosion on campus is the worn paths students make as they find the shortest distance between campus buildings. These by-products (paths) can be useful in understanding organizational behavior as well. What are the path patterns between and among various offices in an office complex? Do these patterns suggest the need for a rearrangement of offices? Leftovers are traces represented by objects not consumed in the behavior. Trash and litter are the most common examples. Many student affairs organizations have resource rooms and break rooms. What are the leftovers associated with the behavior in these rooms? Do the leftovers suggest informal social interaction? Is there just one leftover coffee cup or are there several? What is leftover in the resource room?

Bechtel and Zeisel (1987) use the concept of missing traces to indicate a lack of use in areas where erosion and leftovers are expected but do not show up. Many campus spaces were designed in such a manner that they are never used by people on campus. The documentation of this lack of use, or missing traces, is often helpful to campus student affairs organizations in gaining support for a redesign of the space to better serve the needs of the campus. For example, if a goal of a student affairs organization is to increase the informal social discourse among its staff members, then an ecological scan of places to congregate as a group would be useful. Which sitting walls, benches, coffee rooms, and other spaces afford seating for informal staff gatherings?

Zeisel (1981) uses the concept of adaptation to encompass situations in the environment where a change has been made because the first design did not serve its original intention. Campus adaptation for use would include renovations, expansions, and other changes or improvements. Student affairs organizations are often the campus advocates of access for all students, but they occasionally fail to look at the spaces associated with organizational units of student affairs. Often the attempt by students to adapt a space for an unintended purpose is the first cue that a redesign effort may be needed. For example, how do students approach the reception areas of the various student affairs service units? An observation of students as they approach a reception area can yield information regarding how comfortable or uncomfortable the reception area might be. Are students searching for the correct desk? Are they trying to look around the backs of computer monitors or other pieces of equipment? Again, visual scanning for this type of ecological information not only gives specific insights regarding organizational access issues, but also a sense of the welcoming culture of the organization.

Zeisel (1981) uses the concept of display of self to illustrate how the physical environment can convey messages about individual and group ownership. The Greek letters on fraternity and sorority houses are clear examples. These displays become important to the process of individualizing and personalizing huge spaces. Huge signs are found in residence hall windows marking a floor or wing. These are important traces to understand. No one can enter the campus environment without noting the use of T-shirts to display messages of self and group. From Greek affiliation to academic majors, from attendance at rock concerts to where one spent spring break, all of these are all displayed through T-shirts. Again, these traces can increase understanding of the sociocultural environment on campus because they assist the evaluation and development of new strategic decisions for a student affairs organization. For example, a western campus bookstore was asked to adopt a policy of selling only clothing that was official (university colors and official logo). A walk across campus, quickly informed the scanner, however, that students were finding other off-campus retail shops to buy more creative clothing in terms of colors, logos, and slogans. After a period of reduced sales, the policy was rescinded. The students' desire for personalization went beyond the institutional look offered by the bookstore.

The last category for Zeisel (1981) is public messages. Included in this concept are traces that range from official signs, symbolic public images, and graffiti. Academic buildings often provide clear examples; maybe you find a world globe on top of an international studies building, and or you find an oil derrick on the roof of a petroleum engineering building. These symbols give the public messages concerning the values and interests of campus organizations. Most observers of the campus environment are quite familiar with campus graffiti. It can signal creativity or the meaning of local issues, or it can give insight into prevailing attitudes on complex issues such as tolerance for diversity.

In addition to providing information regarding campus culture, signs and symbols also send organizational messages. Gagliardi (1990) points out the importance of symbolism and artifacts in communicating organizational values. Entrances to student affairs offices provide an example. Do these entrances send welcoming messages or messages of "try and find us"? Are the doors open and inviting, or are students faced with high counters and the back sides of computer monitors?

In summary, the concept of behavioral traces can be a useful tool for the campus student affairs organization's ecological scanning and assessment activities. As Zeisel (1975) states: "The environment is used as a medium of communication. . . ." Understanding this communication can assist in student affairs organizational strategic activities.

To illustrate this methodology, one of this book's authors assisted 17 student affairs graduate students in conducting an ecological visual scan of a university library. The students, as consumers of the library, were instructed to scan the library by photographing those elements that were pleasing and those that were not, elements that send consumer messages, and elements that were examples of the concepts within the behavioral/physical trace method of observation. Over 300 photographs were collected and analyzed by the group of graduate students for major themes. The ecological scan produced an overarching theme that library staff members should give additional consideration to the library as a "building that teaches" as well as the traditional view of the library as a collection of resources. Within this major theme were the following subthemes: (a) greater attention needed to given to the physical condition of the library, (b) many lost opportunities within the building that could be used to teach (empty cases, no organized exhibits, etc.), and (c) many positive "sense of place" spaces in the library that should serve as prototypes for forthcoming renovations.

How Do Student Affairs Organizations Construct the Ecological Scanning Function?

The concluding question is about organizing the ecological scanning/assessment process. Ecological scanning systems range from rather simple to very complex. A beginning system for a campus student affairs organization could be as simple as assigning several staff members to review and abstract information from journals, magazines, and newsletters focusing on issues that affect student affairs organizations. Information generated by the ecological scanning activity could be shared in staff meetings or departmental newsletters. The sharing and discussion of the information can lead to the development of more formal ecological scanning processes.

A more evolved system might include a network of staff members who could engage in ecological scanning, with each performing informal as well as formal scanning in areas dictated by strategic issues of the campus student affairs organization. This ecological scanning information could be used to build a series of scenarios for discussion and consideration. Sharing of information could include an interactive database or other innovative ways of organizational communication. In this mode, the ecological scanning activity could input data regarding trends, events, and emerging issues. Other members of the process could add information and implications for the organization. Leaders in the student affairs organization could also access the system for information and for asking additional questions of the scanners. Finally, the most institutionalized option would be the establishment of an ongoing office or department dedicated to organizing, implementing, and coordinating a student affairs, divisionwide ecological scanning and assessment program. Moving from the informal approach to the institutionalization of a function formalizes the accountability for the ecological scanning effort; it also probably increases the resources for the scanning and assessment process, both in terms of staff members and dollars.

Whatever form the ecological scanning structure takes, the final critical task is to provide information that will be helpful to the strategic decisions

of the organization (Stoffels, 1988). Hitchcock and Willard (2008), in reference to the work of the World Commission on Environment and Development, suggest that the most often quoted definition of sustainability reflects the notion of meeting the needs of the present generation without compromising the ability of future generations to meet their needs. This definition has direct application to campus student affairs organizations. How can current student affairs organizations assess their functioning and make organizational changes that will ensure that future students will benefit from the services and programs that student affairs organizations afford to students? Important in answering this question is the role of organizational assessment, not only the processes associated with its gathering of information, for example, ecological scanning, but also how the information is processed. As has been pointed out in this book in many places, the notion of sharing, open dialogue, and full participation of diverse stakeholders are key elements to organizational sustainability. This is particularly critical in the organizational assessment arena.

Reflective Summary

1. Describe from your own experiences the difference between environmental scanning and ecological scanning.
2. Describe a campus intervention that is (a) person-focused, (b) transactional-focused, (c) environmentally focused.
3. If you were in charge of organizing a student affairs organizational assessment, how would you go about the task?
4. Reflecting on your experience, what would be the top three critical topics for a student affairs organization that could be pursued using a qualitative meta-analysis?
5. If you were asked to do a visual ethnography of a student affairs organization, how would you organize the effort? What are some potential settings to take a camera?

References

Aguilar, F. J. (1967). *Scanning the business environment.* New York: Macmillan.
Altheide, D. L. (1987). Ethnographic content analysis. *Qualitative Sociology, 10*(1), 65–77.
Anderson, D. L. (2010). *Organizational development.* Los Angeles: Sage.

Banning, J. H. (1995). Environmental scanning: Application to college and university housing. *Journal of College and University Housing, 25*(1), 30–33.

Banning, J., & Kuk, L. (2005, November). Campus ecology and college student health. *Spectrum*, 9–15.

Banning, J., & Kuk, L. (2009). The student affairs organizational dissertation: A bounded qualitative meta-study. *College Student Journal, 43*(2), 285–293.

Banta, T. W., Lund, J. P., Black, K. E., & Oblander, F. W. (1996). *Assessment in practice*. San Francisco: Jossey-Bass.

Bechtel, R., & Zeisel, J. (1987). Observation: The world under a glass. In R. Bechtel, R. Marans, & W. Michelson (Eds.), *Methods in environment and behavioral research* (pp. 11–40). New York: Van Nostrand Reinhold.

Bess, J. L., & Dee, J. R. (2008). *Understanding college and university organizations*. Sterling, VA: Stylus.

Bluedorn, A. C., Johnson, R. A., Cartwright, D. K., & Barringer, B. R. (1994). The interface and convergence of the strategic management and organizational environments domains. *Journal of Management, 20*, 201–262.

Brown, A., & Weiner, E. (1985). *Supermanaging: How to harness change for personal and organizational success*. New York: Mentor.

Bryson, J. (1988). *Strategic planning for public and nonprofit organizations*. San Francisco: Jossey-Bass.

Chaffee, E. E. (1985). Three models of strategy. *Academy of Management Review, 10*(1), 89–98.

Chaffee, E. E. (1991). Three models of strategy. In M. W. Peterson, E. E. Chaffee, & T. H. White (Eds.), *Organization and governance in higher education* (pp. 225–238). Needham Heights, MA: Simon & Schuster Custom Publishing.

Chermack, T. J., & Lynham, S. A. (2002). Definitions and outcome variables of scenario planning. *Human Resources Development Review, 1*, 336–383.

Estabrooks, C. A., Field, P. A., & Morse, J. M. (1994). Aggregating qualitative findings: An approach to theory development. *Qualitative Health Research, 4*(4), 503–511.

Felner, R. D., & Felner, T. V. (1989). Primary prevention programs in the educational context: A transactional ecological framework and analysis. In L. A. Bond & B. C. Compas (Eds.), *Primary prevention and promotion in the schools* (pp. 13–49). Newbury Park, CA: Sage.

Gagliardi, P. (Ed.). (1990). *Symbols and artifacts: Views of the corporate landscape*. New York: Aldine deGruyter.

Glass, G. V. (1976). Primary, secondary, and meta-analysis of research. *Educational Researcher, 5*, 3–8.

Harrison, M. I. (1987). *Diagnosing organizations: Methods, models and processes*. Newbury Park, CA: Sage.

Hayden, C. (1986). *The handbook of strategic expertise*. New York: The Free Press.

Hitchcock, D., & Willard, M. (2008). *The step-by-step guide to sustainability planning*. London: Earthscan.

Hough, J. R., & White, M. A. (2004). Scanning actions and environmental dynamism: Gathering information for strategic decisions. *Management Decisions, 42*(6), 781–793.

Jensen, L. A., & Allen, M. N. (1996). Meta-synthesis of qualitative findings. *Qualitative Health Research, 6*(4), 553–560.

Krippendorff, K. (2004). *Content analysis: An introduction to its methodology* (2nd ed.). Thousand Oaks, CA: Sage.

Lawler, E., Nadler, D., & Cammann, C. (Eds.) (1980). *Organizational assessment.* New York: Wiley.

Lieshoff, S. (1993). *Environmental scanning: Charting your way through the data explosion.* Paper presented at the Annual Adult Education Conference, Dallas, TX. (ERIC Document Reproduction Services No. ED 367–238)

Lusthaus, C., Adrien, M. H., Anderson, G., Carden, F., & Montalvan, G. (2002). *Organizational assessment: A framework for improving performance.* Ottawa, ON: International Development Research Centre & Inter-American Development Bank.

Mafrica, L. (2003). From scan to plan: How to apply environmental scanning to your association's strategic planning process. *Association Management, 55*(1), 42–49.

Miller, B. A. (2007). *Assessing organizational performance in higher education.* San Francisco: Wiley.

Moen, R. S. (2003). Environmental scanning makes planning possible: How can you bring emerging issues and trends to the forefront so that you can focus strategic attention on them? *Association Management, 55*(8), 65–67.

Morrison, J. (1985). Establishing an environmental scanning process. In R. Davis (Ed.), *Leadership and institutional renewal* (New Directions for Higher Education No. 49) (pp. 31–37). San Francisco: Jossey-Bass.

Morrison, J. (1987). Establishing an environmental scanning/forecasting system to augment college and university planning. *Planning, 15* (1), 7–22.

Morrison, J. (1993). *Environmental scanning in educational planning: Establishing a strategic trend information system.* Paper presented at the Annual Meeting of the American Educational Research Association, Atlanta, GA. (ERIC Document Reproduction Services No. ED 361–897)

Noblit, G. W., & Hare, R. D. (1988). *Meta-ethnography: Synthesizing qualitative studies.* Newbury Park, CA: Sage.

Paterson, B. L., Thorne, S. E., Canam, C., & Jillings, C. (2001). *Meta-study of qualitative health research: A practical guide to meta-analysis and meta-synthesis.* Thousand Oaks, CA: Sage.

Schreiber, R., Crooks, D., & Stern, P. N. (1997). Qualitative meta-analysis. In J. Morse (Ed.), *Completing a qualitative project* (pp. 311–326). Thousand Oaks, CA: Sage.

Stern, P. N., & Harris, C. C. (1985). Women's health and the self-care paradox: A model to guide self-care readiness. *Health Care for Women International, 6,* 151–163.

Stoffels, J. (1988, November–December), Environmental scanning for future success. *Managerial Planning*, 4–12.

Walvoord, B. E. (2004). *Assessment clear and simple*. San Francisco: Wiley.

Wergin, J. F., & Swingen, J. N. (2000). *Departmental assessment*. Washington, DC: American Association for Higher Education.

Whiteley, M., Porter, J. & Morrison, J. (1989). Developing scenarios: Linking environmental scanning and strategic planning. *Planning for Higher Education, 18*(4), 47–60.

Zeisel, J. (1975). *Sociology and architectural design*. New York: Russell Sage Foundation.

Zeisel, J. (1981). *Inquiry by design*. Monterey, CA: Brooks/Cole.

8

SECURING LEADERSHIP FOR ORGANIZATIONAL FIT—NOT THE OTHER WAY AROUND

Selena Martinez closed the door to her small office and sank into the desk chair. It had been a really long day and she was exhausted. It seemed like such a good idea when the group charged with staff training this year decided to put people in cross-building teams instead of leaving them all day in their workgroups. Every year, the training followed the same agenda, and each year, it seemed like you could predict before starting that all the icebreakers, team-building activities, and review of the division's mottos would not change the end result. Nothing ever seemed to change the fact that people were more interested in figuring out how to get more resources than the other groups or in arguing why they were more important to student well-being and why they really couldn't work on a particular goal of the division because it "just isn't what we do." And yet, at the end of each training session every year, the groups would all come together and do spirited cheers about team work before breaking for the day and heading off to their different residence halls or offices.

This year, after three days of training so far, nothing had changed. No one seemed to understand that things *had* to be different if they were going to be able to do a good job this year. Selena had seen the data on the incoming class of students, and she had been in many meetings with the other associate directors and academic staff members earlier in the summer in which they discussed the ways in which budget shortfalls were going to affect the campus this coming year. Her boss, John Carter, the dean of students, was clear that there would need to be some restructuring plans developed over the year within the division, and some positions might be merged or eliminated. Selena thought that if the staff members could start the year in a different frame of mind and could work more like a team, it would make some of the rest of the changes needed over the year a bit clearer. Dr. Carter agreed to let Selena organize training differently this year after she lobbied him for the opportunity most of the summer. He had developed fall staff training for the last 10 years and always thought the sessions were effective.

Thinking back over the last few days, Selena wasn't quite sure what to do that might turn the last two days of training around. Staff members did not seem to be working well together or even getting to know each other outside their employ-ment groups; the ideas they were generating in response to any of the activities they were given seemed very safe and a lot like the way things had always been done. Selena shook her head, wondering how she might get the staff members to see the importance of working together and working differently. Maybe Dr. Carter was right. He'd said, "After several days of group work, Selena, if there were things that we needed to get done in the next year, I just told them what the goals were. When they had to turn in their results, I turned the work over to their unit directors to lay out the plans with their staff. All this team talk just takes a lot of time and doesn't get you anywhere. I know you're young and full of ideas, and you want me to think you're really cut out to take my place as head of staff training, but trust me. I know what works here." Maybe he was right.

O ver time, leadership has been viewed in many ways: from restrictive and elite to diffuse and widespread. As we consider the complexity of student affairs organizations and how they may be developed for sustainable change, the question of leaders and leadership also needs to be addressed. We have discussed how decision making, change, and general organizational structures have evolved from a top-down orientation to one that may be characterized as flat(ter), weblike, or at least shared; leadership in general and in student affairs in particular has followed a similar path.

Historically, leadership writing began with notions of remarkable indi-viduals who were born into leader roles and were assumed to be leaders because of innate abilities of power and influence. Leadership was viewed as a top-down, lone activity that provided vision and direction to the organiza-tion. Because formal organizational leaders were almost always men, the term *great men* came to describe this body of research and thinking about leaders. For example, in higher education, we tend to think about great presidents who created the colleges and universities that symbolized the early elite institutions in the United States, individuals such as Charles Eliot of Harvard, William Raney Harper of the University of Chicago, and Andrew

White of Cornell University. Today, we might call to mind a more diverse group of presidents (although not as diverse as many would hope) to include individuals such as Beverly Daniel Tatum of Spellman College, Mary Sue Coleman of the University of Michigan, Philip Dubois of the University of Wyoming, Scott Cowen of Tulane University, and Albert C. Yates of Colorado State University. All of these people exercised leadership in the face of significant challenges to their institutions. Although presidential search committees continue to seek "great" individuals to move our colleges and universities forward, it is far more common that the presidents of today rely on teams of senior campus leaders and advisers to help them with decision making, planning, and change. They are not as likely to see themselves as singular leaders, as was the case in the early periods of U.S. higher education.

As scholars began to realize that little scientific proof existed for believing that hereditary factors were the determiners of leadership, they focused on traits exhibited by those in leadership positions. Trait theorists were popular during the first half of the 20th century, and they believed that leaders had superior qualities that differentiated them from others. Hiring based on these determined characteristics was presumed to be a way to increase the likelihood of a great leader. Even though the idea of a checklist of ideal traits has been long rejected, we still see vestiges of these beliefs in search committee evaluations, search firm protocols for identifying candidates, and our own biases about what matters in choosing academic leaders. This is part of the reason why those who are different from previous leaders have such difficulty breaking through (see, for example, *Shattering the Myths: Women in Academe* [Glazer-Raymo, 1999] and *Leaders of Color in Higher Education: Unrecognized Triumphs in Harsh Institutions* [Valverde, 2003]). Volumes of research on those who are "the first" in their institutional setting demonstrate the strength of trait theory, even though it has not held up to closer scrutiny and rigorous research.

Other major historic paradigms of leadership research included a focus on behavior (how one acts as opposed to the traits one possesses) and situational theory, which contends that leaders act differently depending on the situation, and therefore the situation may determine who emerges as a leader. More recently, scholars have framed leadership as a social exchange process, one of influence, and one that focuses on the relationship with followers by whatever term they are known. In much of the writing between the 1950s and the 1990s, the language changed and the emphasis expanded to include others in the leadership relationship, but the apex of power and influence still remained with a central figure—the single leader. The situation sounded better and more inclusive, but there is little research that supports philosophies of practice had been changed, career paths provided significantly greater access for those who were competent but perhaps still not "the same," and for the genuine promotion of collective leadership and responsibility. Even in student affairs, stereotyped as a profession that typifies collegiality and cooperation, there remained *chief* student affairs officers and more traditional pyramid structural hierarchies of administrators within divisions.

As has been noted in previous chapters, the changes in colleges and universities generally, and in student affairs specifically, in growth and complexity challenged these traditional leadership orientations significantly. The job was becoming too big, too involved in broad internal and external work of the institution on behalf of students, too affected by regulatory compliance, and just too encompassing to pretend that a single individual could be that great man or great woman of the past. Even as late as 2003, Ellis writes of her own experiences as a new senior student affairs leader: "At this point [achieving this level position] in their careers, most people have figured it out—it's endless . . ." (Ellis, 2003, p. 16). Now we have the notion of teams and the metaphors of shared leadership, webs, servant leaders, and flattened hierarchies that have become the language of leadership favored by scholars over the last 15 to 20 years (e.g., Bensimon & Neumann, 1993; Helgesen, 1995; Spears, 2002). Authors have examined leadership developmentally (e.g., Komives, Lucas, & McMahon, 2007; Kuhnert & Lewis, 1989), through life stories and critical incidents (e.g., Bennis & Thomas, 2002), ethics and morals (e.g., Brown, 2006; Helmich, 2007), from gendered and cultural perspectives (e.g., Curry, 2000; Kezar, 2009), as it is embedded in the different kinds of institutions in which we work in student affairs (Hirt, 2006; Manning, Kinzie, & Schuh, 2006; Tierney, 2008), and in the different positions found within these divisions (e.g., Taylor, 2007; Wergin, 2007). More continues to be written about leadership than can possibly be absorbed, so the focus in the rest of this chapter will be on how these new images and beliefs about leadership contribute to facilitating and sustaining change in student affairs organizations.

Leadership as Learning

In reframing leadership for facilitating effective organizational change, scholars have cast leadership as learning and doing rather than as a set of skills to be acquired or traits to be possessed. Researchers who examined learning organizations and mental models, such as Argyris and Schön (1978), Senge (1990), Vaill (1996) and others, focused attention on the ways in which administrators make sense of the world, transform organizational reality, challenge the institution's status, and encourage deep organizational and individual change (Amey, 2006; Quinn, 1996). Leaders clarify the identity of the institution through its mission by expressing its core values, providing a strong sense of identity that fosters cultural integration, and helping people be on the same page (Tierney, 2008). They help frame the issues and ways of understanding them for others within the student affairs organization (Eddy, 2003), which is different than just being an effective communicator. Framing is about shaping perceptions and beliefs more than it is necessarily about being a charismatic speaker. As Tierney (2008) indicates, leaders are more likely to be catalysts for perceptual rather than physical change. Although this may sound like a way of placating those without certain forms of power and resources in the organization, it more accurately raises the potential for leadership to exist throughout the division, and therefore the potential for leadership that can sustain and support effective change.

Those in student affairs create learning environments for students that include cultural awareness, acceptance of multiple intelligences, beliefs in different ways of knowing, a value of collaboration, and an identity as professionals who foster growth and development of the whole person. Although resources are important and status might be nice, these outcomes of student affairs leadership truly are rooted more in core values and beliefs (Tierney's [2008] "perceptions") than they are in physical, curricular, or structural changes. We might advocate for overhauls in any of these areas on our college campuses, but student affairs leaders aim to change the foundations of the learning environment and create different core assumptions about students, their learning needs, and how these can best be achieved. If you need to be convinced of this claim, you only need to read any of the volumes of research on student success, access, identity development, service learning, residential colleges, and living–learning environments with an eye toward the leadership implications and recommendations made. Transforming the college and university reality on behalf of students is the mantra of those in student affairs; we may just not have thought about calling this "leadership as learning."

There is a second part to this leadership as learning orientation, however, and that is its insistence that leaders personally have a core value of learning for themselves in order to facilitate learning in others (Heifetz & Laurie, 1997). The leader has to have the opportunity to process intake information and internalize it intellectually in order to consciously incorporate it into approaches to leadership (Kolb, 1984). We speak of authenticity and self-efficacy for students (Baxter-Magolda, 1999), but we often do not claim it for ourselves as professionals. Put differently, the learning college means learning for *everyone* in the organization. In this context, a primary organizational priority for a leader is creating a learning environment, space for risk taking, challenge, and space for the adaptive work that is required to address the complex issues of today's campuses (Heifetz, 1994). Student affairs professionals become active inquirers into their own and others' practices. Bartlett (1990) speaks about this when she writes, "Because knowledge arises within social contexts and in multiple forms, the key to increasing knowledge lies in an effort to extend one's limited perspective" (p. 882): in other words, to learn. Ellis (2003) said it this way: "Many days I can easily take the other side and think through others' perceptions and opinions. But some days I cannot do this alone and need help" (p. 65). And Allen and Cherrey (2002) posit that the new focus of leadership is determining how to lead, how to relate, how to influence change, and how to learn together.

This kind of leadership has little to do with hierarchical position and expert authority. It has everything to do with enabling the best ideas to emerge from wherever they come, through a process of informed and rational dialogue and cognitive interpretation. This sense of examining and reexamining assumptions, viewpoints, and understandings with others resembles the learning communities that we believe foster appropriate growth and development in students; this time, it is meant for leaders throughout the student affairs organization. At the same time, college members still have expectations for title holders within the student affairs organization, but maybe more in times of serious conflict or when institutional bureaucracies and politics get in the way. We could argue that instead of a leader per se, at these times the organization needs an effective manager to handle the structural processes. The leader, then, gets to stay in the role of skilled convener, working to help members realize their full leadership potential.

Leadership as Collective Responsibility

If leadership is not the job of solely the titular head of a university or a student affairs organization, then what are the alternatives? Broadly conceived, one option with great promise for sustained change in leadership is collective responsibility, or how the organization does leadership (Woodard, Love, & Komives, 2000). This shifts the focus even beyond the senior management team, which is often seen as the extent to which the leadership lens needs to be broadened, and takes into consideration those across the institution: midlevel managers and early career professionals—all of us, together. For example, Astin and Astin (2000, p. 12) suggest that "the most effective group leadership effort is the one that can serve as a collaborative learning environment for its members." It becomes both an unexpected form of accountability, perhaps, and a wonderful opportunity to energize and innovate; it also should minimize the victim mentality and eliminate the "when I become the [name the next position up the line]" sense of efficacy. We need to lead now from wherever we are in the organization. Wergin (2007) calls it "leading in place" and lays out clear arguments about why higher education organizations need to cultivate this way of thinking among all members if they are going to be successful.

Leadership as collective responsibility changes many things about the way work in student affairs unfolds. First, it recognizes that we need to work smarter together (Allen & Cherrey, 2002; Vaill, 1996; Wheatley, 2002). There is much to do on our college campuses, and not always with the benefit of substantial traditional resources. So work demands a refocusing on collaboration, synergies created across departments and organizational silos (Amey, Jessup-Anger, & Tingson-Gatuz, 2009), a greater sense of interdependence that has often been lacking in student affairs (Woodard et al., 2000), deeper understandings of the core work in which we are involved, and a recognition of the significant contributions made by others to the work of the student affairs organization. It is no longer sufficient to know the job you have; you also have to understand how each job fits with others to create the whole. Moving in this direction requires changing information flow, reward and work structures, expectations we hold of each other, and other aspects of organizational structure (which were described in chapter 5 of this book). It requires a systems way of thinking and acting that rewards boundary spanners (Morgan, 1999), those willing to step outside their comfort zones to see from other organizational vantage points, and those who will share the accomplishments and take responsibility for those efforts that do not succeed, all done collectively. In this way, we can pool talents, resources, and creative thinking into communities of difference that really afford the greatest strengths to the challenges faced by student affairs organizations. This more holistic understanding also leads to collective efficacy (Bandura, 1996), defined as a group's belief about its ability to organize and enact actions required to achieve its goals.

Before making it sound too much like a cure-all, it is important to note that leadership as collective responsibility is as challenging as it is effective.

The embedded biases about who should be involved, who knows best, who has the authority to make decisions, and so on, are as rife within student affairs organizations as they are within higher education more broadly. Changing these assumptions has significant consequence to perceived status and role within the organization, and it never is as easy as deciding "we now will be a team" or work well together. It is not easy for those who have built careers and reputations based on expert knowledge and being "right" (Senge, 1990) that permeate group discussions and planning meetings to suddenly abandon that sense of expertise in deference to new ideas, alternate approaches to problem solving, and shared leadership.

With the leader's help, then, student affairs professionals need to move toward strategic thinking (Peterson, 1997; Senge, 1990), which requires transitions in how members approach their work and engage with the organization, including each other, on a continuum from knowledge expert to knowledge collaborator. Ellis (2003) states that it is strategic thinking and acting that are important. She adds that "thinking strategically requires you to commit resources, prioritize clearly, and follow through on key decisions. Strategic acts are highly imaginative but don't just happen. Collaboration is typically required" (p. 70). Strategic thinking yields rich rewards, but it is more difficult to implement than reliance on "right strategy" thinking; still, complex problems demand this kind of second-order and adaptive thinking and leadership (Argyris & Schön, 1978; Heifetz, 1994).

When framing leadership as collective responsibility, leaders give the work back to members (Heifetz & Laurie, 1997). This causes members to discuss and work together to understand and change the situations that cause problems the organization faces. They are encouraged to learn rather than only to act, which is something that many in student affairs almost fear doing because the profession is often consumed with "putting out fires" (Woodard et al., 2000, p. 85) rather than stepping back to reflect. Student affairs professionals need to understand, when they are engaged in instrumental learning that controls the circumstances and reinforces existing responses to issues, that it may be most appropriate for technical problems, which are those for which existing solutions might actually work. And they must realize when they need to engage in adaptive work: when they must question basic assumptions, realize solutions to problems are not evident (or at least that past strategies will not work well), and seek learning an adaptive and new response to the situation (Heifetz, 1994). Helping student affairs professionals see this strategy as a primary aspect of their collective goals on behalf of students is a very different orientation to administrative work than we usually talk about, and a very different leadership approach than we typically advocate. This is not to suggest that accomplishing goals is unimportant, especially in today's climate of accountability, but it does suggest that thinking together, critically reflecting, and organizational learning *are* important. They will not occur unless we actually take the steps to make them happen (Amey, 2005; Woodard et al., 2000).

So then the questions become, How do leaders facilitate the sense of validation for individual, unique contributions to the student affairs organization that may be part of the intrinsic motivation for doing good work and being in this profession in the first place, while simultaneously encouraging the development of shared understandings that are essential to collective responsibility? How do leaders motivate others to excel without breeding unnecessary competition, personal attacks, and win-lose approaches to work?

Leadership From Anywhere

Building on the concept of leadership as collective responsibility is the idea that leadership can and does exist anywhere within the student affairs organization. What has been most frequently discussed is the leadership of those at the top of the organization, in this case, senior student affairs officers. But these organizations, like colleges and universities generally, have many leaders, not all of whom are obvious by title or position.

In the middle, leadership is less reliant on position authority and more on influence, social capital, networks and coalitions, institutional knowledge, personal reputations, and interdependence (Amey et al., 2009; Taylor, 2007). Although they are not expected always to provide grand visions for their organizations, midlevel leaders are the conduits of change, connecting vision from the top with implementation elsewhere in the organization, effectively communicating and framing realities for others, serving as information brokers, and facilitating change more so perhaps than any other group of campus leaders (Jessup-Anger, 2009; Morgan, 1999). Taylor (2007) argues that midlevel leaders are essential to creating organizations that are flexible, innovative, people-focused, and accountable, and can sustain change. They find internal contradictions between what we do (our theories in use) and what we say (our espoused theories), and other forms of current and potential organizational dysfunction, and then suggest strategies to address these scenarios and other environmental challenges (Argyris & Schön, 1978; Taylor, 2007; Tierney, 2008).

Midlevel leaders have a Janusian quality, looking up and down, being leader and follower, supervisor and supervisee, goal-setter and implementer, mentor and mentee, transactional and transformational leader (Taylor, 2007). They have to see situations from multiple perspectives, be effective organizational analysts, understand the needs and aspirations of their colleagues deeply, have an orientation toward learning, and possess the facilitative skills to foster leadership as collective responsibility. Because they are in the middle, however, midlevel leaders are often caught between senior leader directives and the realities of implementation experienced by those "on the ground," between generational clashes of values and work ethics, between history and tradition on the one hand and innovation and fresh perspectives on the other. As a result, these unique and important leader roles in the student affairs organization need to be intentionally cultivated and fully supported in order to protect institutional viability. Without a strong core of effective midlevel leaders, the organization limits its future senior leadership pool and stifles interest in taking the initiative among prospective early career leaders. This form of leadership development and succession planning often leads to participation in various professional development opportunities provided by national associations, graduate preparation programs, and regional consortia. It is a critical need in student affairs organizations and a significant leadership commitment for the future.

Finally, leadership in place means that even those in early career positions can be and are leaders in their organizations. A student affairs organization with a leadership culture will promote leaders everywhere, at every level, including new professionals and others who are not in positions of authority. As they enter positions in student affairs, new professionals need to recognize opportunities to develop and exercise leadership. They need to learn to read their unit and/or division, understand its values and beliefs, know the bases of decision making and priorities, determine the other departments and individuals with whom to connect, and enact leadership relevant and appropriate to creating change in the culture of their organization (Amey et al., 2009). It sounds like a tall order for an early career professional, but if leadership scholars are correct, actual structural impediments do not prevent this; leaders are everywhere.

Leading from anywhere means that those in any position or with any power base need to see themselves as co-learners and embrace a form of authentic, shared leadership. Shapiro states that "[l]eadership is an action, not a title, and the ability to lead can be found in every person. Each of us must claim out authority to lead at the right time and in the right place

(Shapiro, 2005, p. 1). Although one may debate Shapiro's claim, it is challenging to disagree with his statement that this leadership approach fundamentally moves the student affairs organization toward a flatter, more inclusive, weblike, multicultural organization than will maintaining a centralized, top-down traditional approach to leadership. To this end, we argue that leading from anywhere is critical to the future effectiveness of student affairs organizations.

Ethical Considerations

The mid-1990s saw the start of a flurry of publications focused not on leadership skills and traits but on actions and how and in what leaders ground their behaviors. *Leading With Soul* (Bolman & Deal, 2001), *Leadership Is an Art* (DePree, 2004), *On Becoming a Servant Leader* (Greenleaf, 1996), and *Leadership by Design: Strengthening Integrity in Higher Education* (Bogue, 1994) are just a few titles that emerged during this time and tried to discern the motivations, guiding principles, ethics, and values that presumably are the foundation of leadership. This writing continues today with titles as diverse as *Competing Values Leadership: Creating Value in Organizations* (Cameron, Quinn, Degraff, & Thakor, 2006) and *Maybe I Should . . . . : Case Studies on Ethics for Student Affairs Professionals* (Hamrick & Benjamin, 2009). The point of these texts is to raise the importance for leaders of reaching deep inside for the values, social conscience, authenticity, beliefs, and spirit (Woodard et al., 2000) that help them navigate the turbulent times and difficult decisions (Barwick, 2007) that characterize student affairs work and higher education today.

It is important to remember that ethics and values are culture-based (Ortiz & Martinez, 2009). Some believe that the values of a culture, in fact, are what define leadership in any setting. This becomes even more critical to understand when we note the rising percentage of our college campuses comprised of domestic students from non-Anglo cultures and international students representing world cultures that are rich and diverse, and not necessarily based on the same value foundations on which our colleges, structures, and rules are based. Matchett (2008, cited in Ortiz & Martinez, 2009) identifies three core ethical principles that should be considered as leaders proceed in their daily work. She argues that we need to understand how a set of rules are applied to different situations rather than just adhering to them; that every decision and action has ethical dimensions; and that we are accountable for our conduct, thereby making ethics not just a personal issue but one associated with others.

When we think through the myriad situations in which student affairs professionals find themselves, and the changing contexts of the decisions they make, ethical leadership gets tested regularly. Promoting social justice, and setting policies on a broad array of issues (admissions, discipline, dress codes, social networks, tailgating, workloads, travel reimbursements, and webinar participation on the job) are just two of the many aspects of work that may cause ethical challenges for leaders in student affairs—not just for how they work with students and each other, but in their own daily decisions. Bogue (1994) reminds us that dignity, curiosity, compassion, candor, courage, and a willingness to serve others are just some of the ethical considerations that should frame the way leaders make decisions today. They mirror aspects we have discussed in earlier chapters of this book as cornerstones of organizations designed for sustainable change.

Authentic Leadership

"Although our profession may seem overrun by women (not necessarily a bad thing), I find myself immersed in a culture dominated by males" (Ellis, 2003, p. 27). Careful examination of the implications of gender, race, ethnicity, sexual orientation, and class for leadership in higher education is beyond the scope of this book; it has and could be the focus of full texts (see, for example, Curry, 2000; Glazer-Raymo, 1999; and Valverde, 2003). As Ellis's comment suggests, student affairs organizations are not yet as diverse and inclusive as we want them to be, at least not where leadership is concerned. We would be remiss not to raise consciousness in this area of scholarship and practice.

We choose to label this discussion authentic leadership because it is rooted in the belief that the experiences of student affairs professionals contribute to who they are as leaders. Decisions they make are connected to who they are and what they value. The great man theories of leadership focused on men, thereby negating the experiences, stories, ideas, philosophies, and truths of women; they were predominately also normed on white men, thereby ignoring the realities of leaders of color. The leadership perspectives of white women and leaders of color are more recently being included in the literature, but progress is slow and uneven, in spite of the prevalence of research on these different identities of students. We continue to need culturally sensitive frameworks with which to study these leaders so that they are not assessed in some deficient way or that we do not conclude that, because their leadership is exercised differently from their white male counterparts, that it is somehow less effective. Rather, we need to consider different measures and evaluation schemas to accurately capture the work of all leaders.

Even though the research and writing is not as strong as it might be, professional associations in student affairs and higher education have recognized the need to support leaders with different identities. The Alice Manicur Symposium and the Multicultural Institute of the National Association of Student Personnel Administrators, the American Council on Education's Women's Network and Center for Advancement of Racial and Ethnic Equity, and the Higher Education Resource Services Summer Institute for Women in Higher Education Administration, for example, all focus on leadership issues and self-awareness for women. These professional development opportunities have evolved over time to be in touch with their respective target audiences, for example, providing women-centered programming as opposed to focusing heavily on how to function in gendered organizations (Amey, 2006). Learning outcomes, including leadership outcomes, are better addressed when learning styles and learner needs are accounted for in program design, and these identity-specific professional development opportunities are a means by which the next generation of leaders is identified and cultivated.

The point we want to make about authentic leadership is its importance to the overall importance of this value to creating student affairs organizations for sustainable change. We profess the critical nature of supporting diverse experiences for our students if colleges and universities are to be effective global learning environments in the 21st century. Yet we have not always attended to how these same beliefs, structures, and actions translate into effective practice for student affairs professionals. There almost seems to be an assumption that, because we work on behalf of students, we must be well supported in that work as professional administrators. Yet research on the gendered, racist nature of higher education persists, and so we hold up the mirror to argue that creating learning environments that also cultivate authentic leadership across our campuses is just as central to the future of postsecondary education as is work we do on behalf of students. These efforts start with the recognition that there is no one-size-fits-all way to enact leadership, and that the leadership we need truly embraces the authentic identities of the individuals who are in positions to create effective change on our campuses.

Building the Mobile

> We have to redefine the nature of leadership. . . . [W]e need to evolve from a power-based model into an enabling model. We need to evolve from control and management into empowerment, and we need to move from . . . a linear, 'we do this and we do that, and then we do that' bulwark kind of model into a mobile where you have an evolving set of constantly changing relationships where you understand and view it in its entirety. We need to move more effectively from power-based relationships into reciprocal relationships. (Amey & Brown, 2004, p. 116)

To build the leadership mobile reflected in the quote above, title holders and individual leaders need to be able to transition from authority to facilitator, and other members of the student affairs organization need to be ready to assume leadership roles and responsibilities. This shift is predicated on the assumption that organizational goals and roles are clear, that trust and effective communication have been established, that others see their potential as leaders, and that all are actively involved in ongoing learning processes. It requires continued assessment of the leadership needs of the group and that the leader regularly makes appropriate adjustments. It also implies that leaders are personally able to make the shift, actually adjusting their own style from authoritarian to servantlike. It means that the leader has to be able to objectify the role and ideas of leadership in order to effectively facilitate the learning processes of others (Kuhnert & Lewis, 1989); one has to be able to separate self from the role.

The type of leadership described in this chapter takes longer, develops more slowly, is fostered through dialogue rather than delegation, and often challenges core beliefs of members and of the leader. It is rarely easy, often exciting, and demands capable leaders fully aware of the need for challenge and support as learning and development occur (Amey, 2005). Yet when pulling together student affairs professionals for group work, we often continue to rely on traditional variables such as seniority, title, and professional expertise for selecting group leaders. We use the same logic when looking to hire and promote the next generation of senior (and even midlevel) administrators. If you are chosen for these traditional reasons, you probably depend on them in your practice rather than being willing to challenge and change the system to incorporate voices from around the division, expertise that comes apart from job title, and creativity that challenges the status quo (Morgan, 1999). But with increased awareness of alternative leadership perspectives, we can build student affairs organizations differently and in ways that will enable deep and meaningful change. After all, student affairs professionals have a "sincere interest and [the] deepest commitment . . . to make their college or university the best possible place for students to learn and grow" (Ellis, 2003, p. 80). Thus, they provide a great resource for populating the sustainable change organization.

Reflective Summary

1. What assumptions do you have about the leadership needs of your organization?
2. In what ways are the members of your organization encouraged to assume leadership responsibilities, or to be "leaders from anywhere"? How do you encourage others do be leaders?
3. How do you define the leadership in your organization? Do your definitions differ depending where one is in your organization (e.g., entry level, midlevel, or senior level professional)?
4. Consider someone you think is an effective leader and one who is not. What are the differences?
5. Think about a challenge your organization has faced. Regardless of how the challenge turned out, how would you describe the challenge in terms of leadership?
6. Why is it important to know what you believe in as a leader? In what ways have your beliefs been tested in your organization?
7. Think about your experiences and identity. How do you think these factors affect you as a leader and your leadership?
8. What activities and steps are included in your leadership development plan?

References

Allen, K. E., & Cherrey, C. (2002). Student affairs as change agents. *NASPA Journal, 40*(2), 29–42.

Amey, M. J. (2005). Leadership as learning: Conceptualizing the process. *Community College Journal of Research and Practice, 29*(9), 689–704.

Amey, M. J. (2006, November/December), Leadership in higher education. *Change*, 55–58.

Amey, M. J., & Brown, D. F. (2004). *Breaking out of the box: Interdisicplinary collaboration and faculty work.* Greenwich, CT: Greenwood Press/Information Age Publishing.

Amey, M. J., Jessup-Anger, E., & Tingson-Gatuz, C. R. (2009). Unwritten rules: Organizational and political realities of the job. In M. J. Amey & L. Reesor (Eds.), *Beginning your journey: A guide for new professionals in student affairs* (3rd ed., pp. 15–38). Washington, DC: NASPA.

Argyris, C., & Schön, D. A. (1978). *Organizational learning: A theory of action perspective.* Reading, MA: Addison-Wesley.

Astin, A. W., & Astin, H. S. (2000). Principles of transformative leadership. In A. W. Astin & H. S. Astin (Eds.), *Leadership reconsidered: Engaging higher education in social change* (pp. 8–17). Battle Creek, MI: W. K. Kellogg Foundation.

Bandura, A. (1996). *Self-efficacy: The exercise of control.* New York: Freeman.

Bartlett, K. T. (1990). Feminist legal methods. *Harvard Law Review, 103*, 829–888.

Barwick, J. (2007). Following the leader and leading the followers. In J. F. Wergin (Ed.), *Leadership in place: How academic professionals can find their leadership voice* (pp. 149–168). San Francisco: Anker.

Baxter-Magolda, M. B. (1999). *Creating contexts for learning and self-authorship: Constructive-developmental pedagogy.* Nashville, TN: Vanderbilt University Press.

Bennis, W. G., & Thomas, R. J. (2002). *Geeks & geezers: How era, values, and defining moments shape leaders.* Boston: Harvard Business School Press.

Bensimon, E. M., & Neumann, A. (1993). *Redesigning collegiate leadership: Teams and teamwork in higher education.* Baltimore, MD: Johns Hopkins University Press.

Bogue, E. G. (1994). *Leadership by design: Strengthening integrity in higher education.* San Francisco: Jossey-Bass.

Bolman, L. G., & Deal, T. (2001). *Leading with soul: An uncommon journey of spirit.* San Francisco: Jossey-Bass.

Brown, D. G. (Ed.). (2006). *University presidents as moral leaders.* Westport, CT: American Council on Education and Praeger Publishers.

Cameron, K. S., Quinn, R. E., Degraff, J., & Thakor, A. V. (2006). *Competing values leadership: Creating value in organizations.* Northampton, MA: Edward Elgar Publishing.

Curry, B. (2000). *Women in power: Pathways to leadership in education.* New York: Teachers College Press.

DePree, M. (2004). *Leadership is an art.* New York: Doubleday.

Eddy, P. L. (2003). Sensemaking on campus: How community college presidents frame change. *Community College Journal of Research and Practice, 27*(6), 453–471.

Ellis, S. (2003). *Dreams, nightmares and pursuing the passion: Personal perspectives on college and university leadership.* Washington, DC: NASPA.

Glazer-Raymo, J. (1999). *Shattering the myths: Women in academe.* Baltimore, MD: Johns Hopkins University Press.

Greenleaf, R. K. (1996). *On becoming a servant leader.* San Francisco: Jossey-Bass.

Hamrick, F. A., & Benjamin, M. (Eds.) (2009). *Maybe I should . . . : Case studies on ethics for student affairs professionals.* Washington, DC: ACPA-College Student Educators International, University Press of America.

Heifetz, R. A. (1994). *Leadership without easy answers.* Cambridge, MA: Harvard University Press.

Heifetz, R. A., & Laurie, D. L. (1997). The work of leadership. *Harvard Business Review, 75*(1), 124–134.

Helgesen, S. (1995). *The web of inclusion.* New York: Currency/Doubleday.

Helmich, D. M. (2007). *Ethical leadership in community colleges: Bridging theory and daily practice.* San Francisco: Jossey-Bass.

Hirt, J. B. (2006). *Where you work matters: Student affairs administrators at different types of institutions.* Lanham, MD: University Press of America.

Jessup-Anger, E. R. (2009). *Implementing innovative ideas: A multisite case study of putting* Learning Reconsidered *into practice.* Unpublished dissertation, Michigan State University, East Lansing, MI.

Kezar, A. (Ed.) (2009). *Rethinking leadership in a complex, multicultural, and global environment: New concepts and models for higher education.* Sterling, VA: Stylus.

Kolb, D. A. (1984). *Experiential learning.* Upper Saddle River, NJ: Prentice Hall.

Komives, S. R., Lucas, N., & McMahon, T. R. (2007). *Exploring leadership for college students who want to make a difference* (2nd ed.). San Francisco: Jossey-Bass.

Kuhnert, K. W., & Lewis, P. (1989). Transactional and transformational leadership: A constructive/developmental analysis. In W. E. Rosenbach & R. L. Taylor (Eds.), *Contemporary issues in leadership* (2nd ed., pp. 192–206). Boulder, CO: Westview.

Manning, K., Kinzie, J., & Schuh, J. (2006). *One size does not fit all: Traditional and innovative models of student affairs practice.* New York: Routledge.

Matchett, N. J. (2008). Ethics across the curriculum. In S. L. Moore (Ed.), *Practical approaches to ethics for colleges and universities* (New Directions for Higher Education No. 142, pp. 25–38). San Francisco: Jossey-Bass.

Morgan, G. (1999). *Images of organizations* (2nd ed.). Beverly Hills, CA: Sage.

Ortiz, A. M., & Martinez, C. R. (2009). Developing a professional ethic. In M. J. Amey & L. Reesor (Eds.), *Beginning your journey: A guide for new professionals in student affairs* (3rd ed., pp. 39–60). Washington, DC: NASPA.

Peterson, M. W. (1997). Contextual planning to transform institutions. In M. W. Peterson, D. D. Dill, L. A. Mets, & Associates (Eds.), *Planning and management for a changing environment: A handbook on redesigning postsecondary institutions* (pp. 127–157). San Francisco: Jossey-Bass.

Quinn, R. E. (1996). *Deep change: Discovering the leader within.* San Francisco: Jossey-Bass.

Senge, P. M. (1990). *The fifth discipline: The art and practice of the learning organization.* New York: Doubleday.

Shapiro, P. (2005). Too many leaders? . . . or do we use the term "leader" too freely? *News & Tools Leadership, 1*(2), 1–2.

Spears, L. C. (2002). Tracing the past, present, and future of servant leadership. In L. C. Spears & M. Lawrence (Eds.), *Focus on leadership: Servant-leadership for the twenty-first century* (pp. 1–18). New York: Wiley.

Taylor, C. M. (2007). Leading from the middle. In R. L. Ackerman (Ed.), *The mid-level manager in student affairs: Strategies for success* (pp. 127–154). Washington, DC: NASPA.

Tierney, W. G. (2008). *The impact of culture on organizational decision making: Theory and practice in higher ed.* Sterling, VA: Stylus.

Vaill, P. B. (1996). The learning challenges of leadership. In Kellogg Leadership Studies Project, *The balance of leadership and followership working papers.* College Park, MD: Academy of Leadership Press.

Valverde, L. A. (2003). *Leaders of color in higher education: Unrecognized triumphs in harsh institutions.* Walnut Creek, CA: Alta Mira Press.

Wergin, J. F. (2007). Why we need leadership in place. In J. F. Wergin (Ed.), *Leadership in place: How academic professionals can find their leadership voice* (pp. 1–20). San Francisco: Jossey-Bass.

Wheatley, M. (2002). The work of the servant-leader. In L. C. Spears & M. Lawrence (Eds.), *Focus on leadership: Servant-leadership for the twenty-first century* (pp. 349–362). New York: Wiley.

Woodard, D. B., Love, P., & Komives, S. R. (2000). *Leadership and management issues for a new century* (New Directions for Student Services No. 92) (pp. 81–91). San Francisco: Jossey-Bass.

9

NAVIGATING THE FUTURE FOR STUDENT AFFAIRS ORGANIZATIONS

Thom Jeffries, a new student affairs professional, sat listening to his vice president for student affairs during a new staff member orientation. This was Thom's first job after graduating from a student affairs masters program. His excitement and eagerness to begin his new career made it difficult for him to focus and listen to what was being said. He believed he had been well trained and now he wanted to get into the field to begin applying the skills and competencies he had developed.

The vice president talked about her own career of nearly 35 years as a student affairs professional and how the role and responsibilities had changed over the years. She talked about the challenges the division faced in the midst of serious budget limitations and the lack of sufficient resources to fully address the challenges that were before them. She noted the changing demographics of the student body, the changing expectations facing higher education from the public and families, the need to partner more with faculty and academic programs in serving students and fostering student learning and student success, and the increasing challenges facing practitioners as societal ills continued to present themselves on their campus. She stressed the commitment of the existing divisional staff members, their strong loyalty to their profession and the institution, and the sacrifices they continue to make to ensure that students can be successful.

Thom's mind wandered to the future and what he might expect as his career unfolded. He wondered what it would be like when he was in the same position as his vice president, reliving his experiences and rallying staff members to face the challenges that would confront them in the near and not too distant future. He wondered if the changes facing the profession would seriously alter its role and mission within the institution. Would the division be organized and designed differently to better address the emerging challenges? Would staff roles and responsibilities be different? Would he have to retool his knowledge and competencies to meet emerging challenges? It was hard to grasp what might be the scope and nature of the issues that awaited him, but he knew that things were not likely to stay the same. Although the idea of continuous change was a little scary, it actually felt good to know that he and his colleagues were able to prepare for this reality.

A s student affairs organizations look to their future, one thing is certain: the situations they face are going to change, and change as a process is likely to be a constant variable in organizational life. What and how organizations will change is not exactly clear. However, there are some indications of where change is headed and what issues might influence organizational change. This chapter will discuss some current and emerging issues facing student affairs organizations and also how leaders and practitioners can prepare their organizations to adapt to change and sustain themselves in a culture of change.

The Inevitability of Change

Given the shifting landscape of higher education and the pressing and changing demands on student affairs organizations, it is clear that change is inevitable. What is not clear is what the change will look like and how it will unfold. What is also not clear is the extent to which student affairs practitioners can effectively take charge of this process and navigate the necessary changes to make their organizations more effective. Student affairs practitioners can either wait for change to come or they can take charge of their own future and begin to design their organizations to be more flexible and adaptive to change.

It is clear that the mechanistic, hierarchical structures of the past are not going to be the most effective models for future organizations. Organizations of the future will need to be designed and built for sustaining change, to be responsive to mission and strategy shifts, to be more effective in the use of their specific technologies, and to enable staff members to be more engaged in the organization and leadership processes at all levels. Staff members will need to be engaged in developing organizations that are more attentive to the external environment. They will need to understand how the culture and structure of their organization can become adaptive and self-adjusting to changing needs. Collectively, each student affairs organization will need to understand how it learns and adapts, and essentially how it can correct and reconstruct itself for change if it wants to achieve success and become more effective.

It is also clear that there will be many factors and issues that will influence the change that is to come. Even though we have no certainty about future directions of change, we have some evidence that some current issues will continue to influence change or may increase their impact on change in the years ahead. The following discussion is a brief review of some of the change-related issues and how they might influence student affairs organizational change.

Diversity and Student Affairs Organizations

Any look into the future for events and/or trends that have relevance to the student affairs organization would see the opportunities and challenges afforded by diversity (Kezar, 2001). As the population of the United States becomes increasingly diverse and the interdependence of the world becomes more apparent, issues related to diversity will become more critical and complex for collegiate communities. The concepts and issues related to diversity come in two forms for the student affairs organization: external environmental diversity associated with the changing demographics of higher education, and intraorganizational diversity.

This first notion of diversity is the more familiar use of the term *diversity* on college campuses. It denotes the increasing diversity related to personal characteristics of the students and faculty and staff members within campus environments. The literature and demographic facts related to this issue are quite clear on three points. First, the diversity associated with race/ethnicity, class, sexual orientation, disability, and other groups that have been historically underrepresented is going to increase on college campuses in the future. Second, these groups have historically been marginalized, and providing access to higher education and creating campus experiences that foster their success continues to be problematic. Third, the complexity and economic realities associated with these issues are likely to continue to be significant educational issues in the future. To what extent will organizations adjust to the challenges that diversity and related issues place on the institution? How will they address the issues of access and at the same time address the political and educational issues associated with vertical equity, providing the same to all, and horizontal equity, providing differently based on need, to an increasingly diverse collegiate population (Stone, 2002)?

Over the years, student affairs organizations have developed myriad campus programs to address the external environmental variable of diversity represented by various member characteristics. Student affairs organizations have been viewed as the leaders related to diversity initiatives and, in many cases, diversity in staffing. As student affairs organizations look to their role in the future, continuing to foster the same organizational alignment for these efforts may not be the most effective option. Taking a new look at the philosophical and organizational underpinnings of these programmatic efforts might be helpful in navigating the future.

For example, Tierney (2008) raised serious questions about the prevailing approach to campus diversity. He suggested that the current thinking associated with the concept of social integration developed by Tinto (1987) misses the critical issue that students within the construct of diversity may not be served by programs that attempt to develop social integration, but they might be better served by programs that "conceive of the universities as multicultural entities where difference is highlighted and celebrated" (Tierney, 2008, p. 66). How collegiate and student affairs organizations view these issues and which of the diversity philosophies are embraced by the campus will have a great impact on student affairs organizational issues. For example, should student affairs be organized to support one multicultural center for all diverse groups, or should there be individual programs and offices for each unique group? Should all programs and services be integrated to include diversity-related issues, or should there be separate offices, services, and so-called safety zones for every diverse group on campus? Should every staff person assume a level of responsibility for diversity efforts, or should these efforts be housed in specific centers or within a specialized office or unit? Should they be assigned the responsibility of experts charged with providing leadership and directing specific programs and services? The latter would be more in concert with Tierney's position. However, others argue that diversity should be infused within the culture and fabric of the organization and that isolation only continues to create an atmosphere of "separate but equal."

Another organizational option would take the issue one step further by asserting that higher educational organizations should assume a leadership role in creating a "new narrative and discourse" that gives voice to diverse communities (Green & Trent, 2005). This role challenges the organization to reorganize at all levels, especially within its leadership levels, to actually demonstrate difference as an asset and to recognize that distinct populations may need to be served differently. This "new narrative" underscores the importance of differences and heterogeneity in the structure and leadership of the organization, as well as within the programs and services it provides. The extent to which student affairs organizations approach such philosophical issues will affect the overall structure and culture of their unit and the organization of the institutions in which they exist.

The second view of diversity, intraorganizational diversity, focuses on issues of diverse membership and structures within organizations. The topic is addressed throughout the organizational literature, particularly the literature that emerges from the organizational ecology perspective. For example, Morgan (2006) offers the following regarding the concept of requisite variety:

> Related to the idea of differentiation and integration is the principle of requisite variety, which states that the internal regulatory mechanisms of a system must be as diverse as the environment with which it is trying to deal. For only by incorporating required variety into internal controls can a system deal with the variety and challenge posed by its environment. Any system that insulates itself from the diversity in the environment tends to atrophy and lose its complexity and distinctive nature. Thus, requisite variety is an important feature of living systems of all kinds. (Morgan, 2006, p. 41)

Organizational diversity should include diversity in structure and diversity in membership. As student affairs organizations structure themselves for the future, being aware of and adapting to the local external environment is critical. Typologies related to diversity of institutional types and cultures do exist; for example, Bergquist and Pawlak (2008) outline six cultures of higher education, and Kuk (2009) and Hirt (2006) outline student affairs organizational models based on organizational type and mission. Understanding the diverse organizational needs of an institution based on type and cultures will become even more pressing as higher education continues to differentiate itself in the market. The student affairs organization, to be viable, must recognize and respond to the uniqueness of its own cultural context; the student affairs organizational structure needs to be able to reflect and contribute to the diverse culture of the campus and to support the mission and goals of the institution.

In addition to paying attention to dimensions of diverse organizational structures, student affairs organizations will need to keep diversity in student affairs organizational membership as a central focus. There is a strong tendency for organizations to hire and retain staff members who think, look, and behave like the organization's leadership. Diversity in membership has often been viewed in many organizations as hiring ethnically and racially diverse individuals, and little attention has been given to understanding the importance of diversity to the health and life of the organization. Diverse members in an organization can bring diverse opinions, knowledge, and perspectives, and they can actually assist the organization to rejuvenate and keep it from atrophy and death. When organizations simply engage in hiring what appears to be diverse individuals, but expect them to think and act like the existing leadership, then the benefits of diversity to the organization are not realized. It is no wonder that diverse employees often leave organizations where diversity is espoused and valued only on the surface.

A strong argument for a deeper organizational position on valuing diversity is the research associated with divergent thinking. Argote and Ophir (2005) point to this research, showing that organizations that are more diverse in membership are also more creative and perform better, consider and assess information in more complex ways, and develop more creative solutions than organizations without diverse membership. As campus student affairs organizations encounter greater diversity in local campus conditions and are concerned about performance and innovation, the willingness to entertain both organizational structural diversity and diversity in organizational membership will be critical (Williams & O'Reilly, 1998). For student affairs professionals, the future will require addressing issues related to diversity in organizational structures and membership, and in adopting a thoughtful and intentional programmatic philosophy built on appreciation of diversity and the celebration of heterogeneity in relationship to the external environment.

Fostering Healthy and Safe Campus Environments

The once-acclaimed ivory tower of the academy has been increasingly seized by acts of violence, disruptive and senseless behavior reflective of the larger society. Incidents such as those at Virginia Tech, Northern Illinois, and the University of Florida, and other violent, disruptive, and senseless acts are becoming more frequent on college campuses, and these incidents are becoming more serious and deadly. Responding to these types of incidents, preventing them from occurring whenever possible, and addressing proactively the closely associated issues of providing a safe and supportive campus environment for students to learn and develop will be central to the role and responsibilities of student affairs organizations in the future. Although extreme acts of violence may actually be rare on college campuses (Kingsbury, 2007), assault; theft; and disruptive, reckless, and mindless behavior are fairly common and can create considerable disruption and destruction within the campus environment. Although prevention and positive development may be the preferred goals, there is no way to predict how students, guests, and others are going to act or respond within the day-to-day life of the campus. As a result, the student affairs organization must be designed to be both vigilant and responsive when needed.

Addressing these issues on a fairly regular basis requires a collaborative, highly responsive, well-trained, self-managing team. It requires an organizational structure that can adapt and make decisions quickly and effectively. These teams need to be able to work across the entire institution and to behave both reactively and proactively simultaneously. They need to be able to address each incident and/or set of behaviors that are presented within the parameters of their unique dimensions and qualities. No two students are the same, and no two behavioral incidents are the same. Cookie-cutter approaches to needed assessments, and emergency and behavioral responses will not work effectively. Ongoing staff development and training will be critical to keeping staff members well prepared to address these issues.

At the same time, the student affairs organization might also consider taking a leadership role in fostering a campus and organizational cultural climate that is healthy and safe for everyone. This will require changing the culture of the campus and student affairs organization so that they express and model positive psychology thinking (Spano, 2008) and also focus on creating community-focused environments throughout the campus. These efforts can go a long way in preventing violent and destructive behavior and can also create healthy and positive learning and work-related environments on our campuses (Banning, 2001; Banning & Kuk, 2008; Petersen & Seligman, 2004; Spano, 2008).

Accountability and Student Affairs Organizations

The demand for accountability from legislatures, government executives, and the general public continues to increase, as do the demands for change, transparency, and greater efficiency. The university is no longer an ivory tower, and its interactions with the greater environment have become critical to its survival and its success.

Students and other constituent groups are increasingly voicing opinions that the functional hierarchical designs of most student affairs organizations are not equipped to respond quickly and effectively to student needs and concerns. Students do not understand nor do they care about the organizational reporting structure: who makes decisions, who has resources, and who reports to whom. What they care about is getting services and seeing results. In their world of real-time information, instantaneous responses, and immediate results, waiting for information and decisions to be funneled up and down a chain of command, or having to submit reams of paper through a bureaucratic maze that takes days or even weeks for a decision is tolerated less and less. They also increasingly expect that their individual needs and issues will be attended to with individually developed solutions.

Students and their families want to talk with decision makers, and they expect that one unit of the organization knows what the other unit in the organization is doing. They expect that faculty and staff members, regardless of which department or unit they work in, or which level on the organizational chart they appear on, are working together to assist them in achieving success. The concepts of academic and administrative turf and siloed functionality, and bureaucratic decision making are not part of their reality and they do not understand or easily tolerate its presence in their college experience.

Parents and taxpayers are demanding that higher education pay closer attention to costs and limit increases in tuitions and fees. Institutional leaders are also beginning to question whether current organizational designs can address the changing philosophical focus of student affairs and remain effective in light of new demands and increasing challenges. As accountability and metrics assume a greater role in institutional decision making, emphasis on being able to measure and to justify the effectiveness of existing organizations, and their programs and services, will increase. Many industrial organizations, which have already downsized, find it difficult to justify a host of midlevel managers, and student affairs organizations are now finding it difficult to demonstrate how midlevel managers enhance and add value to the educational experience of students.

In some cases, issues about what programs and services contribute to a high-quality educational experience will also come up. Should campuses be in the business of providing some services such as health care, counseling, and special population services when they can be obtained in the greater community? Should such services be provided without having students who use them pay the full costs of these services? How should such student services be orchestrated, and how will other units be designed to support students who may no longer be able to access these services on campus? Can some services be redesigned to address student needs in a more holistic manner, and/or can the institution partner with local organizations and companies to provide high-quality services in a more efficient and effective arrangement? These and similar types of questions and organizational issues are likely to come up for discussion and debate. Justification through thoughtful and strategic assessment and designing more creative and efficient ways to organize and deliver services will be critical to student affairs organizations.

In other cases, the existence of student affairs as an organizational unit may be challenged. Some institutions have already done away with student affairs organizations or have eliminated so-called nonessential services and moved the remaining services within academic and/or administrative services. As accountability pressure increases and resources become less abundant, institutions are likely to seek additional means to reduce costs and eliminate nonessential programs and services. How will student affairs units demonstrate and justify their value in achieving student success and providing quality programs and services to students? How will they redesign their organizations to maximize the use of existing resources so that they do not provide unnecessary and low-quality programs and services to students? How will they achieve a necessary and essential level of structure and an organizational culture that is adaptive, responsive, and welcoming so that they can address new challenges and emerging student issues?

Competition for Scarce Organizational Resources

Student affairs organizations are already quite aware that their value to the greater organization is generally considered secondary to the academic units of collegiate institutions. Although they provide valuable programs and services to the collegiate organization and its students, student affairs staff members are rarely given the status and recognition for their contributions to student success at the same level as are academic faculty members. They have a history of having to compete, often unsuccessfully, with academic programs for resources. Over the years, student affairs units have increasingly sought alternative sources of funding to keep from engaging in direct competition with academic units for state appropriations and tuition-based funding. Although these efforts have been somewhat successful in stabilizing student affairs funding in recent years, increased reductions in state support and limits on increases to student tuition and fees will challenge the successful continuation of these efforts. Given the concern for the total cost of acquiring a college education, institutional leaders and governing boards are beginning to address these issues on all fronts. This is likely to have a significant impact on student affairs funding and student affairs organizations in the future.

Although these challenges appear to be gloomy, they could actually provide some exciting opportunities to engage in organizational redesign. For example, if financial restrictions are altered to permit greater flexibility, student affairs units may find that they no longer have to design their organizations based on financial fund sources, which may create opportunities for greater cross-unit collaboration, flatter organizational designs, and attention to the holistic needs of students.

Having to focus on preserving quality, eliminating duplication, and prioritizing needed programs and services may foster greater levels of lateral collaboration and more efficient use of resources. This could spark greater use of nonfunctional designs that may cross current unit boundaries and create greater organizational synergy. It may foster the use of flatter structures, more lateral decision making, and reciprocal cooperation with academic units.

Partnering Across Division and Organizational Boundaries

A continuing challenge to student affairs organizations will be the increasing need to partner with other student affairs units; other academic units within colleges and universities; and with external, community-based entities. Although the focus on student success and learning has increased within student affairs organizations, actual changes in organizational structure and design that would advance and enable this focus have not materialized. Some partnering efforts are occurring, usually based on personal relationships, but they have not become standard practice and are not generally recognized and rewarded within existing cultural norms across the institution.

The current cultural and organizational structures within collegiate organizations make it difficult to create intentional and ongoing opportunities for effective partnerships. The continued dependence on vertical reporting and decision-making processes make cross-unit teaming complicated and difficult to achieve. At the same time, the need for partnerships across organizational boundaries and disciplines is increasing and is likely to become critical to the success of higher education in the future. Student affairs organizations need to find ways to strengthen these partnerships and to design their organizations with a more intentional lateral focus that rewards collaboration and effectively uses self-managed teams.

As student affairs divisions attend to organizational assessment efforts, a focus on creating organizational designs that foster cross-unit and external partnerships will be important. What elements in organizational design will foster cross-divisional teams? How can the organization establish teams that are self-managing and are designed to be learning-centered? How will the organization utilize organizational assessment to provide ongoing information and feedback regarding changes in the environment and foster efficient adaptation to new challenges and opportunities?

Hiring and Retaining Competent and Adaptive Staff Members

One of the greatest challenges that will continue to face student affairs organizations is the ability to hire and retain competent and adaptive student affairs professional staff members. With shrinking and increased competition for resources, there will probably be fewer resources for salaries, benefits, and hiring additional staff members. As the economy grows in the private sector, competition for staff members will make it challenging to attract competent and dedicated individuals to the profession. This will be especially true if salaries are not competitive and overextended workload responsibilities continue to plague student affairs organizations. These issues are likely to be the most challenging to institutions that do not have other benefits and attributes that might draw staff members to want to work for them.

Student affairs organizations will need to be diligent about these issues and seek more creative means for attracting and retaining staff members. They will probably need to create additional means of crafting professional opportunities for engagement, acquired experience, job sharing, cross-training, professional development, and recognitions within their organizations. They need to enable staff members at all levels to have greater involvement in leadership and decision making in the organization. Creating new organizational designs that foster these elements of job enrichment and career opportunity will be critical. Enabling staff members to feel valued and connected to the greater organization will be at the heart of success in student affairs organizations as they adapt and sustain a climate, culture, and structure that support ongoing change.

Enabling Effective Leadership

Leadership will continue to be a critical variable in the organizational success of student affairs. How leadership is viewed and the role it plays within the organization probably need to change. The top-down, control-focused, hierarchical approach to organizational leadership that dominated organizational behavior in the past will not be effective in new versions of successful organizations. With more organic, flatter structures; more cross-divisional, collaborative foci; team-driven decision making; and more flexible and adaptive learning-focused staff members, the leadership role will become a shared responsibility and will depend less on a single vision dictated from the top of the organization. The characteristics of successful leadership will be context-driven and enabled by those who have the expertise, experience, and talent to orchestrate appropriate decisions and realize desired results. Leadership responsibilities will focus more on enabling, coaching, and orchestrating a shared vision and set of values that guide decision making than actually making daily decisions.

Although this new approach to leadership appears to make sense on a theoretical level, implementing it will probably encounter considerable resistance from current and the aspiring leaders within higher education organizations. Power and control have potent addictive properties and are not easily surrendered. Once individuals have power, they often act in ways to covet more not less, and it begins to cloud and define their organizational reality. Sharing power, delegating decision making, and loosening the grip of control are foreign for many organizational leaders. It is not clear what it will take to change this dynamic and if it will even be possible. One place to start is to enable organizational members to be fully engaged in the selection of leaders and to insist that new leaders demonstrate values and past behavior that support new approaches to leadership. New leaders need to bring experience and knowledge of student affairs and of organizational leadership to these roles.

Applying Ethical Principles to Practice

The discussion of ensuring ethical behavior within student affairs organizations is not new; in fact, it has been at the center of the student affairs profession for decades. A number of professional associations have developed guiding ethical principles for the profession. A study conducted by the Council for the Advancement of Standards in Higher Education (Dean, 2006) identified seven ethical principles that are shared by various student affairs professional associations: (a) autonomy, respecting freedom of choice; (b) nonmalfeasance, doing no harm; (c) beneficence, promoting the welfare of others, especially students; (d) justice, being fair and respectful to others; (e) fidelity, being faithful to our word and duty; (f) veracity, being truthful and accurate, and (g) affiliation, fostering community and public good (Dalton, Crosby, Valente, & Eberhardt, 2009, p. 174). Specific ethical principles of practice can be found through contacting the various student affairs–related professional associations. The ethical principles published by student affairs professional associations are intended to guide the behavior and reflect the values associated with professional practice by individuals and their organizations within student affairs work. Although these principles were designed primarily to guide the practice of professionals in their work with students, they should also guide their behavior toward others within the organization, and with others they work with outside the organization. However, the work-related dimensions of ethical behavior within the student affairs literature has not always been very explicit and is also not always attended to within student affairs organizations.

The ethical behavior by staff toward other colleagues, other divisional units, and even outside partners is an important and complex organizational issue and may become more pronounced in the future. Unethical behavior can become pronounced or ethical practices can be overlooked when resources become tight or when decisions must be made that affect individual livelihoods, or the threat of losing a job or gaining a promotion hangs in the balance. Unethical behavior can also surface when individuals or their work units are threatened by proposed changes or the realignment of responsibilities and resources. Such behavior can be at the source of individuals being treated unfairly or unprofessionally, and/or being victimized or being made a scapegoat by others in the organization.

Espousing ethical behavior within an organizational unit and establishing norms and values related to intraorganizational behavior does not indicate that such behavior will be reciprocated. Becoming a victim of unethical behavior can lead to organizational sabotage and other destructive and unhealthy behavior among colleagues and toward the organization. Most important, it can destroy lives and professional careers.

Promoting ethical behavior within student affairs organizations toward colleagues and others outside one's work unit should be attended to as diligently as we advocate ethical behavior toward students. Developing an organizational culture that promotes sound ethical practices toward colleagues at all levels and engaging all staff members in the discussion and creation of organizationally held values and accepted norms regarding ethical behavior is paramount. Being open and transparent about personnel policy and practices, as well as how staff members are treated in terms of rewards and recognition, is essential to modeling ethical behavior. Listening and responding to staff member concerns about work climate issues and holding all members of the organization to high ethical and behavioral standards can help create an ethical environment within the organizational culture. As student affairs professionals assess their organizations, they should be conscious of ethical behavior issues and seek to address them in humane and positive ways at all levels of the organization.

As stated in chapter 3, ethical behavior is an important attribute within the organization–environment relationship. The community process approach gives guidance to the ethical issues associated with the design and assessment of the organizational environment. It suggests that all those who will be affected by the efforts to redesign the organization–environment must have an opportunity for meaningful input into the process (Huebner & Banning, 1987). Kelman and Warwick (1978) suggest a variety of questions like the following (which might be considered when judging the ethical nature of the process to change environments): Who participated in the process? How were diverse interests represented? Who will benefit, and who will suffer? By what means will the decision be implemented, by coercion or by facilitation? Who is involved in the ongoing assessment? (See chapters 3 and 6 for more extensive coverage about ethics related to organizational environment and change.)

Designing Organizations for Change

A first step in becoming equipped to address these challenges is to acquire an understanding of organizational behavior and design theory and how they can be applied in student affairs organizations. Although future organizations will require leaders to attend to their organization's unique element of design so that they can respond to their specific challenges, being intentional and using existing knowledge and research to help craft organizations will enable organizations to be designed effectively. There is no single, uniform way to structure organizations; there are knowledge- and research-based organizational design elements and processes that better equip organizations to be effective and responsive. Organizational design is a complex process that is greatly enhanced by using existing theory and tools to craft an appropriate and effective design for a specific organization. Effective organizational design involves much more than moving organizational units around in the reporting structure.

Second, it is helpful to be able to understand and apply environmental and organizational assessment strategies and tools. It is nearly impossible to know if you have achieved a goal if you do not know where you started or where you ended up. Organizational assessment is a key to unlocking an understanding of organizations, providing the necessary feedback loop among strategy, behavior, and performance. Too often we utilize anecdotal information or personal impressions to make decisions about organizational and individual performance. This approach does not enhance the organization.

Although we may have developed learning outcomes and satisfaction assessments related to our students, student affairs organizations have seldom initiated organizational assessments. If these assessments exist, they are generally orchestrated for accreditation reviews and are not built into the ongoing fabric of student affairs organizational operations. We also seldom use these organizational assessments to understand our environments and to adjust our operations on a regular basis to become more effective or to stay on course toward achieving our goals. Our assessments are often quantitatively focused on questions of what and not as effectively focused on the questions of how or why related to our organization's effectiveness. We may be engaging in assessment, but we may also be asking the wrong questions or not providing the information needed to close the feedback loop that will help us achieve our desired outcomes.

Third, it is critical to understand change as an ongoing process and to gain experience to lead an organization in the midst of sustained change. Many change processes have failed because the leaders within an organization did not manage change effectively, or they did not understand the fact that change is an ongoing phenomenon and not a one-time dramatic event. Although the idea of transformational change is alluring, especially to institutional leaders who want to turn the organization in a new direction quickly, change is more sustaining if it is incremental, gradual, and participatory. Process takes time, and participatory process takes even more time and requires lots of patience. Organizations need to be designed to change and not simply lead into change. Starting and stopping change as though it were an isolated independent event is not very effective. Structure, culture, jobs and responsibilities, rewards, and other organizational systems need to be designed to enable change to occur all the time, as a regular part of the daily operating processes.

For example, a true learning organization assumes that change occurs as a natural part of the ongoing assessment of its daily operations. Individuals and teams within the organization not only regularly gather feedback to improve existing operations, they also assume that there are always better ways to realize the organization's goals. As a result, they intentionally make decisions and reallocate resources to increase the likelihood of change. They do not have to secure approval or provide evidence that a new strategy is needed; change is part of their daily lives and they simply do things differently to see if they work more effectively.

Finally, it is imperative that leaders begin to grasp the true role and responsibility of leadership in organic organizations. They need to understand their role in enabling and coaching others to engage in leadership and ownership related to change and innovation. For leaders at all levels within student affairs organizations, the ability to deal with change and also to understand that change must become sustainable; it must be built into the fabric and culture of the organization because it is paramount to both its survival and future success.

According to Hesselbein, Goldsmith, and Beckhard (1997), organizations of the future should be designed for fluidity and flexibility. They should be mission-focused, value-based, and demographics- and environmentally driven. If student affairs organizations are going to be viable and effective in the future, staff members at all levels need to be engaged in the design and assessment of their organizations. They need to understand and be able to utilize existing theory and research to craft organizations that address the unique challenges that they face, and to be able to shift structure and strategy to adapt to the changing needs and issues in the uncertain future.

This book has attempted to present an introduction to organizational behavior and theory and its application to student affairs organizations in college and university settings. Our goal was to present a variety of related theories, constructs, and models that would enable you to better understand the workings of your student affairs organization and to become more effective student affairs scholar-practitioners within your organizations. Now it is up to you to take what you have learned and begin to apply it within your organization. We trust this book will enable you to enhance organizational effectiveness and to help sustain change in the future.

Reflective Summary

1. What factors might influence change within higher education in the near future? How might these changes impact student affairs organizations and their relationships with other campus units such as academic affairs?
2. How might your student affairs organization effectively deal with the increasing issues of diversity on your campus?
3. How can your student affairs organization respond more effectively to issues of safety and ensuring a healthy campus environment for all members of the community?
4. How should student affairs organizations deal with concerns related to increasing costs for students and also increasing demands for quality, personalization, and efficiency in programs and services?
5. How might your student affairs organization attend to greater demands for assessment and accountability related to organizational effectiveness?
6. In light of increasing change and shifting demands on organizational resources, how should your student affairs organization address issues of human resource and leadership development?
7. What role does ethical behavior play in the organization-environmental relationship within your student affairs organization?
8. How might your student affairs organization effectively apply organization and change theory and strategies to craft an organization that can sustain change and effectively face future challenges?

References

Argote, L., & Ophir, R. (2005). Intra-organizational learning. In J. A. C. Baum (Ed.), *The Blackwell companion to organizations* (pp. 181–207). Malden, MA: Blackwell.

Banning, J. H. (2001). Developing the environmental program. In M. Bartley-Taylor (Ed.), *Higher education housing facilities* (pp. 38–43). Charlottesville, VA: National Association of College Auxiliary Services.

Banning, J. H., & Kuk, L. (2008). *Campus violence: The role of the residence hall.* Retrieved from http://www.reslife.net/html/crisis_0708a.html

Bergquist, W. H., & Pawlak, K. (2008). *Engaging the six cultures of the academy*. San Francisco: Jossey-Bass.

Dalton, J. C., Crosby, P. C., Valente, A., and Eberhardt, D. (2009). Maintaining and modeling everyday ethics in student affairs. In G. S. McClellan & J. Stringer (Eds.), *The handbook of student affairs administration* (pp. 166–186). San Francisco: Jossey-Bass.

Dean, L. A. (2006). *CAS professional standards for higher education*. Washington, DC: Council for the Advancement of Standards in Higher Education.

Green, D. O., & Trent, W. T. (2005). The public good and a racially diverse democracy. In A. J. Kezar, T. C. Chambers, & J. C. Burkhardt (Eds.), *Higher education for the public good* (pp. 102–123). San Francisco: Jossey-Bass.

Hesselbein, F., Goldsmith, M., & Beckhard, R. (1997). *The organization of the future*. San Francisco: Jossey-Bass.

Hirt, J. B. (2006). *Where you work matters: Student affairs administration at different types of institutions*. Lanham, MD: University Press of America.

Huebner, L., & Banning, J. H. (1987). Ethics of intentional campus design. *NASPA Journal, 25*(1), 28–37.

Kelman, H., & Warwick, D. (1978). The ethics of social intervention: Goals, means, consequences. In G. Bermant, H. Kelman, & D. Warwick (Eds.), *The ethics of social intervention* (pp. 3–33). New York: Wiley.

Kezar, A. J. (2001). *Understanding and facilitating organizational change in the 21st century: Recent research and conceptualizations. ASHE-ERIC Higher Education Report, 28*(4). New York: Wiley.

Kingsbury, A. (2007, April 30). Toward a safe campus. *US News & World Report, 142*, 48–52.

Kuk, L. (2009). The dynamic of organizational models within student affairs. In G. S. McClellan & J. Stringer (Eds.), *The handbook of student affairs administration* (3rd ed., pp. 313–332). San Francisco: Jossey-Bass.

Morgan, G. (2006). *Images of organization*. Thousand Oaks, CA: Sage.

Petersen, C., & Seligman, M. E. P. (2004). *Character strengths and virtues: A handbook and classification*. Oxford, UK: American Psychological Association & Oxford University Press.

Spano, D. B. (2008, January–February), Nurturing institutional culture of caring. *About Campus*, 7–23.

Stone, D. (2002). *Policy paradox: The art of political decision making*. New York: Norton.

Tierney, W. G. (2008). *The impact of culture on organizational decision making: Theory and practice in higher education*. Sterling, VA: Stylus.

Tinto, V. (1987). *Leaving college: Rethinking the causes and cures of student attrition*. Chicago: The University of Chicago Press.

Williams, K. Y., & O'Reilly, C. A. (1998). Demography and diversity in organizations: A review of 40 years of research. *Research in Organizational Behavior, 20*, 77–140.

ABOUT THE AUTHORS

Linda Kuk is associate professor of education and program chair for the graduate program in College and University Leadership at Colorado State University. Prior to her faculty role, she served as vice president for student affairs for more than 22 years at Colorado State University; the Rochester Institute of Technology, in Rochester, New York; and the State University of New York at Cortland. She brings diverse experiences to her post, from her consulting work in China to sitting on numerous community boards of directors. She has served on the National Association of Student Personnel Administrators (NASPA) Board of Directors as Region II vice president, the NASPA Foundation Board, the NASPA Journal Board, and the American College Personnel Association Board of Directors. She also serves on the editorial board of the *Spectrum Journal*. In October 2003, she was named Alumni of the Year for the College of Education at Iowa State University, and in March 2004 she was named a Pillar of the Profession by the NASPA Foundation. Linda earned a PhD in professional studies at Iowa State University, and a master's in education and a bachelor's with distinction in social work from Colorado State University. She has written and presented on varied subjects in the area of higher education administration, organizational behavior, gender studies, and career/professional development, and she serves as a student affairs organizational consultant.

James H. Banning (Jim) is professor of education at Colorado State University. He is an environmental psychologist who studies institutional learning environments from the perspective of campus ecology, with a focus on the role of the physical environment. Jim holds a PhD in clinical psychology from the University of Colorado, Boulder. He has served as vice chancellor for student affairs at the University of Missouri, Columbia, and vice president for student affairs at Colorado State University. In the student affairs field, he is seen as a pioneer in the campus ecology movement. He co-authored the recent book, *Education by Design: Creating Campus Environments That Work.* Jim teaches courses in qualitative inquiry, qualitative data analysis, ethnography, and environmental psychology, and his current interests focus on a sense of place, the concept of third place, and restorative environments.

Marilyn J. Amey is professor of higher education and chair of the department of educational administration at Michigan State University; previously, she was a faculty member at the University of Kansas. Marilyn worked in residence life, student activities, student unions, and summer conference coordination, as well as for a state lobbying agency for private colleges and universities. She served two terms as a NASPA Faculty Fellow and has been a member and Chair of the NASPA Dissertation of the Year Committee. Marilyn earned her PhD in higher education and a master's in public administration from Penn State University, has a master's degree in college student personnel from Ohio State University, and a bachelor's degree in elementary and special education from Wittenberg University. She recently co-edited a third version of *Beginning Your Journey: A Guide for New Professionals in Student Affairs,* published by NASPA, and has written extensively on leadership, administrative and governance issues, and community colleges.

Also available from Stylus

Becoming Socialized in Student Affairs Administration
A Guide for New Professionals and Their Supervisors
Edited by Ashley Tull, Joan B. Hirt, and Sue Saunders

"An important resource for new professionals."—***Marilyn J. Amey***, *Professor and Chairperson, Department of Educational Administration, Michigan State University*

"A valuable addition to the profession. In this volume, Tull, Hirt, and Saunders have brought together experts on the socialization experiences of new professionals. Graduate students can anticipate their first years on the job, and new professionals will find accurate descriptions of their circumstances and useful insights for adjusting to full-time work. Supervisors and mentors can use *Becoming Socialized* to construct environments where individual responsibility for professional development can meet workplace expectations and commitments to high quality job performance in service of students."—***Kristen A. Renn***, *Associate Professor of Higher, Adult, & Lifelong Education, Michigan State University*

A Day in the Life of a College Student Leader
Case Studies for Undergraduate Leaders
Sarah M. Marshall and Anne M. Hornak
Foreword by Susan R. Komives

"Politics. Divided loyalties. Ethical dilemmas. Peer conflicts. Supervisory issues. These are just a few of the complexities student leaders must navigate in their daily lives on college campuses. In order to better prepare students to constructively engage in such experiences, [this] book offers a litany of case studies designed to generate meaningful dialogue and critical analysis of realistic campus-based student experiences with leadership. In sum, the specificity and flexibility of this book make it a valuable contribution to faculty and administrators seeking to help students wrestle with the nexus of leadership theory and practice. It offers a much-needed contribution to the student leadership literature."—***Journal of College Student Development***

Demonstrating Student Success
A Practical Guide to Outcomes-Based Assessment of Learning and Development in Student Affairs
Marilee J. Bresciani, Megan Moore Gardner, and Jessica Hickmott

"This volume is a wonderful addition to existing resources on assessment in student affairs. Institutional illustrations and examples add robustness to this book through detailed treatment of central topics in outcomes assessment."—***John H. Schuh***, *Distinguished Professor, Iowa State University*

"The book is practical, concise, and convincing. I can't wait to get the guide into the hands of our student affairs managers. *Demonstrating Student Success* takes the intimidation factor out of the critically important task of outcomes-based assessment. The concepts and best practices are presented with the student affairs practitioner in mind with ready to use approaches and plans."—***Paul Dale***, *Interim President, Paradise Valley Community College, Phoenix, Arizona*

22883 Quicksilver Drive
Sterling, VA 20166-2102

Subscribe to our e-mail alerts: www.Styluspub.com